Functional Pottery

Functional Pottery

Form and Aesthetic in Pots of Purpose

Robin Hopper

Chilton Book Company · Radnor, Pennsylvania

Library of Congress Cataloging in Publication Data
Hopper, Robin.
  Functional pottery.
  Bibliography: p. 247
  Includes index.
   1. Pottery. 2. Implements, utensils, etc.
I. Title.
TT920.H66 1986   738.2   85-48270
ISBN 0-8019-7451-8

1 2 3 4 5 6 7 8 9 0   5 4 3 2 1 0 9 8 7 6

To lovers of pots, whomever they may be

Contents

Preface

Making pottery is a timeless occupation, and the best of pots through the ages have a quality of timelessness about them that transcends chronological and cultural boundaries. Their appeal is universal. The essence of form, the movement of a brush, the quality of surface, the hidden meanings, and the integration with mankind's daily existence over several thousand years, all add to the significance of the art.

This book is about pots of purpose—their forms, meanings, and functions. I hope that it will stimulate new vigor and understanding into the process of making pots for use. It is not a history book, although approximately a quarter of it is given to historical concerns. It is not a design book, although a similar space is concerned with design. It is not a "how to" book, although almost half of it does concern this aspect. It is also not a contemporary this-is-the-state-of-the-art-of-functional-pottery book, although this is included too. It is a book that concerns the development, design, and making of utilitarian pottery, and the thought processes behind it. It is primarily a "why to" book that attempts to draw together the many diverse approaches to making domestic, functional, or utilitarian pottery. It is about a process of discovery.

This book is, in effect, a compilation of essays, arranged in four parts, each having its own introduction. The concerns of the parts are: (1) historical, cultural, and ethnic variations; (2) form, growth, and design; (3) practical and analytical approaches for the working potter; and (4) a view of eight contemporary clayworkers.

There has been little written on the art of making functional pottery, perhaps because in the past making utilitarian wares has largely been viewed as a means to an end rather than an end in itself. In the contemporary art arena, pottery has been looked at as the poor cousin to painting and sculpture, in much the same way that the graphic arts once were viewed. Pottery is neither painting nor sculpture, although it has elements of both. It is significant that in many of the world's languages there is no word for *art*. Art is the result which comes from the activity known as *craft*. There may be good art or bad art, the quality being largely dependent on the combination of skill, understanding, emotion, and intent.

Pottery has concerns that are quite different from most other media of expression. First is its process of transformation from maleable mud to hard ceramic. Second is its associations with the rigors of daily life and the rituals of religious life. Third is in its multiplicity of uses. Fourth is in the infinite variety of form that may be created. Fifth is in its range of technical variation, giving a possibility of expression that is at least equal to all of the variants of painting and graphics, from watercolor to oils, and from etching to photo-lithography. And lastly, the degree of skill that is needed to bring all these concerns to the focal point of a finely made piece of work.

In his book *The Lesser Life,* William Morris, the great nineteenth-century designer-craftsman says:

I should say that the making of ugly pottery was one of the most remarkable inventions of civilization.

He was talking about the visual monstrosities of the Victorian (nineteenth century) period of industrial pottery production. This period of questionable aesthetics heavily influenced North American art pottery of the early twentieth century. A hundred years after the Victorians, we still have a remarkable abundance of visual pollution all around us.

In compiling the illustrations and writing this book, it is my hope that potters might be both stimulated by, and take courage from, the past in the search for an individual style, and to look at the making of pottery with fresh vision. Through looking at objects from the past, finding out a little of their genesis and the needs of their makers, we may establish the similarities and differences of thought between those cultures that we are attracted to and our own work. Through an awareness of form and the forces that both create and control it and its proportions, we may find the distinct direction that each individual potter must travel. Through an analysis of use and usefulness, we may establish the parameters that help us to produce work that satisfies needs. And through a knowledge of the paths of others we may establish an individual identity for ourselves.

Pottery is an art form with its roots based in science. In his collection of essays, "The Visionary Eye," Jacob Bronowski observed the following:

All created works, in science and in art, are extensions into new realms. All of them must conform both to the universal experience of mankind, and to the private experiences of each man. The work of science or of art moves us profoundly, in mind and in emotion, when it matches our experience and at the same time points beyond it. This is the meaning of truth that art and science share; and it is more important than the differences in factual content which divide them.

Pottery is undoubtedly the most scientifically based art form, and at the same time one of the most universal experiences of mankind. Makers of pottery for use are part of a continuum from man's earliest experiences in fired clay in a search for usefulness, truth, and beauty. In the words of the poet, John Keats:

Beauty is truth, truth beauty,—that is all Ye know on earth, and all ye need to know.

Historically, pots were seldom made with specific considerations or analysis of how they might best perform their duties. However, since the early Twentieth Century edict of Walter Gropius and the Bauhaus movement that "form follows function," both potter and public have become much more aware of how things work most efficiently through the study of ergonomics. In the short term, this will probably affect how the work suits the marketplace. In the long term, the potter must decide whether to make pots to suit specific functions, or to find, or allow the buyers of his or her work to find, functions to suit the pots that he or she wishes to make. In reality, most of us probably do a little of both.

Acknowledgments

I wish to thank all the people who have helped and encouraged the development of this book, the many students, potters, teachers, and buyers of pottery who consciously or otherwise have caused me to think that it was a worthwhile task. My thanks go especially to Judi Dyelle, for her patient reading and rereading of the manuscript, her help with photography, her constant analysis and discussion of concepts in the book, and with the task of compiling the Bibliography from a mass of books and a pile of notes.

I also wish to thank the many readers who have made valuable suggestions and observations: Mick Casson, Allan Crimmins, Sue Hopper, Les Manning, Philip Rawson, Dianne Searle, Tom and Ginny Marsh; also, the potters who make up the portfolio section and who have helped with the reading: John Leach, Gwyn Hanssen Pigott, Bruce Cochrane, Tom Turner, Stanley Mace Andersen, Walter Keeler, Denise Goyer, Alain Bonneau, and Eilene Sky. I thank the many people who have allowed me to photograph objects from their private collections, and the staffs of museums and art galleries which were so helpful, including the Art Gallery of Greater Victoria, the Brooklyn Museum, the Montreal Museum of Fine Arts, The Metropolitan Museum, the Boston Museum of Fine Art, the Field Museum in Chicago, the Asian Art Museum and the De Young Museum of San Francisco, the George R. Gardiner Museum of Ceramic Art in Toronto, the Vancouver Museum, the Nelson-Atkins Museum of Art, Kansas City, Missouri, and the National Museum of Greece (Heraklion). I couldn't have done the project without the help of Tom, the intrepid typist, or without the support of the Canada Council, whose Jean A. Chalmers Fund helped in the cost of photography.

To all who have shared in this gestation, my sincere thanks.

Part One

Made to be Used

Opposite:
From Jost Amman and Hans Sachs, *Eygentliche Beschreibung
Aller Stände auff Erden* [*The Book of Trades*]
(Frankfurt am Main: Sigmund Feyerabend, 1568.

INTRODUCTION

Part One is a short exploration of the growth, development, and change in utilitarian or domestic pottery made throughout history. It relates particularly to form, function, and detail. It is heavily illustrated with photographs and drawings of pots from a variety of cultures. In the space available, it is impossible to do more than give a taste of, and hopefully whet the appetite for, the incredible wealth of historical pottery that graces the museums of the world. I have selected photographs of objects which emphasize the intent of this book. They are mainly arranged in groups which focus on form and details: spouts, handles, feet, and lids. They come from a wide geographical range, but by no means can be thought of as all-encompassing. Each is a fine example of a specific style of work which will, I hope, prompt the reader to look further into the styles he or she is most attracted to.

This book is not intended to be a chronological survey, rather an outline of what pots are and what they do. The forms of functional pottery through history may be used as a reference for potters of today to learn from and draw from to produce new work, as potters of the past often did. Each major culture had its own chronological growth and history, often in competition and contemporary with other cultures. These cultures were independent on one another prior to the development of trade routes around the Mediterranean Sea, through the Middle East to the Orient, and among various areas of the Orient. Later, they were to become linked through trade, war, religion, and the migration of peoples from one area to another.

Since the beginning of the current craft revival in the 1950s, clayworkers seem to have had a huge ambivalence toward the study of ceramic history. One large segment has been deeply concerned with understanding the paths that have been trodden from the beginning of pottery making, stepping back, as it were, in order to go forward. Another large segment of the clayworking community tends to remove itself from and ignore all that has gone before. This group attempts to live and create in a vacuum, where the medium is the only thing that matters and contact with things past is at best irrelevant, and at worst counter-productive and an infringement on personal growth. Total isolation from all outside stimulus is virtually impossible, since the nature of the artist's imagination is to get ideas and concepts from a variety of sources, no matter how unlikely or trivial they may seem to anyone else. The mundane processes of daily living bring one into contact with things to cook in, eat and drink from, wash or urinate in; things that can definitely form object images in our minds, leading to a potentially wide source of inspiration for future development. The familiarity that we may have with everyday household objects can easily lead to further visions. All forms of functional object have developed and changed throughout history, as new needs or fashions came into being, requiring different objects to suit different purposes. Mankind has always learned from his past; not always very well, one has to admit, but he has used the past to forge new tracks into the unknown.

The history of pottery making goes back at least 8000 years, to Neolithic times, when the nomadic hunter settled to the life of crop farming and animal husbandry. Exactly where and when pottery making first developed nobody can be quite sure. What is most likely is that it developed spontaneously in different places during roughly the same period of time. Ceramic history could be a great deal older than what is currently accepted. Recent finds in Australia claim archaeological remains containing rudimentary ceramics dating back

30,000 years. The area usually credited with being the cradle of civilization, that of the Mesopotamian basin in the Middle East, is also credited with having the first pottery-making cultures. Japan possibly has a ceramic history at least as long as any in the Middle East. One recurring fact is that, in what are often labelled primitive cultures, the quality of claywork and its decoration had become exceptionally well-made and sophisticated at such an early period in man's cultural history. Regardless of where the actual first developments took place, the rudimentary forms from early pottery-making cultures also have an astonishing similarity.

Archaeologists generally agree that, like most of mankind's major discoveries, the earliest pottery probably developed by accident. There are two basic theories of development. It may have come from observations of the way the earth became baked around firepits, with the subsequent experimentation of making and firing pinched clay pots. On the other hand, it may have come from the accidental burning of clay-lined baskets. Baskets were the original storage containers. They were made from grasses, reeds, roots, or soft, pliable tree branches, primarily for carrying and storing grain and seeds, the major part of the diet at that time. Baskets are anything but impervious to the loss of small seeds, which easily find their way through the basket weave. After a while inner coatings of clay were probably smeared into the baskets to prevent loss. Some of these mud-lined baskets were possibly accidentally burnt, leaving a fired clay lining. Pottery could even have developed from the process of wrapping foods in a skin of clay and placing them in the embers of a fire, or on heated rocks, to cook. This method was common among the Indians of North America, and may also have been the precursor of the common cooking pot. From these simple beginnings has developed an art form which has served mankind for thousands of years, for his daily needs from birth to the grave, and beyond. Throughout man's pottery-making history he has developed a huge repertoire of shapes and surfaces to fill his many needs. This book is mainly concerned with those needs, and of the development of the shapes and details which were made to fill them.

Origins

Clay is one of the earth's most abundant raw materials. It is constantly developing from the decomposition of certain igneous rocks. The earth's crust, to a depth of at least four miles, is primarily composed of igneous rocks, which decay and break down as they become exposed to weather conditions. Clay is in fact forming more quickly than it is being used. Since it is a common material over most of the earth's surface, pottery making probably emerged in sporadic developments, quite isolated from one another.

Throughout the civilized history of mankind, after the gradual change from nomadic hunter and gatherer to settled farmer and animal breeder, clay has probably been the most consistently used material for improving the quality of life. Ceramic objects made since Neolithic times have included figurines and sculptures; lamps; bricks of all kinds; walls; roofing; flooring and decorative tiles; granaries; feeding troughs; chimney pots; pot stands; ovens; kilns; tannurs; beads; sickles; hoes; wall hooks; molds for foods; molds for pots and figures; molds for metallurgy; crucibles; waterwheel jars; drains; dovecotes; beehives; churns; latrines; sling stones; spitholders for cooking; potter's wheels; pipes for smoking; pipes for water, irrigation, and sewage; cuneiform writing tablets; ostraca; execration figures and bowls; jar stamps; ossuaries; coffins; libation vessels; tax measures; tokens as coin substitutes; medical pastilles; gaming pieces;

toilets and wash basins; and an endless variety of vessels.

Looking at pottery in museums, or as illustrations in books, one can't help but be amazed by the huge and subtle diversity of forms that man has molded clay into, for a wide variety of possible uses. Beyond the natural instincts of enjoying the purely manipulative quality of the material, and the function which is required of the formed objects, ceramic form has been influenced and altered by many factors and forces.

Pottery developed as a response to the needs of mankind. Pots became containers and dispensers: pots of purpose. The forms that they took developed for a variety of reasons: the use required; religious associations; as a substitute emulating other, more precious, materials; geographical and climatic considerations; and the many variations in cultural customs. Once the basic needs became evident, forms were developed and made to serve them. The variety of ceramic vessel forms that have been created is almost infinite.

Religious associations also had a profound effect on form development. Pots were made for fertility rites, deflowering of young girls, ritual libation vessels for the pouring of wine or oils, usually over sanctified ground, through to flower vases for temples and shrines of many Oriental countries. They also include pots made for funeral rites and ceremonies dating far back into the earliest of cultures. In Ancient Egypt, rulers and other people of power were embalmed and mummified after death. Their internal organs, or viscera, were removed during the embalming process and were later interred with the mummy in four canopic jars, surmounted with modeled heads of the jackal (the stomach), the baboon (the lungs), the falcon (the intestines), and the human (liver).

Clay form has been greatly influenced by objects made from materials other than clay. Functional objects in use by different strata of any society might simultaneously have included objects made in gold, silver, bronze, pewter, copper, stone (mainly onyx, alabaster or limestone), glass, wood, bone, leather, roots, reeds and grasses, or clay. Not all these materials were used by all cultures, but in each culture there was a hierarchy of materials that were used, mainly as a symbol of status. Clay was usually at the lower end of the status scale and often used to simulate objects made in a material of a higher value (see page 28). Chinese porcelain was perhaps the only early ceramic development which was afforded the recognition of being a material of substantial value. In some cultures, notably in India, pottery was the disposable material, like today's paper, Styrofoam, or polystyrene. In some parts of India, everyday pottery was thrown away after use, either as a measure of hygiene or by religious doctrine, or both.

Geographic and climatic considerations are responsible for many form variations. Firstly, the availability of clay, and the types of available clay, determine to some extent the objects that can be made in any given area. For instance, there may be only alluvial or silty red clay, or buff clay with a large amount of sand in it, as one finds in many parts of the Middle East and Africa. The pottery there is of a very direct nature with little opportunity for excessive manipulation. In other areas, where there may be an abundance of highly plastic clays, pots of a much more fluid nature may develop. Plastic clays will usually tolerate a great deal more manipulation, and therefore more complex forms are likely to emerge. Different pots are made at high altitudes than those made at sea level, not only because of the clay content but also because of the firing variations at higher altitudes.

Climatic conditions have also played an im-

portant role. In hot countries water is a precious commodity. Pots made for storing water are usually shaped to conserve it from excessive evaporation; therefore, they usually have comparatively narrow necks. Water is either tipped out, or lifted out with a small ladle or dipping pot attached to a string. A vessel may even be a totally enclosed form with just a minute spout and small filling hole (Fig. 1.1). The forms themselves may be quite extended and bulbous to expose a maximum of surface to condensation on the outside of the pot, in order to keep the water cool inside. There are usually a considerable number of insects in hot countries, which are kept out of the containers by various cunning devices, such as enclosed forms, objects that fill from the base, strainers, and many anti-insect lid and spout variations. In cold or temperate climates, forms of cups and bowls are often more closed than open so that hot foods don't cool too quickly, and the pots can also be a source of heating for the hands. Other climates will undoubtedly have their special effects.

Mankind's varied cultural customs and living habits have yet other influences on the development of form in functional pottery. The way that the pottery is used, and in what sort of environment, has a strong effect on the way that the bases of ceramic objects are made, for instance. In cultures which use tables, the base of the object needs to be flat, or nearly flat. In other cultures which may have little use for tables, pots may be hung

Fig. 1.1 Indian and African water jars.

FIBRE RING.

Fig. 1.2 Pre-Columbian vessels from Peru. Designed for easy carrying and to prevent insects from entering.

Fig. 1.3 Mycenaen. Late Helladic side-spouted, necked jar with basket handle and insect strainer. Buff clay with decoration. Height, 27.4 cm. Courtesy of the Brooklyn Museum: Museum Collection Fund.

from branches, walls, hooks, or ceiling joists: pots used in this way often have pointed bases. In yet other cultures, the objects may be placed directly on earth or sand floors: in this case, we often find pots with rounded bases that can be made to tip or roll easily in use. These forms would often be set on a braided fiber ring, or even a ceramic ring, to facilitate tipping (Fig. 1.4) In a further development of form, pointed or round-based pots were half-buried for the storage of liquid that needed to be kept cool. It is much easier to bury, or half-bury, a pot with a rounded base than one with a flat base. In some places, where the contour of the ground was uneven, tripod or multiple feet were developed to keep the piece stable.

Carrying methods also have a strong bearing on form. In many cultures, particularly in Africa, objects are made with round bases to fit onto the head, separated and kept secure by a ring of fibrous material. In others, particularly in mountainous parts of South America, the pots were carried on the upper part of the back, or slung behind the neck by a rope or cloth sling placed through the pot's low level handles and around the person's fore-

head. The handles that were the support loops for the slings were carefully contoured so that they had no sharp edges that might cut the fabric. Their placement was also critical to good support and mobility (Fig. 1.6).

The ways and means of preparing and serving food and drink have also had their effect on form development. In early primitive societies, food was mostly consumed in its raw or uncooked state. The diet of early civilizations consisted of little more

Fig. 1.4 Braided fiber rings.

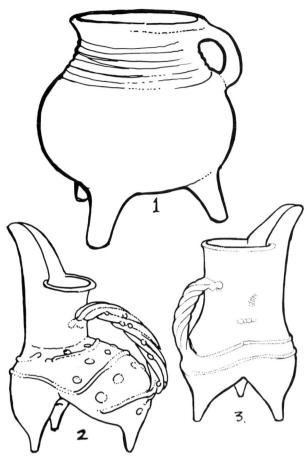

Fig. 1.5 Tripod vessels: (1) Cooking pot, 13th–14th century *A.D.*, North Germany; (2) and (3), spouted vessels, 2000–3000 *B.C.*, China.

Fig. 1.6 Aryballus, Inca; burnished earthware. Height, 8¼". Courtesy of the Metropolitan Museum of Art (1978.412.68).

than various forms of grain with the occasional portion of meat or fish, and beer made from fermented grain to wash the food down and aid digestion. The earliest forms of cooking were by either direct cooking of meat or fish by impaling bits of flesh on sticks and holding them in front of a fire, or by a form of steaming. This was done by heating rocks in a depression in the ground, or by placing hot rocks in a basket. In both cases, the rocks were covered with a thin layer of damp leaves, or seaweed, and the food placed on top. This was then covered with further layers of leaves, and sometimes earth or sand to contain the heat and steam. Both of these simple cooking methods were, and are still, common to many areas; other timeless methods are cooking on top of embers, as well as on both charcoal and peat. As cooked foods became

more widespread, different ways of cooking also developed.

Pottery was developed to serve these needs, although in some cultures, notably India and Islam, iron, copper, and brass cooking pots were preferred. Of all the pottery that we can see in the museums of the world, cooking pots are perhaps the least in evidence, most likely because of their fragility from continual use, but also because they may not have been held in high enough esteem to be placed in tombs to accompany the deceased in the afterlife. Most of the pots that one finds in museums were made to be used rather than just to be looked at. Often they had a special significance, and were mainly used for the less damaging actions of daily life. With a gradually changing role from utility to contemplation at certain periods of history, the pots of some cultures attained a glorified role and were made expressly to be looked at. This happened particularly in England, Europe, and Czarist Russia from the mid-eighteenth to the mid-nineteenth centuries, where a large volume of interior ceramic accessories had little or no function other than a decorative one. Among these one would find mantelpiece garniture sets, obelisks, and centerpieces, often based on structures and forms from the Classical world of Egypt, Greece, and Rome.

In many cultures, simple pottery forms were often endowed with spiritual or symbolic significance which has become lost with the passing of time. Vessels generally are the universal feminine symbol, the womb of the Great Mother, shelter, protection, preservation, nourishment and fertility. They also represent inwardness and inner values. Bowls represent giving or offering, and fertil-

ity. The seven small bowls placed on a Bhuddist shrine represent the seven offerings for an honored guest: flowers, incense, illumination, perfume, food, water for drinking, and water for washing with. Lidded forms, covered jars, boxes, urns or bottles represent the feminine principle of containing, enclosure or the womb. The chalice, cup or goblet represents the source of inexhaustible sustenance or abundance, the heart and salvation, plenty, immortality and receptivity. The ewer is a symbol of purity, and of washing the hands in innocence. Gourd-shaped vessels represent mystery and longevity. The vase, water-pot, and pitcher symbolize the cosmic waters, the Great Mother, fertility, perpetual harmony and the heart.

Even games have had their effect on shaping some pottery forms. In Classical Greece, a game called "Kottabos" was played using the wine cup

Fig. 1.7 Variations on Classic Greek and Apulian drinking vessels: kylix, skyphos, kantharos, and mastos. Kylix, courtesy of The Montreal Museum of Fine Arts; skyphos, courtesy of the Brooklyn Museum: loaned by Miss Iris C. Love.

or kylix. The kylix is a stemmed cup with elegant handles. In the game, a finger was crooked through the handle and then, with a flick of the wrist, the dregs of remaining wine were flipped at a target across the room. If the aim was accurate, the thrower dislodged a flat metal disc from the top of a metal stand, which then fell to the floor with a resounding crash. Both the shape of the cup and the handle had some effect on the efficiency of the game, and the resultant kylix form was one of great elegance. Variations on the kylix form have been abundant since the neo-classic period of the eighteenth century (Fig. 1.7).

A piece of pottery, then, is an amalgam of many things. In the late twentieth century, we may not be aware of many of the attributes, considerations, and hidden meanings that are built into pots of old, or of their importance to the cultures that made them. More often than not, we are only aware of the form or surface itself, and of one culture's forms in relation to those of another. Through television, books, and magazines we have become aware of the two-dimensional graphic image of what a pot may be, often becoming more interested in profile and surface than with inner qualities. Much of the pottery of the western hemisphere has become more concerned with the clothing that goes over the body, than with the basic form itself. In some oriental cultures the pot is seen as soul, where volume and form grow from the depths within, and the outside shape is a direct result of the inner form. Perhaps in the western hemisphere, we are more concerned with appearances than with truth or meaning; with clothes that obscure the form rather than glory in it. Maybe by contemplation and study of the uses and meanings of pots of the past, we can infuse a greater understanding and content into our own developing works.

Thirty spokes share the wheel's hub;
It is the centre hole that makes it useful.
Shape clay into a vessel;
It is the space within that makes it useful.
Cut doors and windows for a room;
It is the holes that make it useful.
Therefore profit comes from what is there;
Usefulness from what is not there.

From *Tao-Te Ching* by Lao Tsu. New Translation by Gia-Fu Feng and Jane English. New York: Vintage Books.

2

Functions, Methods, Shapes, and Details

The regular functions of life for which mankind has generally developed and used clay vessels are eating, drinking, storage, carrying, serving, cooking, lighting, washing and perfuming, planting, decoration and the rites of death. Individually, each variant of use suggests and controls some aspects of the shape of the object.

POTS OF PURPOSE

Eating

The utensils for eating from have always been either flat or bowl-shaped, starting with leaves and the cupped hand. When pottery was developed, the natural forms were emulated, and remain the basic forms to this day. In most western cultures, the use of leaves for plates has long since passed, but there are still many cultures in other parts of the world where the leaf is the ultimate plate: useable, disposable, and biodegradable. The use of leaves and flowers for serving food, and for making offerings to deities, has left a legacy in both the form and decoration of a great variety of plates and shallow bowls, where veined, floriated, and foliated edges and forms are common (Figs. 2.1 through 2.3). The bowl form is an extension of the natural cupped hand, originally made to feel comfortable when placed in the hand. Pottery bowls from many world cultures have a special and almost imperceptibly contoured surface with slight ridges that fit the hand. In more recent times, in so-called sophisticated society, it has become the norm to eat one's food at a respectable knife and fork's distance from the ware. The sense of touch among people who seldom hold the plates and bowls they eat from has become considerably diminished as a result. Perhaps as a further consequence, the tableware made for mass consumption is less and less enticing to pick up and nestle.

Drinking

Vessels used for drinking probably developed from the shape of the cupped hand, shells, or from the horns of animals. Early historical pottery examples can easily be found which draw on these elementary forms. Horn and shell forms often had small double or tripod feet to allow for stability, a design detail which later probably led to the development of the stemmed drinking vessel, goblet, or chalice. Pottery refinements and form also develop consistently from the process of making, and the fluidity of the clay. Although refined and beautifully formed and handled cup shapes were made on the island of Crete as early as 1750 B.C., the development of the cup and saucer most likely comes from the civilized and sophisticated court customs of the Tang and Song dynasties in China, where the cup and stand were in use for drinking rice wines. For the most part, the oriental cup has no handle. Cups made for later Ming and Qing dynasty export trade to Europe carried a wide range of handle styles to satisfy the elegant European demands of the day. These styles were embellished in European copies to all manner of confections. The fads and fashions of specialized beverages, such as coffee, tea and chocolate, also had their effect on the styles of pottery made to suit different needs.

Storage

After Man the Nomad settled, one of his earliest needs was to store the bounty of the summer's harvest, to allow him to get through the cycle of autumn, winter, and spring, before fresh crops were again available. His initial storage containers were most likely granaries built like small houses on stilts, much as they still are in parts of Africa. The place-

Fig. 2.1 Porcelain bowl, celadon. Yuan, 14th century A.D., China. Height, 5½". Courtesy of the Asian Art Museum of San Francisco: The Avery Brundage Collection.

Fig. 2.2 Stoneware bowl, celadon glazed. Sawankhalok, 14th–15th century A.D., Thailand. Height, 3¾". Courtesy of the Asian Art Museum of San Francisco: The Avery Brundage Collection.

Fig. 2.3 Stoneware plate. Yuan, 14th Century A.D., China. Height, 2". Courtesy of the Asian Art Museum of San Francisco: The Avery Brundage Collection.

Fig. 2.5 Hajiki jar and stand. Earthenware, painted with red pigment. Mid-Kofun period, Japan. Height: jar, 6"; stand, 5¼". Courtesy of the Asian Art Museum of San Francisco: The Avery Brundage Collection.

Fig. 2.4 Greek rhytons, 600–450 B.C. Based on the form of a drinking horn (center).

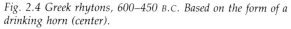

Fig. 2.6 Stem bowl with flange foot. Buff-colored earthenware. Sialk culture, mid-fourth millenium, Persia. Height, 9.1". Courtesy of the Asian Art Museum of San Francisco: The Avery Brundage Collection.

Fig. 2.7 Cup and saucer with Samgam decoration; celadon-glazed porcelaneous stoneware. Koryo dynasty, 12th–13th century A.D. Height: cup, $3\frac{1}{16}$"; saucer, $2\frac{3}{8}$". Courtesy of the Asian Art Museum of San Francisco: The Avery Brundage Collection.

Fig. 2.8 Terra cotta beaker. Romano-Britain, 2nd century A.D. Height, 3". Courtesy of the Fine Arts Museum of San Francisco: given anonymously through the Docent Council and de Young Museum Society.

ment off the ground helped to keep them free of vermin. This detail might well have been the starting point for a large variety of both storage and cooking vessels that use the tripod base form. Granaries, often up to ten feet high, were usually made with a clay and straw mix. In tropical climates with little rain, there was no need to fire them. In more temperate and colder zones, however, large storage containers needed to be resistant to rain, snow and frost. Ways of making and firing large storage jars were developed in areas such as Crete, where jars up to 6 feet high and 3 feet wide have been unearthed at the palaces of Knossos and Phaistos (Fig. 2.11). These jars were usually placed in interior locations. Perhaps the most important single vessel type throughout history has been the water storage pot. Depending on whether it is carried back and forth to the well, or is static in the house and filled with water from a smaller carrying pot, its shape is quite variable. Its many variations

Fig. 2.9 Mug, salt-glazed stoneware. Westerwald, late-17th-century, Germany. Height, $5\frac{1}{4}$". Courtesy of the Royal Ontario Museum.

Fig. 2.10 Jar, lead glaze with copper. Eastern Han, 225–220 *A.D.*, China. Courtesy of the Montreal Museum of Fine Arts: F. Cleveland Morgan bequest.

Fig. 2.12 Wine jar, Changgun white porcelain. Yi, 17th–18th century *A.D.*, Korea. Height, 36.2 cm. Courtesy of the Asian Art Museum of San Francisco: The Avery Brundage Collection.

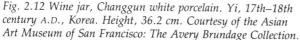

Fig. 2.11 Storage jar, 6 ft. high. Knossos, Crete, ca. 1800 *B.C.*

in form generally have one common theme—a fairly narrow neck to keep evaporation to a minimum and to keep insects out.

Carrying

Pots made for carrying are basically of three types: those that are balanced on the head, usually on a fiber ring; those that are slung by a rope or cloth; and those that are held in the hand and carried by various forms of handles and lugs. Some were made to be carried by two people, and have substantial side handles to allow this. The placement of handles on head-carried pots is usually low down, and the forms themselves are made wide and low, with a low center of gravity to allow ease of both lifting and carrying. Forms intended for hand carrying over long distances have handles placed high up,

Fig. 2.13 Ring-shaped Sueki bottle. Late Kofun, 6th century A.D., Japan. Height, 12". Courtesy of the Asian Art Museum of San Francisco: The Avery Brundage Collection.

often over the top of the pot, bale fashion, to minimize the likelihood of spillage. Some forms, such as pilgrim flasks, have been flattened for easy carrying, and sometimes attached to a belt or shoulder strap. They were often made to emulate the form of silver or leather bottles, or flat gourds. These were the historical equivalent to the hip-flask, for liquid sustenance on long journeys.

Cooking and Food Preparation

Cooking pots developed in extreme variety, due to the wide range of foods being prepared, as well as the variety of cooking methods. Historically, food preparation has mainly used a variety of bowls, grinding mortars, sieves, colanders, and pouring vessels, depending on the types of food being prepared. Early cooking methods were described in the last chapter, but with the development of more sophisticated control of cooking methods, particularly with the invention of the enclosed oven, different styles of cooking developed. Food may be baked, boiled, steamed, broiled, roasted, poached, fried, stewed, or casseroled. With the variations in cooking methods, the need for alternate forms of pottery grew. Some cooking pots function best when made wide and shallow, whereas others are better tall and bulbous. Some need lids, spouts and handles, while others don't. Some pots are to contain mainly liquids; others, mainly solids. Some cooking utensils are obviously better in materials other than ceramic, such as tin-coated copper or heatproof glass, but these are comparatively recent developments in man's culinary and epicurean heritage.

Serving

Cooking and serving are closely related. With more and more variation and sophistication in cooking, the attention to presentation and serving became

Fig. 2.14 Bellarmine bottle, salt-glazed stoneware. Rhineland, 16th century A.D. Height, 12". Courtesy of the Royal Ontario Museum: anonymous gift.

Fig. 2.15 Casserole with cover; burnished earthenware with impressed pattern. Nigeria. Courtesy of the Royal Ontario Museum.

Fig. 2.16 Vessel and cover, burnished earthenware with impressed pattern. South Congo. Courtesy of the Royal Ontario Museum.

Fig. 2.17 Animal-shaped vessel, buff earthenware. Amlash culture, 1,000–800 B.C., Iran. Height, 5¼″. Courtesy of the Asian Art Museum of San Francisco: The Avery Brundage Collection.

much greater, with the attendant requirement of a huge range of pottery variations. Often these were made emulating other, more precious, materials such as gold, silver and glass, but equally often they used pottery serving dishes made in the forms of leaves, fruits, vegetables or even animals, birds and fish (Fig. 2.17). Much current industrially made pottery is a throwback to these imitative formal developments, in particular, to those made in the eighteenth century.

Lighting

Mankind's need for illumination and night-time security was originally met with the discovery of how to make fire. Fire is not easily contained for interior use except in large spaces. The invention of braziers and fire pits later made fire more convenient and safer, and the discovery that animal fats and oils, and vegetable oils, could burn in a contained space gave rise to the various forms of oil lighting. The addition of small grass or fiber wicks gave small amounts of localized light, which was long-lasting and eminently portable. Multiple holes for wicks gave more light for larger areas. The forms of oil lamps (Fig. 2.21) devised in various cultures have also influenced the forms of many other types of pottery, from flower vases to sauce-boats.

Washing and Perfuming

Pots for washing are usually in the form of large bowls, depending on what is being washed. They may be for food preparation, toiletries, and personal hygiene, or the washing of the deceased before burial, cremation, or mummification. In some cultures, washing was often a ritual affair, where servants were employed in the bathing, perfuming, and oiling of the nobility. Apart from the bath, which in some cultures was ceramic, small pots were used in the process for perfumes, oils, and unguents, often having forms designed for hanging from a belt or chatelaine. The ritual of washing the deceased often gave the pots a symbolic significance. It is suggested by archaeologists that in the pre-Columbian Mimbres culture of the American Southwest, bowls used for cleansing the dead were ritually "killed" at the tomb by breaking a small hole in the base, and releasing the spirit. The

Fig. 2.18 Figure of a woman, earthenware. Amlash culture, 1,000–500 B.C., Iran. Height, 11". Courtesy of the Asian Art Museum of San Francisco: The Avery Brundage Collection; gift of the Asian Art Foundation of San Francisco.

Fig. 2.19 Jar, earthenware. Jomon period, 2000–1000 B.C., Japan. Height, 11¾". Courtesy of the Asian Art Museum of San Francisco: The Avery Brundage Collection.

Fig. 2.20 Handwarmer, earthenware. Meiji period, late 19th century, Japan. Height, 20.4 cm. Courtesy of the Art Gallery of Greater Victoria: Fred and Isabel Pollard Collection.

Fig. 2.21 Oil lamp shapes.

bowl was then placed covering the head of the deceased (Fig. 2.22).

Funereal Use

From the earliest times of pottery making, mankind has used the ceramic form in relation to the burial of the dead, either as a ceramic coffin, ossuary, or ash jar. The funerary or canopic urn features in many cultures, and in many forms (Figs. 2.23 through 2.27). In various places, the funerary urn has modeled ancestral or other effigy figures. In others, the figurative additions relate to deities. The forms themselves vary considerably, depending on the source. The different methods of disposing of human remains varies from culture to culture. For the most part, only figures of political, religious, or social importance were given glorified funeral rites. After cremation, the ashes were usually scattered unless the deceased was sufficiently important for the remains to be interred in a reliquary or shrine. In other cultures the deceased might be put out for nature to take care of, on anything from an ice floe to a desert sand dune.

Planting

The growth and regeneration of plants for both indoor and outdoor use has been done with the use of ceramic containers since time immemorial. Pots for planting directly into are usually shaped as a cylinder which flares toward the top. The rea-

Fig. 2.22 Two bowls, Mimbres classic period, 1000–1150 A.D., New Mexico.

Fig. 2.23 Large vessel with features of the God Bes. Dynasty XXVI, Egypt. Height, 16.2 cm. Courtesy of the Brooklyn Museum: Charles Edwin Wilbour Fund.

sons for this shape are the ease of removal for re-potting, planting out, or root pruning, and to accommodate the normal shape of the root system of most plants. Plant containers have also been specifically developed for bulb culture, particularly in Delftware from Holland. Many vase forms have developed for a single specimen plant, corm, bulb, cutting, or for the special growing of dwarf plants or bonsai (Fig. 2.28).

Decoration

Pots whose sole function is to be decorative have also been in evidence for several hundred years. The major growth in this area started in Ming dynasty China, followed by the Ching dynasty, and spread to Europe through international trade, particularly in the late seventeenth and eighteenth centuries, arriving at a time when European court culture was ripe for change. The impression on the courts was such that European pottery and later porcelain companies, mostly attached to the royal households of Europe, developed heavily the "Chinoiserie" styles in the field of decorative ceramics for interior use. All manner of huge vases and lidded containers, obelisks, centerpieces, garnitures, and sculptural pottery forms served as embellishments for palaces and stately homes. They were often confections, developed from a combination of oriental and classical Mediterranean origins, and often showed an uneasy amalgamation of both.

This short historical overview gives a glimpse at how pottery forms are affected by *use*. Purely decorative pots have total freedom of expression, while functional considerations impose compromise in both form and aesthetic development in pots that are made to be used. The various needs

Fig. 2.24 Funerary urn with male figure. Mosquito, Columbia. Height, 39 cm. Courtesy of the Brooklyn Museum: Frank L. Babbott Fund.

Fig. 2.25 Funerary urn, Fukien ware. 10th century, China. Height, 22.5 cm. Courtesy of the Art Gallery of Greater Victoria: Chen King Foh Memorial Collection.

that domestic pottery serves predetermine to some extent the forms that were and are made. Within all of these basic forms there has usually been considerable room for invention, variation, and improvisation within a theme.

Fig. 2.26 Funeral urn, Ch'ing-pai glazed porcelain. Koryo, 13th century A.D., Korea. Height, 10¾". Courtesy of the Asian Art Museum of San Francisco: The Avery Brundage Collection.

MAKING METHODS

The other major factor in the development of pottery forms is *process*. In order to further consider the forms themselves, it is necessary to have some knowledge of the process of making pottery, as this also partially controls the end result. Although the majority of this book is related to the process

Fig. 2.27 Funerary vase and cover, stoneware. Yuan dynasty, 12th–13th century A.D., China. Courtesy of the Asian Art Museum of San Francisco: The Avery Brundage Collection.

Fig. 2.28 Crocus pot, hard paste porcelain. Pinxton, ca. 1800 A.D., England. Courtesy of the George F. Gardiner Museum of Ceramic Art.

of throwing clay objects on the potter's wheel, there are several other production methods in common use for making pottery. There are many cases where the body of a pot may be thrown, pressmolded, or slip-cast, with handbuilt appendages and details added to the basic form. With many pots made from a combination of methods, it is often very difficult to tell where one method ends and a new one starts. As new technology and more techniques became available, potters took full advantage of their creative opportunities to explore them.

The processes of handbuilding pottery are basically three in number, with many slight variations employing common techniques. The basic three are pinch pots, coil pots, and slab pots.

Pinch Pots

Pinch pots are the primal pottery-making method where clay is literally pinched from a maleable mass and, through a series of squeezing movements, molded into shape. The method is generally limited in scale to what will fit comfortably in the hands. Larger pots may be made by joining two or more pinch pots together. The technique of pinching can be adapted to forming pots from squeezed and flattened clay balls, or short lengths of clay, which are then built up like scales to the required form.

Coil Pots

Coil pots are the most widespread form of handmade pottery in most cultures around the world, from the earliest times to the present. Coil pots are made from lengths of clay that have been rolled between the hands, or on a flat surface, or even extruded. The length and thickness of the coils varies considerably, dependent on the scale of the required object. Coils are often flattened into ribbons which are then joined to one another. The process of making the pots requires the individual coils to be laid one on top of the other, generally with a great deal of careful joining between one layer and the next. Almost any shape can be made with the coil process. Forms are often made on some kind of saucer, part of a gourd, or a curved pottery shard as a primitive turntable or wheel.

Slab Pots

Slab pots are made with clay in a sheet or slab form. The slabs may be used in either a stiff boardlike consistency or in a soft state. In the stiff consistency, pottery forms are often constructed from pieces cut from the clay sheets using a template for accuracy. The prepared pieces are stuck together with slip or water. Soft clay slabs may be formed in or over molds, or used in a free way, exploring the soft qualities of clay.

Pressmolding

Pressmolding is an extension of slab-building, done by pressing slabs or pieces of clay into or over molds to create a form. Pressmolds have been in existence for at least two thousand years, and have usually been made of bisque-fired clay. The forming uses clay in a soft plastic state. Molds may be in multiple parts to allow complex forms to be made. They may also be carved to produce repeatable low-relief surface decoration. Molds for pressmolding can be either single hump or drape for simple forms, or multiple pieces for more complex forms.

Extrusion

For some objects, clay is pressed through an extruder as a long tube or sheet. An extruder is essentially a simple machine fitted with various dies which shape the clay as it is forced through under pressure. Until comparatively recent times the extruder has mainly been used for the making of tiles and pipes. Contemporary potters often use the extrusion principle to develop a variety of shaped, tubelike forms.

Slip Casting

Slip casting uses clay in its liquified form, poured into a mold that is usually made of plaster. It is a comparatively recent technique which has been in common use for less than 200 years, and is essentially an adaptation from the pressmolding technique. The liquid clay is poured into the mold, then left for a short time for a clay skin to attach itself to the mold walls. The excess liquid clay is poured off, leaving a thin cast skin which draws away from the mold as it shrinks. Casting is one of the major industrial making processes.

Thrown Pots

The potter's wheel was developed at least 4000 years ago in the Middle East, possibly in Egypt or Syria. It has been in more or less constant use ever since. It is one of the most flexible tools ever devised by man. As a vertical lathe, where only one end of the material is attached, it allows almost any variable of symmetrical form to be developed with comparative ease. It is a deceptively simple tool, being basically a flat or nearly flat circular surface made to revolve by a power source. This may be from the human hand or foot, electricity, or belts driven by water turbine or animal movement. The clay is attached to the damp wheel and, while rotating, compressed to a central position. From there, it is pulled up into a variety of forms. The pulling up is done with the revolving clay being pressed between the hands with the fingers in various positions, while being kept moist by the use of water or liquid clay slip. The throwing process is a semi-fluid one, where the clay becomes sensitive to the slightest internal and external pressures. The form is made fatter by pressure from the inside and made narrower by pressure from the outside. Most wheels are capable of a variety of speeds that are used at various times during the throwing action, usually fast at the start, and slowing as the form nears

completion. In skilled hands, the wheel is a fast and efficient production tool that demands continuous practice, as well as the utmost sensitivity, to get good results. The wheel is also often used in a semi-mechanical process called jigger and jolleying, where a mold holds one surface, while the other surface is formed by a template that cuts and compresses the revolving clay, at the same time pressing it firmly down into or over the mold form. Jiggering is one of the major industrial methods for producing tableware and flatware.

Other Methods

The above are the most used pottery-making methods on a worldwide scale, although there are others common to industry, but not common for the craft potter. These are mainly processes that utilize hydraulic presses to form clay objects from either plastic clay or moist clay dust. They require a mold that forms the outside and another that forms the inside, with the clay sandwiched between the two and squeezed into shape under high pressure.

THE DEVELOPMENT OF SHAPE

The most natural and elementary vessel is the cupped hand, or both hands cupped together as one. As one of our basic built-in tools, it is used for scooping, holding, carrying, eating, and drinking from. It is the basic form from which the earliest pottery took shape. The primal pottery form is where a thumb or finger has been pushed into a responsive lump of clay to form a cavity capable of holding something. From this most basic of forms, all other pottery forms have developed. The primal form became thinned through pinching the clay between the thumb and fingers, initially in a form loosely resembling cupped hands. Primal pots of most cultures are remarkably similar, like the object that occurs when anyone experiences clay for the first time: usually a round based, slightly flaring, short cylinder. With experience in forming the clay, discovery of its wide range of potential uses, and the response to fulfilling various needs, the basic form developed in a multiplicity of different ways.

In his fine book on aesthetics and appreciation, *Ceramics,* Philip Rawson goes into the growth, development, and change of pottery form in more depth than I have space for here. I would recommend that anyone who is making ceramics of any type read his inspired and perceptive writings on pottery. I am merely touching on things with which he deals in depth.

Figures 2.29 through 2.31 show how the development from the original primal form may have occurred. The primal form has three basic offshoots: first, the rounded bulbous vessel; second, the cylindrical form; and third, the shallow bowl. From each of these, there develops a family of related forms, which, in the main, also have related functions. If we call these types 1, 2, and 3, type 1 are forms mainly used for storage and pouring; type 2 are mainly related to drinking and pouring; and type 3 are mainly related to food preparation, eating, serving and cooking. The outlines of pots in these drawings are easily recognized pottery types from many different cultures, through an extensive

time period. The drawings may be read both horizontally and vertically, to compare and contrast profiles. Although drawn profiles and photographs give some idea of what a pot may be, it is not until one holds a pot, and rotates it in one's hands to feel the movements and rhythms left by the potter's fingers, that one can begin to appreciate the complexities that may be there. If one adds to this the various social, symbolic, and ideological content that may be included in the ware, we will probably come to the conclusion that individually we know little about the total qualities of the objects that we may be visually stimulated by and wish to emulate.

DETAILS

The details of pottery forms are found in their extremities and appendages: the top and bottom, and any additions. In this book I am not particularly

Fig. 2.29 The development from primal form through ovoid form. Used mainly for storage and pouring vessels. Based on drawings by Philip Rawson.

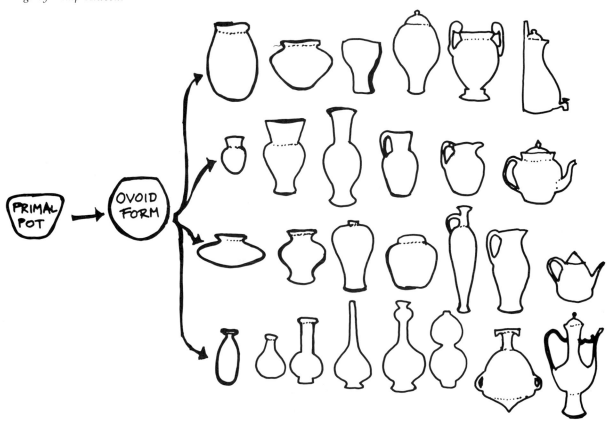

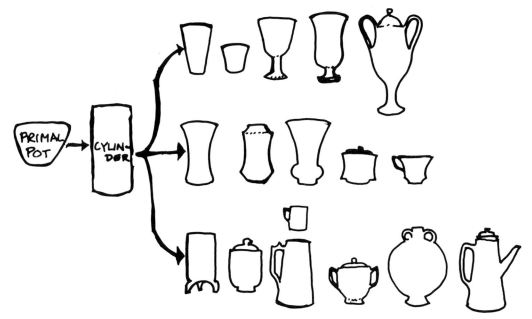

Fig. 2.30 *The development from primal pot through cylinder. Used mainly for drinking and pouring vessels. Based on drawings by Philip Rawson.*

Fig. 2.31 *The development from primal pot through bowl. Used mainly for eating, cooking, and serving. Based on drawings by Philip Rawson.*

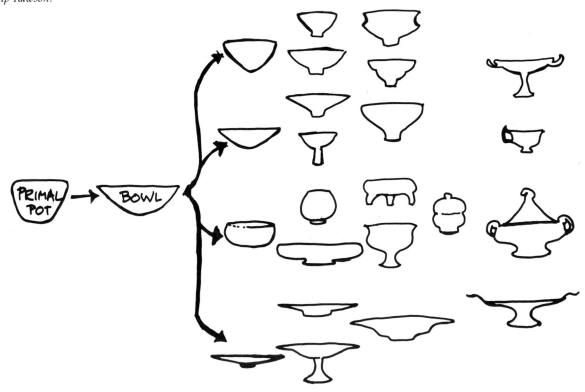

concerned with their glaze coating, decoration or color, exept where the decoration is an integrated element of function. An obvious example of this would be the chicken or phoenix-headed ewer shown on page 33. A pot's extremities of form are the base or foot, and the rim or lip. In either case they may both be part of an extension; the foot by a stem, tripod or multiple foot, and the rim by an extension of the neck. Appendages are parts that are either stuck on or complete the form by their intended use. They may include feet, spouts, lids, knobs, handles, and lugs. The scale of a pot is often determined by the size of the details and additions in relation to the whole. For example, small knobs on a big form can give it a monumental quality. Through history there are many ways that the treatment of the variations of extremity and appendage have been explored and attended to.

The mechanics of making details are discussed at length in Chapter 12. Here we are more concerned with some of the historic and aesthetic considerations.

Feet

The simple base of a pottery vessel may be extended and given more importance in the overall form in many ways. Feet may be cut away from the base of the thrown form by trimming or turning, by the use of a knife, wire, or trimming tool, or profile cutter. Feet may be added on by throwing or handbuilding methods. They may give great variety by creating graceful or solid terminations to lines of form. They may be added to make lifting and holding easier, or just to develop a greater stability. The bottom of pots with untrimmed bases are usually pushed to a concave form. Pinched or thumbpressed bottom edges were in common use in Medieval English earthenware and fourteenth-century German stoneware pottery (Fig. 2.32).

Spouts and Pouring Lips

The form used for pouring has every variation, from the nonexistent to the heavily exaggerated spout. In many cultures, pouring vessels have no special lip, except for a slight sharpness to the inside of the top rim, to cut the flow of liquid. The pouring lip or spout has historically been one place

Fig. 2.32 English Medieval jugs with thumb-pressed bases.

where the potter has given full rein to his inventive freedom. Rims and added-on spouts have been thrown, cut, pulled, modeled, squeezed, beaten, bent, and cajoled into an astonishing variety of functional stream-producing edges. See Pouring Forms, page 68.

Lids, Covers, and Knobs

The earliest form of lid was probably a large flat stone, placed over the opening of a vessel to keep dirt and insects out. The other early cover was simply a skin tied down onto small, loopy handles. From these simple beginnings, all manner of covers have developed to fulfill simple needs. Apart from keeping out dirt and insects, lids also help to cut down on evaporation, control the spillage of contents, keep out air in pickled food or fermented liquor storage containers, allow selective pouring to be achieved through small apertures, and generally enhance and terminate a form with a flourish. Lids that are wider than the simple span of a hand usually have a knob or handle to make the grasping action easier. Knobs and finials are another point of consummate interest for the fancies of the potter, from the use of knobs which carry religious or spiritual overtones, such as the common lotus-bud, or lotus flower knob found on many pots from China, to the miniature Stupa, or Bhuddist shrine found on some Korean pots. The Lotus plant is full of various symbolic meanings almost universally, from Greece and Rome to the Far East. On the other hand, there are many modeled references to both mythological beasts, such as dragons, and the spoils of war, such as decapitated heads or effigies. These often occur on spouts and handles too. (See Lidded Forms, page 100). Handles are often used in place of knobs, where they may be seen as miniature bridges across a depression or valley.

Handles and Lugs

Handles and lugs vary from the almost imperceptible to the exuberant and major component of the overall form (see Handled Forms, page 112). Handles on some objects are often vestigial references to past customs, such as the tying down of lids or skin covers. In others, they may be a combination of carrying device and spout for either pouring or drinking from. As with other details, the handle is a place where play and interest may be focused. Apart from doing its job of lifting, carrying, tipping, and suspending, it is often a major point of interest in the overall form, tying disparate sections of a form together in a linear fashion. Handles both take off from points of emphasis, and cause a point of emphasis to develop by the process of their movement.

Prior to any additions being made, the basic unadorned form of any vessel usually takes care of itself, once its considered use and its process of production are decided upon. Between the top and bottom diameters of a round object there stretches a line which is the profile. One may think of a profile as an elastic line that may be expanded or contracted at will by pressures from inside or out. The line may be fluid, with no marked angular changes, or it may have many points of angular change. Points of angular change are usually called articulation. In some cases, where the profile of the form might resemble the head-on view of a boat, the change in linear direction is often called a carination.

Pottery is full of references to the human body.

Fig. 2.33 Pre-Colombian Inca water jar and cooking pot. Note the strong and finely placed handles.

Parts of a pot may be referred to as lip, neck, throat, shoulder, belly, waist, and foot. They are often endowed with human characteristics and qualities; strong, robust, rotund, fat, vigorous, sensuous, virile, pregnant, weak, mean, thin, slight, tight, loose or jolly. Smooth, soft, fluid, elegant lines are spoken of as feminine, while articulated angular lines are spoken of as masculine. Once the form is taken care of, the fun and interest for both potter and user alike lies in the details.

The vessel is an extremely complex entity. It not only does a job of some kind, but also displaces space as does sculpture, and often has surfaces that resemble paintings. It is integrated with the rigors of family life in a way that painting and sculpture seldom are. With all its body references, and the symbolic attributes which are historically attached, such as giving, receiving, nurturing and cleansing, perhaps pottery should be thought of as the ultimate human art form.

Pottery Forms
in Imitation
of Other Materials:
An Historical Collection

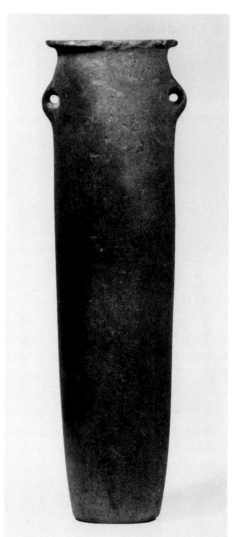

Basalt vase. Egypt, Nagada II. Height, 28.9 cm. Courtesy of the Brooklyn Museum: Museum Collection Fund.

Cycladic stone water jar. Greek, ca. 2500 B.C. Height, 22.2 cm. Courtesy of the Brooklyn Museum: Museum Collection Fund.

Pottery jar, following form and handle styles of stone vessels. Egypt. Height, 14 cm. Courtesy of the Brooklyn Museum: Museum Collection Fund.

Pottery jug, painted to resemble stone. Egypt. Height, 21 cm. Courtesy of the Brooklyn Museum: Charles Edwin Wilbour Fund.

Pot with cover, imitating bronze forms; buff stoneware. China, 3rd century B.C. Height, 22.4 cm. Courtesy, Museum of Fine Arts, Boston.

Vessel in the shape of a stag; earthenware. Marlik style, 10th century B.C., Iran. Height, 11". Courtesy of the Asian Art Museum of San Francisco: The Avery Brundage Collection.

Tripod form with animal-shaped handles in imitation of bronze; earthenware. China, 5th–3rd century B.C. Height, 19.1 cm. Courtesy of the Asian Art Museum of San Francisco: The Avery Brundage Collection.

Jar with carinated shoulder, typical metallic form. Ban Kao type, Thailand. Height, 23 cm. Courtesy of the Asian Art Museum of San Francisco: gift of Joy French Black.

Covered vessel, stoneware. Old Silla period, 5th–6th century A.D., Korea. Height, 10½". Courtesy of the Asian Art Museum of San Francisco: The Avery Brundage Collection.

Jar in the form of a leather bag, Sueki ware. 6th century A.D., Japan. Height, 5¼". Courtesy of the Asian Art Museum of San Francisco: The Avery Brundage Collection.

Saddle gourd (traveling flask); green glazed earthenware. Liao Dynasty, China. Height, 9¼". Courtesy of the Asian Art Museum of San Francisco: The Avery Brundage Collection.

Cup in the form of a tree trunk, stoneware. Yixing ware, 1573–1619 A.D., China. Height, 2½". Courtesy of the Asian Art Museum of San Francisco: The Avery Brundage Collection.

Phoenix headed ewer in imitation of repoussé metalwork; earthenware with three-color glaze. Tang dynasty, China. Height, 33 cm. Courtesy of the Montreal Museum of Fine Art.

Covered box; hard paste porcelain. Frankenthal, ca. 1770 A.D., Germany. Courtesy of the George R. Gardiner Museum of Ceramic Art.

Pair of baskets; soft paste porcelain. Worcester, ca. 1765 A.D., England. Courtesy of the George R. Gardiner Museum of Ceramic Art.

Covered bowl and stand; soft paste porcelain. Chelsea, ca. 1765 A.D., England. Courtesy of the George R. Gardiner Museum of Ceramic Art.

Vessel in imitation of bone; burnished earthenware. Mayan, 550–950 A.D., Mexico. Courtesy of the George R. Gardiner Museum of Ceramic Art.

3

Ethnic Variations and Historical Eclecticism

Pottery from different areas reflects not only cultural, religious, geographical, and social variations, but also exhibits a surprising degree of regional variation within quite small areas. The stylistic variations of different domestic wares are often most profound in the surface enrichment, but subtle changes in the forms and details certainly have their place. In Nigeria, until a few years ago, a central watering place or well would bring together women from a number of small villages. They carried their pottery vessels on their heads, and often the pots would be quite different stylistically from villages placed a mile or two apart. Each carrier's home village was immediately known by the style of her water jar. Unfortunately, much of this variety has now given way to the use of plastics and metal containers. The same sort of regional variation takes place in other countries having a long-standing pottery-making tradition. If one were to look at all of the variations in contemporary folk pottery in Spain or Mexico, for instance, and select a type of form that is produced for the single purpose of liquid storage, the subtlety of variation would be considerable. Figure 3.1 shows a variety of "cantaros and botijos," vessels for wine storage, coming from different regions of Spain.

A similar comparison could easily be made with the forms produced for most utilitarian pottery. Figure 3.2 shows a small selection of traditional cooking pots. They are all variations on a theme, and are made to suit different styles of cooking using both open and lidded, or closed, vessels. Whether any one variation performs its job better than another is questionable, but the excitement in the diversity of form is obvious. The efficiency of the various types of cooking pot generally derives from an acute awareness of the foods being cooked. Until comparatively recent times, in many cultures—particularly in what are now referred to as Third World countries—household pottery was made by the women of the society. In some cases it still is, yet in other cultures it is an entirely male affair. Once the combined female skills of both cooking and potting were developed, it would be quite easy to adjust and improve the efficiency of forms as it was observed that one variant seemed better than another. These changes would probably go on until the most satisfactory solution was arrived at to suit a specific food or range of foods.

Food, in all its universal variations of diet and cooking, is perhaps most responsible for the variety of pottery forms that exist. In most cultures of Europe, at least until the Middle Ages, the diet consisted largely of grain, usually made into a form of gruel, plus onions, mutton, and beer. Food in parts of the Americas consisted of tomatoes, potatoes, maize, fish, and game. In the Far East, rice formed the major part of the diet, augmented by seaweed, soybeans, fish, and eggs. Although the diet in different parts of the world is quite varied, the vessels used for its preparation and cooking are essentially either open or closed, varying not so much in the form, but more in the quantity that a given vessel might hold. The forms used varied in subtle ways, often influenced by the maleability of the clay being used. The character of the product usually seemed to depend on what segment of society the pottery was made for. High quality wares, usually glazed or highly refined, were usually associated with nobility or officialdom; low quality wares, usually unglazed and unrefined, were usually associated with the general population.

Regional and cultural variations are more pronounced in pottery used for serving and for decoration, where it is not subject to the same degree of damage. Pots made for these functions are usually more lavish in form, with many decorative details, and may be adorned with a wide variety of surface enrichment techniques.

THE RITUAL OF THE KITCHEN AND THE TABLE

The large amount of pottery that has been produced through man's history has been either for cooking, or eating and drinking. These daily rituals are at the core of life itself, and can vary from the mundane to the exalted. Pottery vessels used in the rituals can be likewise, depending on the degree of importance of the event taking place. In many cultures, there is regular pottery for daily use, and then there is the "best" for special occasions. There are also many myths, customs, and superstitions that have been built up around pots in use, such as the Orthodox Judaic tradition of one set of pottery for cooking and eating meat, and another for dairy products, and the ritual breaking and renewal at Passover; and the tradition in some parts of India, of breaking household wares after use following the dictates of both Buddhist and Jain religions.

HISTORICAL ECLECTICISM

Throughout mankind's pottery-making history, he has always been quick to absorb and adapt forms and decoration from cultures other than his own.

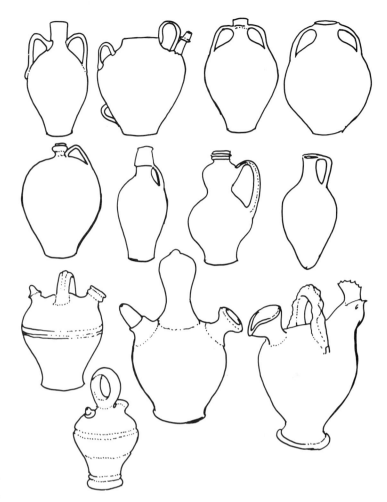

Fig. 3.1 Regional variations in cantaros and botijos from Spain.

These adaptations have been most pronounced in the Old World cultures from countries bordering on the Mediterranean sea, through the Near East to the Far East. They are found most particularly in areas directly affected by the land trade routes from China to Persia, and the sea routes that took in most of the eastern hemisphere and ports of Europe. Another, more sinister, effect of changes in influence comes from war and subsequent domination, where the land of one culture is occupied by the forces of another. Sometimes the occupying force has a strong effect on cultural change, such as the effect that Imperial Rome had on its provinces and dominions, particularly in the northern areas. At other times the reverse is the case, such as the effect of Korean pottery on the Japanese. The Shogun Hideoshi, whose armies invaded Ko-

Fig. 3.2 Traditional cooking pots from France, Italy, Britain, Mexico, and China.

poussé metalworking techniques were well developed in Egypt from at least 1500 B.C., and in classical Greece and Rome much later. The repoussé technique is done by hammering the metal to produce patterns in low relief from the body of the form. The method used to produce a similar result in clay was a process of pressmolding, usually using multiple-piece molds. The nature of metalworking often produces angular forms that can be made with relative ease from beaten or rolled sheets of metal. Cultures with strong metalworking traditions have often produced ceramics with an affinity for angular forms, or forms reflecting metallic origins (see Pottery Forms in Imitation of Other Materials).

With the continual peddling of goods backward and forward across the trade routes, recognized styles of work became blurred by the interaction and integration of new and varied techniques and technologies. Porcelain was developed in China in the early Tang dynasty toward the end of the sixth century A.D. Trade between China and Islam was relatively brisk during the Tang dynasty, and the porcelain wares being transported from China were infinitely more refined than the earthenwares being made in Islamic countries. Islamic potters tried, in self-defense, to copy the porcelains but had neither the necessary raw materials nor the chemical knowledge or firing technology to do it. Their copies led to the development of tin opacified glazes that to the layman gave a similar appearance to brush-decorated porcelain. The wares could be painted over the glaze with a result that looked like porcelain. Through the trade routes the development of both porcelain and tin-glazed wares was spread to the Mediterranean, and subsequently all over Europe, where further copying and development went on. The shipping routes from China and Japan also brought a wide variety of pottery to Europe from the sixteenth century onward, strongly affecting the stylistic development of European pottery. It became fashionable in certain circles to collect the wares of China and, where fashion dictated the "rightness" of one type of ware, those who produced other types were likely to find themselves out in the cold. So styles once again became very highly copied and plagiarized. Almost inevitably, when one culture is superimposed with an alien one, a hybrid develops; much of what

rea in 1592 but came away with only a small amount of plunderings and a number of Korean potters, had developed a love of Korean pottery for the tea ceremony. The forced abduction of Korean potters, and their subsequent pottery work in Japan, gave rise to changes that altered the history and development of Japanese pottery from the late sixteenth century onward.

Since early times in the development of trade from one culture to another, there has always been an exchange of influences. In the ceramics of most cultures, these varied influences are quite obvious, such as the copying in clay of objects made in repoussé-decorated metals, like silver and gold. Re-

Fig. 3.3 Bowl painted with birds and calligraphy. Earthenware with decoration painted under turquoise glaze. Iran, 12th–13th century A.D. Height, 6". Courtesy of the Asian Art Museum of San Francisco: The Avery Brundage Collection.

affects the development and visual stimulus of present-day potters are hybrids of the past.

New forms and decorative techniques generally take quite a long time to become assimilated, but when they do, there is usually a blurring of the origins that gave rise to that form, which makes tracing the changes in historical pottery form something of a detective adventure. One looks for clues and makes an investigation aiming at a long-term buildup of evidence, often through a series of informed hunches. One assumes some things based on an acquired knowledge of various cultures and their development. Accumulated assumptions and

educated guesswork may lead to authentication of the truth or originality behind an object, but doesn't prove the directions that a potter of the past may have traveled in forming his work. We can infer all manner of ideas, but as we can no longer speak to the potter concerned, we can never be quite sure just what historical influences, if any, there may have been in his work. If it is as complex as it seems to evaluate and authenticate works from the past, think how difficult it will be for archaeologists and historians of the future to form educated guesses on the multiple eclectic influences on potters of today!

Footed Forms: An Historical Collection

Egyptian two-footed vase, polished red ware. Metropolitan Museum of Art, Rogers Fund, 1910 (10.176.113).

Incense burner with three legs; glazed porcelain. Jingdezhen, 18th century, China. Height, 11 cm. Private collection.

Tripod form; cord-marked grey earthenware. Neolithic, 2000–3000 B.C., China. Height, 9″. Courtesy of the Asian Art Museum of San Francisco: The Avery Brundage Collection.

Wine pot with three feet, handle, and spout in the form of a chicken head; stoneware. Yue ware, 6th–7th century A.D., China. Height, 18 cm. Private Collection.

Below left: Incense burner; stoneware. Shoji Hamada, 1894–1978, Japan. Height, 8.5 cm. Courtesy of the Art Gallery of Greater Victoria: Fred and Isabel Pollard Collection.

Below right: Jar; red earthenware with lead glaze. Han dynasty, ca. 100 A.D., China. Height, 15.7 cm. Courtesy of the Art Gallery of Greater Victoria: gift of Mrs. Mary Morrison.

Bowl on a pedestal foot; tin-glazed earthenware with luster decoration. Deruta, 16th century A.D., Italy. Courtesy of the George R. Gardiner Museum of Ceramic Art.

Tripod vessel with legs surmounted by monkey heads; burnished red earthenware with ochre and red pigments. 300–800 A.D., Mexico. Courtesy of the George R. Gardiner Museum of Ceramic Art.

Tripod jaguar effigy plate with rattle legs; burnished earthenware with polychrome decoration. Guancaste, 1200–1500 A.D., Nicoya. Courtesy of the George R. Gardiner Museum of Ceramic Art.

Tetrapod vessel. Mayan, 250–550 A.D., Mexico. Courtesy of the George R. Gardiner Museum of Ceramic Art.

Tripod vessel with the head of a ruler. Mayan, 250–550 A.D., Mexico. Courtesy of the George R. Gardiner Museum of Ceramic Art.

Stem cup; stoneware. Lonquan, 14th–15th century A.D., China. Height, 11 cm. Private collection.

Spittoon; soft paste porcelain. Worcester, ca. 1765, England. Height, 11.8 cm. Courtesy of the Art Gallery of Greater Victoria: Ann and Joseph Pearson Collection.

Opposite: Warrior vase; earthenware. Mixtec culture, 1000–1500 A.D., Oaxaca, Mexico. Height, 10½". The Fine Arts Museums of San Francisco: museum purchase, Phyllis Wattis Fund.

Above: Rhyton in the form of a lion; earthenware. Pre-Hittite, 1870 B.C., Turkey. Height, 7½". The Fine Arts Museums of San Francisco: gift of Alma de Bretteville Spreckels through the Patrons of Art and Music.

Four-panel pedestal plate; earthenware. Panama. Height, 7½". The Fine Arts Museums of San Francisco: gift of Dr. and Mrs. Larry Otis.

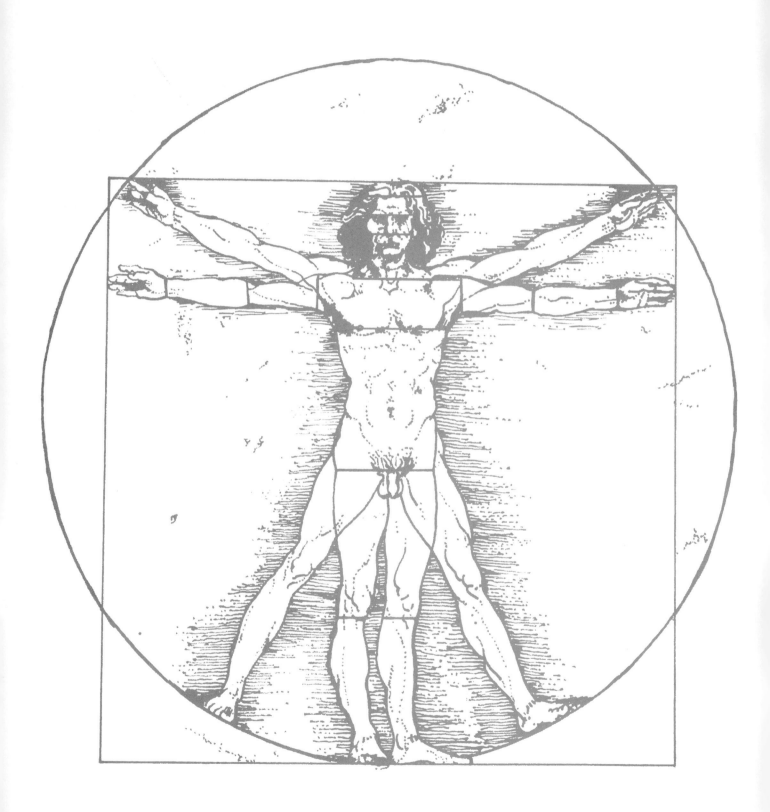

Part Two

Form, Proportion, Relationships: The Measure of All Things

INTRODUCTION

Man is the Measure of All Things.
—*Protagoras, Fifth century* B.C.

The essays which make up Part Two analyze form and proportion, and their relationship to each other and to us. They consider form from organic, geometric, architectural, and human origins, relating them to the production and development of functional pottery. You may question why and how these relate to the contemporary process of making pots. All I can say is that some thirty years ago, when I was a student and starting to formulate ideas on aesthetics for any type of pottery, my personal research led me into some areas which have been a source of constant use and growth ever since. At that time I didn't know just how important to my personal growth they would be, and many things learned are soon forgotten. However, some facts bury themselves deep in the brain and reemerge almost in an intuitive way to control and guide one's thoughts and ideas. I have never been a mathematician, but have always been interested in form. The more one looks at form, the more one realizes how closely allied to mathematics it really is. It all seems quite abstruse and unconnected to clay. One has to realize that mathematics is at the core of life itself, and permeates everything that we are and do. For me personally, it has given a foundation of understanding and developing form for both functional and one-of-a-kind pottery that has served and continues to serve me well. Pottery is, at the same time, the most abstract and the most domestic of the arts.

Experiencing the fluid process of making pottery on a wheel may seem far removed from considerations of a mathematical or architectural na-ture. Yet we all work with geometric forms. Our wheel sends clay in a spiral from a circular base, and our finished results are as miniature architecture, beset with many of the same structural problems as full-scale buildings. In reality the interaction between seemingly formless clay and mathematics starts as soon as the ball of clay hits the wheel. It becomes a spinning mass revolving on an axis—a microcosm of our own planet spinning in space. Each ball of clay represents a new world, governed by natural laws and sciences. These essays hope to explore some of them.

Webster defines *geometry* as: "the branch of mathematics that deals with points, lines, surfaces and solids, and examines their properties, measurement, and mutual relations in space." Two-dimensional images such as circles, squares, triangles, etc., are called *plane geometry*. When a circle is transformed into a three-dimensional object, it becomes a sphere. This is called *solid geometry*. Looked at in its most abstract form, pottery is solid or three-dimensional geometry, much as oranges, the earth, sun, and mineral crystals are. The interaction of solid geometrical forms creates compound form. The potter working on a wheel seldom creates pure geometric solids, as did the power that created oranges, planets, or mineral crystals. The forms are more or less geometric. Geometry and Universal Symbols deals with these aspects, and is echoed in the essay, Forms and Forces, Nature and Growth.

The principles of solid geometry and the development of ceramic forms are closely integrated. Potters often feel the process of throwing to be an organic movement. So it is. But the forces of constraint (gravitational force toward the center), confronting the force of movement (centrifugal force outward from the center), sandwiching clay between them, invariably causes a form with a geometric basis, no matter what shape that form eventually ends up with. The whole process of throwing is a balance between these forces.

The force which a potter uses to counteract the centrifugal forces of clay on a revolving wheel is similar to the forces which mold planets in space. In the case of the potter, the hands control this outward movement by pressure toward the center of the form. In the case of the earth, the force of gravity contains the outward thrust. Without these external pressures, the pot would probably spin itself off the wheel, unless its axis is absolutely true, and the planet would gradually disintegrate, with earthen projectiles hurtling off into space.

Gravity affects the way things grow and the way things are built. Thrown pots combine growth and building. They are structures which grow in a spiraling organic way from a soft inorganic mass. When the soft forms become hard and are fired, they become like Lilliputian architecture with arches, buttresses, cantilevers, and domes. These forms are subject to the forces of gravity, vacuum, and pyroplastic deformation (deformation under the effects of heat). Forms and Forces, Nature and Growth is an essay that explores these relationships.

A structure is composed of interrelated parts forming an organism or organization. Pots are structures, as are the people who use them. Pots are solid geometrical structures, and people are solid anatomical structures. Pots and people go together. Consideration of how the structure of a pot relates to the configurations of a human frame are often overlooked by potters. The essay Pots and Anatomy deals with this topic.

The parts of a structure may be related to each other by proportion. If we take the adult human frame, for example, we find that the average head is one-eighth of the body height, the eyes are halfway between the chin and the top of the head, and the navel is more or less halfway between the soles of the feet and the middle fingertip of the upstretched hands. Many such examples of proportion can be found. An innate understanding of pro-

portions like these is central to much artistic endeavor. The relationship or proportion of one part of a form to another part of the form can be either harmonious or discordant. According to Webster's dictionary, "*aesthetics* is the study or theory of beauty, and of the psychological responses to it; specifically the branch of philosophy dealing with art, its creative sources, its forms and its effects." The struggle to balance proportions of an object in a harmonious way is part of what aesthetic concerns are for the potter. Throughout history, various forms of proportion have been developed which can help in making decisions of an aesthetic nature. These are explored in the essay Proportion and Ratio.

Roots, Growth, Rhythm, and Balance is an essay that looks to the development of harmony between many things, and in essence is the focal point of the functional potter's art. Balance is the midpoint between two opposing forces. Among other things, it represents the point of compromise that all producers of functional pottery must come to grips with. Aesthetics change from one culture to another and it would be impossible to understand all of the variations. Most potters are eclectic by nature and are emotionally drawn to many things and forms. They may be forms from nature or industry, from pots or basketry, or just about anything that might cause the mind to visualize what may be thought of as a "new form." With an art form that goes back for six to eight thousand years at least, it is almost impossible to do anything radically new, even though it may seem like it to the potter struggling to develop his special identity. This essay looks to some of the springboards in the creation of new forms.

I am not suggesting that every person working in clay will profit from these ideas and guidelines, since we are all different and the intellectual interplay of mathematics is certainly not for all. However, if I can give my readers insight into considerations which have strongly affected my work, then it may possibly help them with theirs.

Geometry and Universal Symbols

Geometry is full of figures which have symbolic meaning far beyond the obviously simple graphic outline which we see as circle, square, triangle, rectangle, and oval. In many cultures there are a host of hidden meanings in these two-dimensional or *planar* figures, and in their three-dimensional or *solid* counterparts. To what extent these hidden messages were understood by the cultures concerned can only be a matter of guesswork. To us now they may or may not be relevant, depending on the attitude and perceptions of the maker and the viewer. Most of the time when we make pots, or any objects, we are either unaware of these symbols, or they are so deeply imbedded in the back of the psyche as to be outside the process of making forms with which we may be completely preoccupied. It may be interesting to know a little of the symbolism of these forms and figures, as they had definite meaning for our forebears, and may well have unconscious meaning for ourselves and the viewers and buyers of our work. Most symbols come from an association of ideas, and these may well relate to our works in clay.

SYMBOLISM IN GEOMETRIC FORMS

Circle

The *circle* represents totality, wholeness, the self-contained, original perfection, eternity, timeless-ness, movement, celestial unity, water, dynamism, manifestation, completion, fulfillment, God, the heavens, and all cyclic movement. As the sun, it represents masculine power, but as the soul or psyche, it is the feminine maternal principle. A circle with a dot at its center depicts a complete cycle and cyclic perfection, and in astrology it depicts the sun.

Square

The *square* represents the earth, as opposed to the circle of the heavens, earthly existence, static perfection, immutability, integration, the totality of the Godhead—three sides being its threefold aspect and the fourth being totality. It also denotes honesty, integrity, straightforwardness, and morality. It is the fixation of death as opposed to the dynamic circle of life, while in architectural symbolism it represents the fixation of the buildings of agricultural and sedentary peoples in opposition to the dynamic and endlessly moving circular formation of nomadic tents and encampments. It represents limitation and therefore form. In Pythagorean philosophy, the square represents the soul.

Triangle

The *triangle* represents the threefold nature of the universe: heaven-earth-man; father-mother-child; man as body-soul-spirit; and the mystical number

Fig. 4.1 Universal symbols.

three. The equilateral triangle depicts completion. The upward-pointing triangle is solar and symbolizes life, fire, flame, heat, the masculine principle, the linga, the spiritual world, and the trinity of love, truth, and wisdom. The downward-pointing triangle is lunar and represents the feminine principle, the matrix, the waters, cold, the natural world, the body, the yoni, and the Great Mother as genetrix.

Rectangle

The *rectangle* is the lateral development from the square, and represents the same things. In its upright form, it represents the masculine principle, the linga or phallus, resurrection, and the renewal of life.

Oval

The *oval* in its upright form represents the female life symbol, the vulva. It has many similar meanings to the circle.

INTERRELATIONSHIPS OF GEOMETRIC FORMS

In many cultures these various forms are incorporated into architecture, art and artifact. Perhaps the most complete is in the Japanese sacred stone tower, from which both the five-storied pagoda and stone garden lantern were to develop (Fig. 4.2). The five parts symbolize the five elements of the universe in ancient Japanese cosmology: sky, wind, fire, water, and earth. A simplified three-part version symbolizes spirituality, consisting of heaven (the triangle), earth (the square or rectangle), with man (the circle) between them.

Universal symbols in combination with one another take on a mass of different meanings. For those interested in the symbolism of forms, names of several books on the subject may be found in the Bibliography.

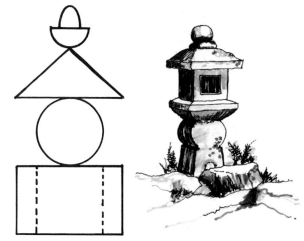

Fig. 4.2 Japanese stone lantern, employing basic geometric forms.

If we look at these plane geometrical figures in their solid forms, we find sphere, cube, pyramid or cone, cylinder or parallelipiped or prism, and ellipsoid. In their three-dimensional forms they maintain their original planar symbolism (Fig. 4.3).

Geometric solids are basic forms of beauty, and have been appreciated as such by different

Fig. 4.3 Plane geometric figures to solid geometric figures.

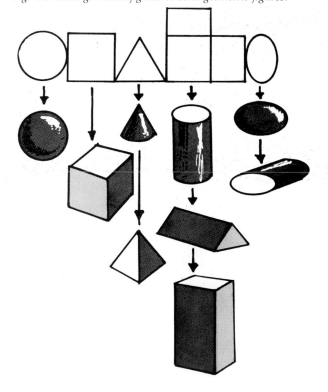

cultures throughout the world at all periods of time. We can call these *pure forms*. They are just as beautiful now as they ever were, and the forms of objects which are based on geometric solids, or combinations of geometric solids, generally receive greater visual appreciation than those which are not. When these forms are cut into sections, they retain elements of beauty found in the basic form. The most obvious of these sections would produce hemispheres, parabolas, truncated cones, discs, domes, and arches.

Geometric solids form the basis of most of the world's architecture. Architecture is the art of enclosing space. Pottery is, in essence, miniature architecture, displacing and enclosing space by the development of three-dimensional forms. Spheres, cylinders, domes, arches and cones are forms which may be equally associated with both architecture and pots. Architecture and pottery have much in common; they can be the purest or the most debased of forms (Figs. 4.5 through 4.8).

The development of complex forms by the interaction of these solids is infinite in variety, and the following two-dimensional drawings give a small idea of the complexity that can develop (Fig. 4.9).

One thinks of forms as being *positive*, and the spaces around and between them, and between the main form and its details, as *negative*. In producing the composition that is a piece of pottery, an understanding and awareness of the interplay between positive and negative shapes can have a profound effect on the potter's ability to visualize form. Negative shapes that are left between a pot's handle and its main form, for instance, are part of the overall outline. If the negative shapes are visually satisfying between one part of a form and another, the total aesthetic quality is enhanced, since everything has been considered. Negative spaces can be further used to echo or contrast with other aspects of the form. Ideas for new forms can easily develop from looking at the negative spaces be-

tween a group of similar forms (Fig. 4.11). Developing an awareness of positive and negative shapes, like any other form of aesthetic understanding, is a slow process, but an important one to learn, as it deals with the totality of composition—how all parts relate to one another. Looking at objects upside-down also gives a fresh view that concentrates the senses. One becomes aware more quickly of relationships of form that are either pleasing or not. A lack of awareness often leads to visual battles taking place within a form, and an inability to correct visual problems.

Perhaps the easiest way to clarify some of these forms and relationships is to look at a few of the objects shown in Part One, and analyze their form and structure. In doing this analysis, I am not trying to intellectualize the objects as geometrical solids, but show how these geometric volumes affect the way that we see objects, and what a large percentage of the world's population perceives as beautiful form. The essay Proportion and Ratio (Chapter 6) also reflects this.

The relationship between historic pots in the photographic sections and those being made by studio potters today is not really that distant. I don't suppose for one minute that the potters of old sat down with drawing compass and ruler and concocted a variety of pleasing outlines. Most of the process of developing useful forms came from diverse cultural backgrounds, and the needs of a particular society at that particular time. They produced pots that were eminently suited to particular functions, and for the most part did it with no intellectual overtones. The fact that they are as aesthetically pleasing as they are is probably due to an intuitive joy in form and proportion.

The only valid reason here for intellectualizing over and analyzing forms is to try to bring things down to a basic simplicity, from which one can perhaps grow with a fresh view. The combination of the discovery of porcelain manufacture, mass-production methods and a revival of interest in the classical world of art and architecture brought about a new vigor. The Industrial Revolution to some extent reestablished some classical values and formed a counterpoint to the simple potter whose work showed the quality of materials and process. As with all new directions, the Industrial Revolu-

Fig. 4.4 Hemisphere, parabola, truncated cone.

Fig. 4.5 Forms where the major volume contains a sphere or hemisphere. Pots made by the author.

Fig. 4.6 Forms where the major volume is contained within a
square or rectangle. Pots made by the author.

Fig. 4.7 Forms where the major volume is contained within the
outline of a parabola. Pots made by the author.

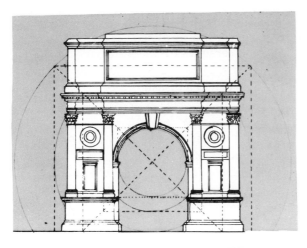

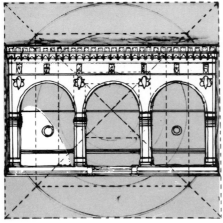

Fig. 4.8 Two architectural designs determined by the proportional scheme of the circle and square. Top: the arch of Titus, Rome, 81 A.D. Bottom: the Loggia Dei Lanzi, Florence, 1376.

Fig. 4.9 Montage of forms using the circle, square, triangle, and ellipse.

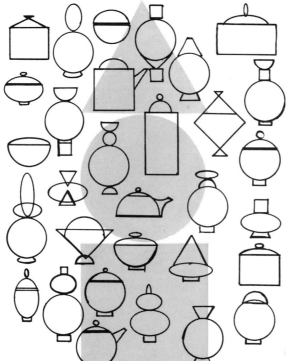

POSITIVE   NEGATIVE

Fig. 4.10 Form showing positive and negative spaces.

Fig. 4.11 The use of negative space to develop new forms.

Fig. 4.12 Looking at objects upside-down often helps to develop satisfying relationships in proportion from one part to another.

tion brought with it both good and bad. One of the bad aspects has been the massive volume of questionable ceramics that has since cluttered our world with visual debris and ugliness. Unfortunately, this has had a disastrous effect on people's ability to see innate qualities of form. Pure forms capture an essence of beauty, and a form of innocence missing from the majority of pottery produced since 1850 A.D.

Perhaps it is time to individually take another look at where our forms have been, where they may be going and why they may be going that

Fig. 4.13 The form of this ewer is a combination of circles and truncated cones, also called a double gourd shape. The curvature of the spout is the same as the handle and also the same as the negative shape of the waist of the pot. Courtesy of the Brooklyn Museum: Museum Collection Fund.

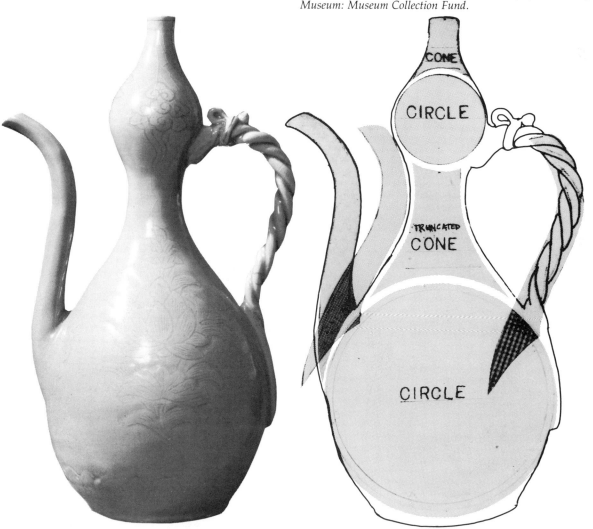

Fig. 4.14 This jug is a combination of geometrical forms. The negative space between the handle and form contains a circle. Jug, silhouette ware; late 12th century, Persia. Courtesy of the Montreal Museum of Fine Arts.

way. The eclecticism that we potters practice in the development of what we consider to be new forms may be a type of seduction. Once seduced, it is difficult to be pure again. The road is not necessarily one that leads to ruin, but one needs to be acutely conscious of its direction. For many, purity is not a comfortable state, possibly because they either enjoy the clutter of visual debris which surrounds us, or have never been able to see beyond it. For these people, the luxurious and opulent, or the chintzy, froufrou nostalgia of the late Victorian period might be just their idea of heaven. On the other hand, many people enjoy the classic no-nonsense purity of a perfect form, like living in a white cube, unadulterated by extraneous material. Most of us probably fall somewhere between these extremes, and while the work that we produce will at times reflect both extremes, we are comfortable in our niche in the middle.

5

Forms and Forces, Nature and Growth

When casually looking at or thinking about nature, one doesn't usually see or think of forms as structured as those found in geometry. One tends to think of things of nature as random or organic, meaning amorphous or formless. Nothing could be further from the truth. All matter has form, from its molecular structure up. When people talk of organic forms they usually mean those seemingly disorganized, not-quite-geometrically-true, assymetrical objects of nature which often become the idea source for pottery that is handbuilt, as opposed to being made within the constrictions of a potter's wheel. Spheres, cubes, cones, pyramids and ellipsoids somehow don't seem to fit. They are too pure. Yet all of these geometric solids are there in nature in abundance if one goes looking for them. We live in a world of wonders, but often pass through seeing nothing.

Mineral crystals give us the majority of the angular solid forms, as can be seen in Fig. 5.1. Spherical and ellipsoidal forms are found in abundance in the shapes of fruits, vegetables, suns and planets (Figs. 5.2 and 5.3).

A great deal of organic growth is twisting or spiral, and may be seen as analogous to the spiraling growth of a pot being formed on a wheel. From the rhythm of wedging to the final pull on the wheel, clay goes in a spiral form. Sometimes the spiral movement affects the way things work, as the thrown clay twists slightly during firing. The twisting of long necks or spouts are examples of this (see Part Three, page 146), as is the vortex motion of liquid coming from the finger ridges of a thrown spout. Spiral or helical growth in nature is found in many flowers, seed pods, pine and fir cones, animal horns, ferns, coiled snakes, the tentacles of an octopus, ears, shells, movements of water, galaxies, clouds, cells, fingerprints, or any form of vortex (Fig. 5.3).

The *spiral* is another of man's symbols which has been in use since paleolithic times, appearing in pre-dynastic Egypt, Crete, Mycenae, Mesopotamia, India, China, pre-Columbian America, Europe, Scandinavia, Britain and Oceania. It represents solar and lunar powers, the air, the waters, the increase and decrease of the sun, the waxing and waning of the moon, birth and death, fertility, and the manifestation of energy in nature. The *double spiral* represents all rhythms of nature, the yin and yang, androgeny, and the continuity between cycles.

Forms, whether they are geometric or organic, man-made or the product of nature, are the potter's stock-in-trade. Everything that he or she produces has form. For most of the last essay I was referring to form stripped down to its essence: pure form. In reality, most functional pottery cannot be just pure form, since it is expected to do something and thus usually requires ancillary parts and attachments such as handles, lugs, lids, knobs, feet,

Fig. 5.1 Angular forms in nature.

spouts, or pouring lips. If a relatively pure form is the basis for the object concerned, the likelihood is that it will probably be visually pleasing. However, when one adds various parts to make it function, one is then creating a composition of interacting or interlocking forms. At this point, the making of a functional object assumes a new direction, becoming sculptural or architectonic.

Concerns that the potter has to deal with at this point relate to the combination of aesthetics and function. How long does a spout have to be to function both visually and physically? What angle should it be from the body? Is it to be a thin tube or a truncated cone? Where does a handle have to go? What relationship has a lid or cover to the overall form? If there is a spout, handle, and lid on the pot, how do these relate to each other,

as well as to the form? Some of these aesthetic questions will be looked at in the next essay, Proportion and Ratio, but in concert with the problems of aesthetics and function there are also some considerations of a purely technical nature.

Depending on their placement, handles and spouts are, to some extent, unsupported extremities. They are loops or thrusts of clay growing away from the basic form. If a clay is fired to a maturing point that approaches vitrification, or turning to glass, as most properly fired pottery clays do, the clay will soften and begin to sag and slump. At this point a combination of both pyroplastic deformation and the force of gravity takes over. If a spout is excessively long, and placed at a near horizontal angle, it will possibly begin to slump. The same thing is true of the excessively large or loopy handle. The basic principles here are similar to those in architecture, related to cantilevered structures. In the historical pots of many cultures, one notices supporting structures which hold the spout from drooping (see Figs. 5.8, 5.11, 5.12). There are two ways of resolving the possible problem of these drooping details, both of which are common in architecture, particularly in bridge design. The jutting section of the form is either supported from above, like a miniature suspension bridge, or has a wide base that forms a graceful self-supporting curve, similar to cantilevered bridges which have a solid base moving to a relatively thin center point.

The structure of a bowl also needs a self-supporting curve, or it may well collapse or deform. It is rather like a bridge, but upside down and in reverse. A bowl is usually marginally thicker in the center than at the outside edges. This thickness lends support to the curve, where the interior base flows into the walls with little or no perceptible angular articulation in the form. There is a clear flowing line, like a hemisphere, or half an ellipsoid. If the foot is improperly placed, the bowl may slump. If the structure is right it can support a huge form, as the trunk of a tree supports a framework that thins toward its edges.

The architecture of a dome is similar to the form of a lid, especially if the lid is quite wide. The shallower the dome, the less it will support itself. Domed forms have to be self-supporting or they will likely fall in. If they are not self-supporting, they have to have some form of buttress to absorb stresses and tensions. We don't often put buttresses on pots, but there are times when the pot itself performs the function of a buttress (Fig. 5.10). For example, casseroles often have handles on the sides and carry a lid. If an arched or domed lid sits on a gallery on the inside of a stoneware casserole, and is fired in place, the form of the pot will absorb much of the downward pressure that can occur as the clay softens and the lid begins to slump. Firing the lid in place does two things in actual fact: first, it stops the lid from slumping and, secondly, by being there, stops the likelihood of the pot warping into a slightly oval shape from the added side weight of the handles. It is much like a roof on a building which not only covers and protects whatever is inside, but also helps to stop the walls from falling

Fig. 5.2 Curvilinear forms in fruit and vegetables.

in or out! Roofs and lids are both details of their respective forms that we tend to take for granted, but to have a building that works and a lidded pot that functions well, these details need thorough consideration.

Gravity is the force that tends to pull all bodies in the earth's sphere toward the center of the earth. Combined with the effects of heat, it is responsible for most accidental deformation that occurs in a kiln, as the objects slump downward. Gravity is also the force to be reckoned with when one lifts and pours from a vessel such as a teapot. The volume of liquid contains a center of gravity. The placement of a handle can improve or impede the use of the teapot, and can radically alter the amount of strength needed to lift the pot and pour out the liquid. Handles on pots fulfill much the same func-

Fig. 5.3 Spiral forms in nature.

Fig. 5.4 The spiral.

tion as levers do in mechanics. They should make the object easier to use.

The principles of leverage as they relate to functional pottery apply primarily to objects that are to be poured from: pitchers, teapots, coffee pots, etc. If one makes a 2½″ cube of solid clay, it will weigh approximately 1 pound. To lift that cube requires no great strength or output of energy. However, if one were to put the cube on one end of a 12″ wooden ruler, and try to lift the ruler by only holding the opposite end, the apparent weight would seem to be many times the actual weight. If this principle is applied to a pouring vessel which in itself weighs only a little, it may seem to be far heavier than it actually is, and thus awkward to use.

In the great majority of cases, handles are placed on pouring vessels in such a way that energy needed to use the object is two or three times what is necessary, and therefore puts excessive strain on the user's wrist. If one takes any pouring vessel and looks at how far the center of the weight (also the center of gravity) is from the handle in a horizontal direction, one can easily judge how awkward that object will be in use. The center of gravity of a pouring vessel can easily be found by doing a small exercise. Make a small thin cardboard profile cutout of the object complete with handle, draw a vertical line from the center of the base to the center of the top (Fig. 5.13). Then take the cardboard form in the right hand and tilt it so that there is a vertical line from the bottom left part of the base, through to the center top part of the handle. Draw this line. Where the two lines cross (point A) is the center

Fig. 5.5 The double spiral.

of gravity, and also the point of balance. The further the handle is from the center of gravity, the more awkward the object is to pour from. Conversely, the closer the handle can be to the center of gravity, the easier it will be to use.

For maximum efficiency in use, the placement of handle and spout are subject to the following simple law: Find the center of gravity. Then draw a line from the center of the handle through the center of gravity to the extremity of the pot. The spout should be at right angles to this line for efficient leverage and, therefore, easy action.

A pouring vessel designed with these principles should pour freely by being hung on a finger or thumb with little wrist action being needed. If followed, this law will always enable liquid to be poured from a vessel without its appearing heavier than it actually is.

To what extent a potter may have to compromise his artistic concept of a pouring vessel by the use of such a law is a private decision. It becomes a balance between visual aesthetic and ease of function. With a great deal of thought devoted to the framework in which the potter has to operate, he or she can accommodate both. It is an interesting problem.

The forces of nature often have an unseen effect in our work, but if one can bear these effects in mind it will possibly help in the production of good work. Often when one has made something, one senses that there is something wrong, but it is difficult to put a finger on the problem. Analysis of both form and function will usually help to correct things. Most of the time, a potter works in isolation with only his or her own aesthetic sensitivity to fall back on. Our time of study is limited in various ways, and we are thrust into the world to do our work with a less than complete understanding of forces that control it. We make our own aesthetic decisions without the backup facility of a teacher to assist. Often, through limitation or lack of study, we feel intimidated by the work we want to do, and end up copying what somebody else has already done. Who is to say that the person copied is any more proficient than the copier? The clone is then at a point of double deficiency: first, a lack of his own creative input, and second, an inability to analyze what works. As the Chinese

Fig. 5.6 Curvilinear forms in architecture.

Fig. 5.7 Curvilinear forms in household objects.

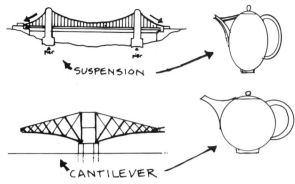

Fig. 5.8 Various methods of support.

Fig. 5.9 Thickening of lower curves supports weight and thrust of bowl.

Fig. 5.10 Lid acts as a buttress to hold form in place.

Fig. 5.11 Spouted pitcher, painted pottery. 8th century B.C., Iran. Height, 12". Courtesy of the Asian Art Museum of San Francisco: The Avery Brundage Collection.

Fig. 5.12 Olive oil jar, earthenware. Tunisia. Private collection.

Fig. 5.13 How one finds the center of gravity.

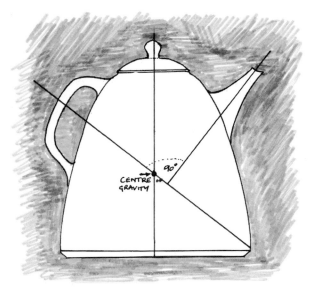

Fig. 5.14 The angle of the spout in relation to the handle and the center of gravity.

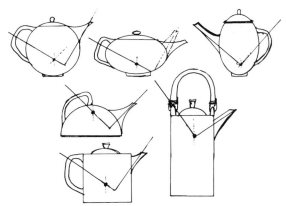

Fig. 5.15 The optimum placement of spouts and handles.

philosopher Confucius is reputed to have said in the sixth century B.C.:

The superior man knows what is right,
The inferior man knows only what sells.

The more that one becomes aware of the many concerns relevant to the making of functional pottery, the more one will develop an intuition and deep understanding of how things relate. If we learn to ask "why?" before "how?", we are well on the way to understanding the problems that we set for ourselves, and possibly becoming superior.

Pouring Forms:
An Historical Collection

Effigy bowl, vulture. Veracruz, Mexico. Courtesy of the Metropolitan Museum of Art: Michael C. Rockefeller Memorial Collection; purchase, Nelson A. Rockefeller Gift, 1961 (1978.412.81).

Jug. 17th Century A.D., England. Height, 22.5 cm. Courtesy of the Vancouver Museum: Department of Decorative & Applied Arts.

Ewer with bird's head spout; earthenware, black decoration under a turquoise glaze. Kashan, 12th–13th century A.D., Islamic. Height, 9¼". Courtesy of the Asian Art Museum of San Francisco: The Avery Brundage Collection.

Jug; handbuilt earthenware. ca. 1800 A.D., Mexico. Height, 21 cm. Courtesy of the Art Gallery of Greater Victoria: gift of A. H. Gordon.

Oinochoe (oil jug); unglazed earthenware. Possibly Cypriotic, 750–550 B.C., Greek. Height, 16.7 cm. Courtesy of the Brooklyn Museum.

Beak-spouted bottle. Middle Bronze Age, 2000–1500 B.C., Cyprus. Height, 36.7 cm. Courtesy of the Montreal Museum of Fine Arts.

Jue, earthenware. Late Shang dynasty, 13th–11th century B.C., China. Height, 4¾". Courtesy of the Asian Art Museum of San Francisco: The Avery Brundage Collection.

Left: Pitcher; salt-glazed stoneware. 18th–19th century A.D., England. Private collection.

Opposite: Double-gourd shaped bottle; porcelain, blue and white. 14th–15th Century, Annam. Height, 6". Courtesy of the Asian Museum of San Francisco: The Avery Brundage Collection.

Spouted bowl. Shigaraki, contemporary, Japan. Collection of the author.

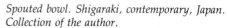

Ewer; porcellanous stoneware. Tang dynasty, 8th century A.D., China. Height, 9½". Courtesy of the Asian Art Museum of San Francisco: The Avery Brundage Collection.

Ewer; porcelain, celadon. Song dynasty, 11th–12th century A.D., China. Height, 9". Courtesy of the Asian Art Museum of San Francisco: The Avery Brundage Collection.

Ewer; green-glazed earthenware, lotus bud knob on lid. Liao dynasty, 907–1126 A.D., China. Height, 6¼". Courtesy of the Asian Art Museum of San Francisco: The Avery Brundage Collection.

Opposite: Phoenix headed ewer; porcellan stoneware. Probably 10th century A.D., C Height, 37.2 cm. Courtesy of the Brookly Museum: Frank L. Babbott and Ella C. Woodward Fund.

Ewer with lid; porcelain. Qingbai ware, Song dynasty, 12th–13th century A.D., China. Height, 6". Courtesy of the Asian Art Museum of San Francisco: The Avery Brundage Collection.

Chicken headed ewer; stoneware. Yue type ware, Six dynasties, 200–600 A.D., China. Height, 7". Courtesy of the Asian Art Museum of San Francisco: The Avery Brundage Collection.

Lusterware pitcher; earthenware. Staffordshire, early 19th century, England. Private collection.

Ewer; stoneware. Koryo, 14th century A.D., Korea. Height, 10¼". Courtesy of the Asian Art Museum of San Francisco: The Avery Brundage Collection.

Ewer; porcelain with enamel decoration. Imari ware, Edo period, 1615–1868 A.D., Japan. Height, 14.7 cm. Courtesy of the Montreal Museum of Fine Arts: Miss Adeline Van Horn Bequest.

Coffee pot and milk jug; porcelain. Capo di Monte style, ca. 1840–1880 A.D., Italy. Height, 17.8 cm. Courtesy of the Art Gallery of Greater Victoria: Gift of Mrs. Rosita Tovell.

Jug; soft paste porcelain. Worcester, ca. 1775, England. Height, 12.8 cm. Courtesy of the Art Gallery of Greater Victoria: Ann and Joseph Pearson Collection.

Sauce boat; soft paste porcelain. Worcester, ca. 1770, England. Courtesy of the Art Gallery of Greater Victoria.

Teapot with lid; soft paste porcelain. Worcester, ca. 1770–1780 A.D., England. Height, 17.5 cm. Courtesy of the Art Gallery of Greater Victoria: Ann and Joseph Pearson Collection.

*Jug; earthenware. Mycenean, 1400–1100 B.C.,
Greek. Height, 21.7 cm. Courtesy of the
Montreal Museum of Fine Arts: gift of
F. Cleveland Morgan.*

*Bridge-spouted jug; earthenware. Minoan,
2000–1800 B.C., Greek. Courtesy of the
Brooklyn Museum: loaned by Mr. and
Mrs. Thomas S. Brush.*

Jar with spout; earthenware. Near East, ca. 1000 B.C., Luristan. Height, 20.3 cm. Courtesy of the Montreal Museum of Fine Arts: gift of E. Rokhsar.

Cylindrical wine jar. Qing dynasty, Kangxi period, 1662–1722 A.D., China. Height, 16½". Courtesy of the Asian Art Museum of San Francisco: The Avery Brundage Collection.

Melon-shaped teapot; stoneware. Yixing ware, Ming dynasty, 1609 A.D., China. Height, 2⅝″. Courtesy of the Asian Art Museum of San Francisco: The Avery Brundage Collection.

Spouted jar; earthenware. Mesopotamia, 1200–600 B.C., Luristan. Height, 19.3 cm. Courtesy of the Montreal Museum of Fine Arts: gift of E. Rokhsar.

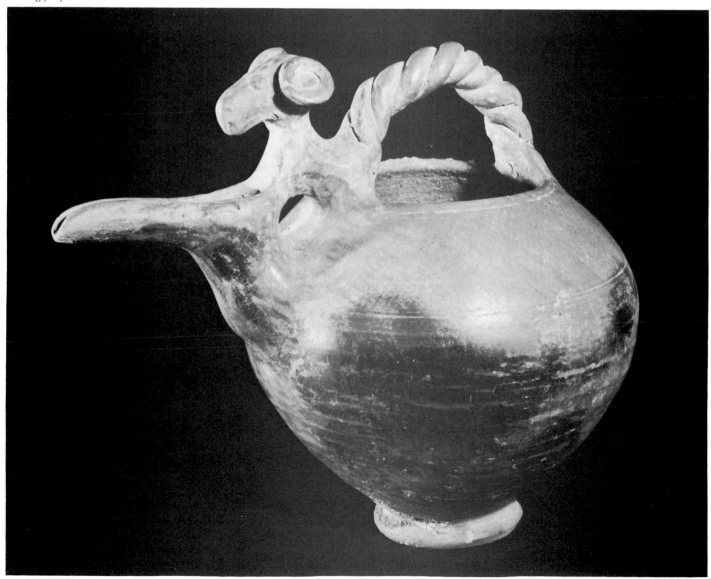

*Spouted pitcher; earthenware. ca. 10th century
B.C., Iran. Height, 6½". Courtesy of the Asian
Art Museum of San Francisco: The Avery
Brundage Collection.*

*Above: Spouted vessel; burnished grey earthen-
ware. ca. 1200 B.C., Iran. Height, 17.5 cm.
Courtesy, Museum of Fine Arts, Boston.*

Pair of covered ewers; hard paste porcelain. Meissen, ca. 1730 A.D., Germany. Courtesy of the George R. Gardiner Museum of Ceramic Art.

Teapot; tin glazed earthenware. London, early 18th century A.D., England. Courtesy of the George R. Gardiner Museum of Ceramic Art.

Teapot; hard paste porcelain. Meissen, ca. 1720, Germany. Courtesy of the George R. Gardiner Museum of Ceramic Art.

Spouted vessel in the form of a house; earthenware. Central Andes, Recuay, 100–300 A.D., Peru. Courtesy of the George R. Gardiner Museum of Ceramic Art.

Painted whistle vessel; earthenware. Central Andes, Lambayeque, 900–1250 A.D., Peru. Courtesy of the George R. Gardiner Museum of Ceramic Art.

Pitcher with feline spout; burnished earthenware. Mixtec, 1200–1500 A.D., Mexico. Courtesy of the George R. Gardiner Museum of Ceramic Art.

Owl vessel; burnished earthenware. Chimu culture, coastal Peru. The Fine Arts Museums of San Francisco: Gift of Herbert Fleishhacker.

Proportion and Ratio

Proportion is the power that brings out the smile on the face of things.

—*Le Corbusier*

The dictionary definitions of proportion and ratio are as follows:

Proportion: A portion or part in relation to the whole. The relation between things or magnitudes, as to size, quantity, numbers, etc. The relationship between parts or things, especially harmonious, proper, or desirable relationship; balance or symmetry.

Ratio: The relation between two similar magnitudes, in respect of quantity, determined by the number of times the one contains the other.

If one looks at an object from a long distance and one is unable to visually pick out the details of the object, the first thing that the eye and brain combine to do is to look at the ratio of height to width, and somehow relate these to previous experiences and ratios. As the brain does this shuffling act, it will ask itself what are the particular relationships that this object may have that can define what it is that the eyes are looking at. From previous experience the brain can tell whether the distant form is a house, car, person, sculpture, animal, or whatever else, by an unconscious process which recognizes ratios, proportions, or forms. We don't have to think about these ratios; they have become intuitive. As we look at the world around

us, we intuitively analyze ratios of one shape against another. This unconscious process occurs to us much more than we may realize. Concern with ratio and proportion has been a major preoccupation with philosophers, artists, architects, and mathematicians for at least two thousand years.

A famous Greek philosopher-mathematician named Eudoxus is said to have carried a walking stick with him, which he asked friends to visually divide into two parts at whatever point they sensed to be the most pleasing. Much to his satisfaction, the great majority of people chose a point at or close to the same place on the stick. From this he deduced that most people are spontaneously drawn to the same ratios.

This is a useful way of testing people's feeling for ratios. Ask a number of people to divide a line so that a pleasing relationship exists between the two parts. Figure 6.1 shows the results of such a test. The divisions are all at or very near the same point. If one averaged a large number of these divided lines, one would get the result in Fig. 6.2. The division of the line into two unequal parts finds that the ratio of the whole length to the longer part is the same as the ratio of the longer part to the shorter part. Most people find this to be a particularly happy division, where neither part is too large or too small. We can say that their relationship is harmonious. A division in the center would lack interest, and a division with one part very

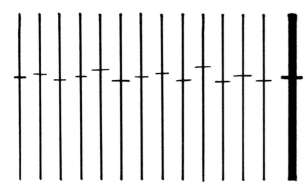

Fig. 6.1 The results of the line test.

Fig. 6.2 (Heavy bar at right) the average of the divided lines.

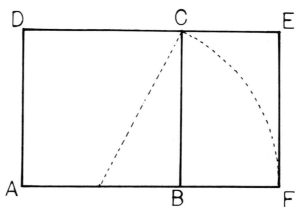

Fig. 6.4 The Most Favored or Golden Rectangle. To construct a Ø rectangle, take a square (A, B, C, D) at a halfway between A and B. Mark the center of an arc whose radius touches at point C. The arc will cut an extension of line AB at point F. Raise a perpendicular from point F to meet an extension of line CD at E. The rectangle A, F, E, D has a ratio of short to long sides of 1:1·618.

short and the other very long would be unbalanced.

A similar test, also dating back to classical Greek times, can be applied to rectangular shapes. A series of different rectangles are arranged as per Fig. 6.3, with their ratios marked beneath, i.e., 1:1 = a square, etc. People are then asked to choose the one which they feel is the most perfect shape, with the greatest harmony between the short and the long sides. With this test, an overwhelming number of people will pick one particular rectangle (G), or the immediate and very similar neighbors (F) or (H). If you compare the ratio of the short to the long sides of the rectangle, you will find it to be the same ratio as the two parts of our previously divided line. Unconsciously, it is also the ratio found between the top of a standing person's head and their navel, and from the navel to the ground. The pleasing proportions of the divided line and rectangle became basic to the development of Greek architecture and pottery of the period 550 to 350 B.C.

Another important mathematical feature which was developed for land surveying in Ancient Egypt, and possibly came from earlier cultures, was the use of a knotted cord to measure both length and surface. The cord had 12 equally spaced knots, probably a cubit apart. A cubit is the distance from the elbow to the end of the outstretched middle finger, more or less 18 to 20 inches. The cord is angled at the fourth and eighth knots, as in Fig. 6.5, and forms a right-angled triangle. The right-angle triangle and knotted cord ideas were taken back to Greece by a philosopher, mathematician, and olive oil tycoon named Thales of Miletus. He operated along the coasts of Asia Minor between 600 and 550 B.C., and in his travels came into contact with the old folklores of mathematics and astronomy. The Greeks at this period were a su-

Fig. 6.3 The test for the most pleasing rectangle.

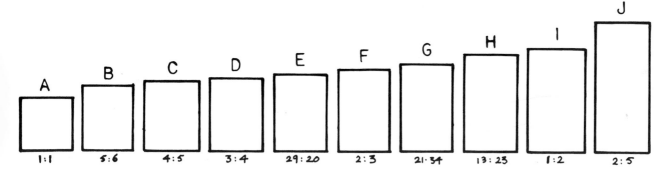

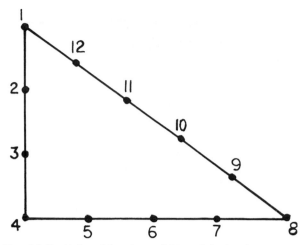

Fig. 6.5 Knotted cord forming a right-angled triangle.

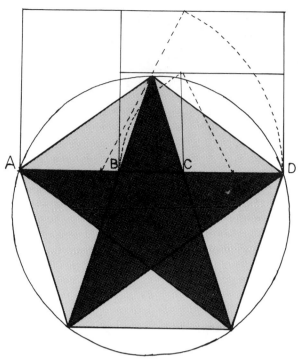

Fig. 6.6 Geometric shapes containing Golden Mean relationships. The pentagon, or five-sided figure, a Greek holy symbol, and the pentacle or five-pointed star—a symbol used in magic. All relationships can be expressed by Ø. It is easy to see why the Greeks thought the pentagon a perfect shape.

premely logical group, and the knotted cord with its right-angled triangle became the focal point of an endlessly fascinating series of geometrical forms and relationships, explored and debated by such men as Pythagorus, Eudoxus, and later, Euclid. During this time, some of the world's finest architecture was built using simple geometry as a base. The science of arithmetic, with addition, subtraction, division, and multiplication, was not developed until some time later.

Back to the line and rectangle. If you compare the two parts of the divided line, or the two sides of the most favored rectangle, you would find that the longer is approximately 1·618 times as long as the shorter. In other words, the ratio between them is 1:1·618. About the year 300 B.C., Euclid, the father of modern geometry, first noticed many interesting qualities about the number 1·618. Since then, it has always been considered to be an important number, and mathematicians have given it the name Ø, pronounced fie. The Artists of the Renaissance called it the Divine Proportion. Not only did the Greeks use the Ø proportion rectangle or Golden Rectangle for their architecture, but they also used the Pentagon, which contains a number of Ø relationships, as a holy symbol. This fascinating number which is also known as the Golden Mean, Golden Section, Golden Ratio, Golden Number, or Golden Rule, is also a significant factor in the living world. We find that natural organisms, including the human body, contain an astounding number of Ø re-

lationships. In preferring proportions based on Ø we are therefore following natural laws. It is these natural laws which create intuitive preference for pleasing forms and relationships.

Architects, artists, musical composers, and craftsmen have always sought to establish pleasing relationships in their works, some of which can be expressed by ratios. Plans and drawings of the architecture of the past show how preoccupied architects have always been with the problem of ratio, not only of the overall shape of a building, but also of the smaller shapes within it. They considered the ratios of doors and windows, and related them to the ratios of the outside walls. They also calculated the height, length, and width of each room in relation to one other. A building was a complicated system of ratios. In order to make it possible to arrive at a pleasing set of proportions, they often related their measurements to Ø. In many cases they found Ø by instinct, as many people do in the line and rectangle tests mentioned earlier. In other cases all the relationships were worked

Fig. 6.7 *The width of the widest part is equal to one-third the height. The top and base are two-thirds the width of the shoulder. Lekythos, Greece. Height, 28 cm. Courtesy of the Montreal Museum of Fine Arts: Gift of Miss Mabel Molson.*

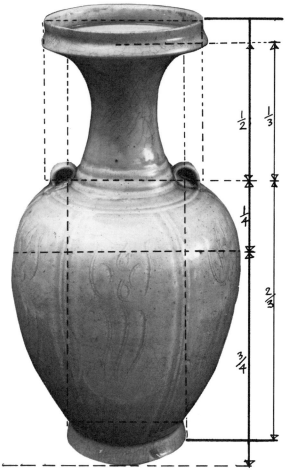

Fig. 6.8 *The width of the top is equal to the height of the neck. The width beneath the lip is equal to the width of the foot. The width of the form where the foot joins is half the width of the widest part. The widest part is approximately half of the height. Vase, porcellaneous stoneware, China. Courtesy of the Montreal Museum of Fine Arts.*

out mathematically. In this way they created structures whose ratios were related to each other and, through $\emptyset$, to the living world.

As stated earlier, mathematics and living things are closely related, and numbers related to living things have often been thought to have magic powers. The number 1·618 or $\emptyset$ is one of those numbers. Another series of numbers which has a close con-

nection to $\emptyset$ is this: 1, 1, 2, 3, 5, 8, 13, 21, 34, 55, 89, 144, etc. This series is called the *summation* series, since each succeeding number is the sum of the two which precede it. It is also known as the Fibonacci series, after Leonardo (Fibonacci) da Pisa (1170–1250 A.D.), the mathematician who first used it. There are a number of interesting things about this series. If you examine the ratios between any number in the series and the preceding one, 34 and 21 for example, and work out their ratio by dividing the higher number by the lower, 34 ÷ 21 = 1·619. If one repeats this with higher numbers in the series, 144 ÷ 89 = 1·6179. You will notice that the higher you go in the summation series, the closer the ratio will be to the Golden Mean of $\emptyset$. Mathematicians know that however high you go in the series, $\emptyset$ is never reached exactly, but is remarkably close and consistent. The summation series is not just an interesting series of numbers. As with $\emptyset$, these numbers are closely related to nature, and are found in an uncanny and infinite number of places.

If one looks at plants such as daisies, chrysanthemums, pyrethrums, sunflowers, and fir cones, it quickly becomes obvious that there are spiral patterns. In fact there are two sets of spirals, one in one direction and one in the other. The number of petals, sepals, or seeds differ from one spiral to the other, but almost always relate to the adjacent numbers of the Fibonacci series. In a pyrethrum you will usually find 21 right-hand spirals, and 34 left-hand spirals. In sunflowers, different varieties will have combinations of 34 and 55 spirals, 55 and 89 spirals, or even 89 and 144. A fir cone has sets of 5 and 8, a daisy 13 and 21, and a small flower like a ranunculus or buttercup has 2 spirals in one direction and 3 in the other.

All these numbers are part of the summation series, which, as explained earlier, is closely connected to the Golden Ratio $\emptyset$. We can see that many of the relationships that we could previously only sense, can in fact be expressed and measured in mathematical terms. Nature is a logical system, and only a study of mathematics will reveal certain of its secrets.

The Golden Mean is not the only proportionate system used by man, of course. There are various others, the most recently developed one being the Modular System of Swiss architect Le Corbusier. This is a system of ratios designed for the practice of architecture. However, all systems have some similarity to either the Golden Mean or the Fibonacci series. Perhaps the most obvious of these systems is that used in the traditional architecture of Japan, where the controlling module for the size of rooms, and ultimately the size of buildings, is the *tatami* or floor mat. The tatami is considered as the space needed for a person to live in—making man the module. A tatami is a mat made of rice straw, always measuring 3 shaku by 6 shaku. A *shaku* is approximately 12 inches. As you will notice, the mat has a ratio of 1:2, found early in the summation series. The size of the mat controls the room size, and consequently one finds rooms sized as 3 mat, 4 mat, $4\frac{1}{2}$ mat, 6 mat, and so on. Figure 6.10 shows how these mats would be placed. This controlling module has the effect of giving the rooms and buildings great harmony, similar to the harmony seen and felt in the great buildings of Classical Greece, such as the Parthenon and Erechtheon in Athens. Greek architecture is an attempt to create an image that, like Greek poetry, music, or ceramics, expresses the idea that proportion is one of the highest values of human life.

In the pottery of both ancient Greece and Japan, although outwardly the absolute antithesis of each other, we can find strong mathematical relationships. To a large extent, the pottery associated with ancient Athens, generally called Attic pottery, was conceived and made according to preordained mathematical proportions and ratios. These were the same ratios that controlled the architecture and were based on the Golden Mean. The harmony between the building and the objects used in the building must have been quite delightful since they related to each other, and also to the users, as they were derived from mathematical principles based on the form of man. The elegance and sophistication of aristocratic Greek life was also related to both the drawings on the pottery, and the frescoes and relief sculpture that adorned the palaces.

In Japan, unlike Greece, any mathematical relationship between pots and architecture is much more complex to discover. However, it is there, and is a subject which could do with a good deal of research.

To really understand these relationships it is necessary to understand much of the background of Japanese aesthetics, particularly coming from the religions of Zen Buddhism and Shintoism. These are the two main faiths of Japan. They both relate closely to natural laws, and most people relate to both faiths, and through them to a love and deep intuitive appreciation of nature. Shintoism looks after birth and life, while Zen looks after death and afterlife. Zen is a derivation from Chinese Buddhism, brought to Japan in the eighth or ninth century A.D. Gardens, flowers and rocks were part of the meditative aspects of Chinese Buddhism. With

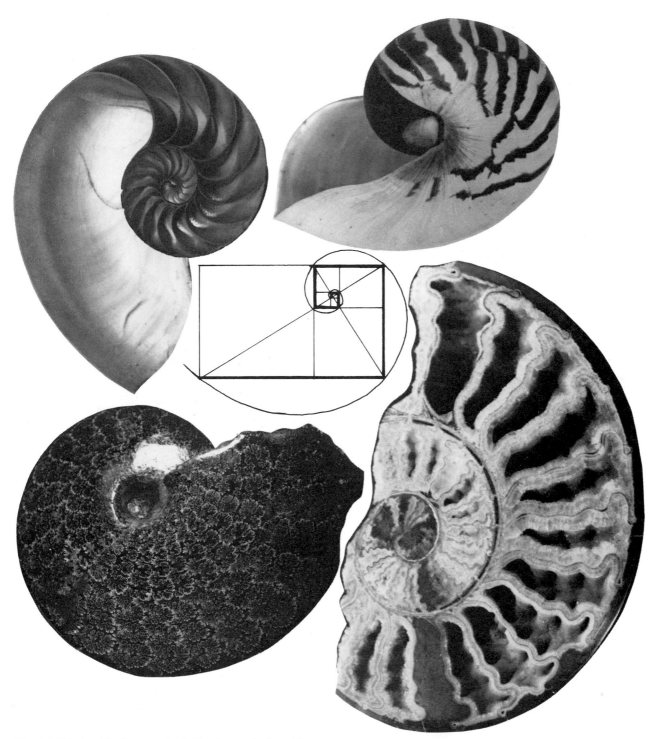

Fig. 6.9 Relationships between the Golden Rectangle, logarith-mic spiral, chambered nautilus, and ammonites.

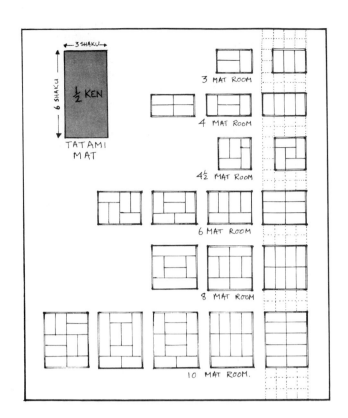

Fig. 6.10 Placement of tatami mats in traditional Japanese architecture.

Fig. 6.11 Classical forms in Greek architecture and pottery.

the growth of Zen Buddhism, particularly in the fourteenth to sixteenth centuries, garden making developed as a powerful art form. Although it appears to be quite natural, the Japanese temple or shrine garden is actually a heavily manicured and mathematically organized space. The placement of rocks is part of a geometric outline, usually equilateral or right-angle triangles. They are generally placed in groupings of three or five. Both shapes and numbers should be quite familiar. The overall effect is one of peace and harmony.

This harmony is further noted in the development of the teahouse and tea ceremony, *cha-no-yu*. The Japanese tea ceremony is the ritual celebration of the simple joys of life. This ritual evolved from the traditions of Zen Buddhism, which teaches the value of limits by the discovery of "greatness in little things" (Okakura, *The Book of Tea*). It is a meditative process, bound up with natural law, that recognizes and worships the imperfect, purposely leaving something unfinished for the play of the imagination to complete. Teahouses are usually set in gardens, often with wall openings or windows which give a tantalizing partial view of the garden. The relationship of inside and outside is very important here. Bringing the outside in brought about the Japanese styles of floral arrangement. Originating as altar offerings in the temples, floral art contained many symbolic meanings in various geometrical relationships. The flower containers probably had a mathematical relationship to the space in which they were used, as did the utensils of the ceremony, creating an extraordinary harmony within the small space of the teahouse. The teabowl had a special relationship with both the space and the user. The teahouse combination of objects of beauty and natural simplicity, in a space of harmonic relationships, with the peace and serenity of a meditative process, must have given the Samurai warriors of the Feudal Lords a sense of total tranquility and thusness before battle. It does much the same for businessmen today, and there is still the same reverence for beautiful objects being used in this way.

The Tatami mat module has a relationship of 1:2. This is the same ratio as the standard 8' × 4' sheet of wallboard, plasterboard, or plywood that are in use today as the basic forms of interior wall

Fig. 6.12 Flower vase, stoneware. Edo period, 1615–1868 A.D., Japan. Height, 25.1 cm. Courtesy of the Art Gallery of Greater Victoria: Fred and Isabel Pollard Collection.

covering. To some extent, this is the module which has standardized much of the world's contemporary domestic architecture. Standard ceilings are 8' high, for example. For economic use, both of the material and the time used in cutting and fitting,

Fig. 6.13 Bowl, stoneware. 18th century, Japan. Height, 18.5 cm. Courtesy of the Art Gallery of Greater Victoria: Gift of Mrs. T. C. Davis.

rooms and buildings are often designed with this module in mind. In theory we should have much better-looking house architecture that we actually do, since the module has a harmonic relationship.

It would be an interesting exercise to make pots which were designed to fit into contemporary architecture, using pleasing proportional systems, as the Greeks and Japanese did. Most urban living environments are a clutter of unrelated forms, since they are a combination of what is available for a given purpose, but with little continuity. They have little or none of the serenity that seems necessary to and compatible with a busy life away from the home, be it fighting battles or doing business. If the relationship between objects and environment could be made more harmonious, it might well have a very beneficial effect on the psyche of the people who use them. This is not necessarily an impossible limitation on aesthetic choice. In music the composer has only a limited scale of notes of predetermined value, but the possible configurations within these limits is almost infinite.

So what do all these proportionate systems have to do with making functional pottery? One can look at this in three ways. First, the object itself. All three-dimensional forms have a relationship of height to depth to width, even in the simplest thrown cylinder. As soon as one alters the form by any articulation or movement, one alters the basic proportions, and thus the relationship between one part and another. When one adds spouts, lids, handles, and feet, the relationship becomes more and more complex, and the proportion between the parts of the object, in conjunction with the basic form, becomes the power that makes that object pleasing or otherwise. Secondly, we must be aware of the proportion of the object, in relation to its function. Some objects need to be big and some need to be small. Thirdly, one can look at the object in relation to other objects, as well as to the space in which it will serve its function.

Figures 6.12 through 6.16 show forms where a particular proportion has been developed both for visual and functional ends. The considerations of proportion in conjunction with the physical feel when holding the form can add immeasurably to the qualities that any object may have.

To suggest conformity to any particular pattern of ratio and proportion would seem to suggest sameness; it does not. By having an awareness of proportion, and its relationship to the work that we do, and to the environments that will house our works, we can and do enhance the quality of the surroundings and, by extension, the quality of life. Although a pot with a good form and pro-

Fig. 6.15 *Stem bowl, stoneware. ca. 1810, Japan. Height, 14.5 cm. Courtesy of the Art Gallery of Greater Victoria: Fred and Isabel Pollard Collection.*

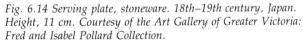

Fig. 6.14 *Serving plate, stoneware. 18th–19th century, Japan. Height, 11 cm. Courtesy of the Art Gallery of Greater Victoria: Fred and Isabel Pollard Collection.*

portion isn't necessarily more efficient than a bad one, it is certainly infinitely more pleasant to live with.

As Sir Herbert Read stated in his book, *The Origins of Form in Art:*

> *What I am searching for, in conclusion, is some formula that would combine individual initiative with universal values, and that combination would give us a truly organic form. Form, which we discover in nature by analysis, is obstinately mathematical in its manifestations—which is to say that creation in art requires thought and deliberation. But this is not to say that form can be reduced to a formula. In every work of art it must be recreated, but that too is true of every*

work of nature. Art differs from nature not in its organic form, but in its human origins: in the fact that it is not God or a machine that makes a work of art, but an individual with his instincts and intuitions, with his sensibility and his mind, searching relentlessly for the perfection that is neither in mind nor in nature, but in the unknown. I do not mean this in an other-worldly sense, only that the form of the flower is unknown to the seed.

Fig. 6.16 Analysis of functional objects made by the author.

Pots and Anatomy

Functional pottery is made for people to use and many potters feel that the pot isn't complete until it is physically used for its job. If it is to do its job totally, it should be efficient, easy to use, comfortable in the hands, and give pleasure to the user at the same time. One should consider how it is to be used and what parts of the human anatomy will be in contact with it for optimum satisfaction on all counts. Judging by a large volume of pottery that one finds in the marketplace, a great number of potters and pottery manufacturers seldom consider the anatomy of the user when making their wares.

Figures 7.1 through 7.3 show X-rays and photographs of the human head and hands. These are the parts of the body that generally come into contact with utilitarian pottery. Showing photographs of how objects may relate to the human frame isn't nearly as good as testing it on oneself, to find what may or may not be comfortable in use. Just how does a cup, mug, or goblet rim feel between the lips? How does a handle feel? How many fingers fit comfortably between the handle and the body of the object? How many fingers are needed to comfortably lift the object without any undue strain? Would the handle be better if it were curved in another way?

MOUTHS, LIPS, AND NOSES

Most forms of eating and drinking vessels come in touch with the mouth and lips. The lips are fleshy muscular tissue covered with a highly sensitive thin skin. They are particularly sensitive to objects being placed between them. The surface quality, thickness, curvature and width of the object are all sensed very quickly, and an instant reaction of pleasure or displeasure is sent to the brain. Ultimately the interpretation of this message might mean the difference between a piece that is enjoyed or one that is avoided.

The shapes and sizes of mouths are infinitely variable, but basically consist of two lips, the upper one of which generally protrudes slightly more than the lower. The distance from the bottom of the upper lip to the bridge of the nose averages 3" to $3\frac{1}{2}$". In between, of course, comes the nose. The sizes and shapes of noses also vary infinitely. If one is to make comfortable drinking vessels, this distance is an important consideration. If the opening of the vessel is more or less than 3" to $3\frac{1}{2}$", it will probably feel awkward in use. If it is larger than this dimension, the rim will probably force the mouth into an uncomfortably wide shape, causing it to dribble. At the same time, it will probably

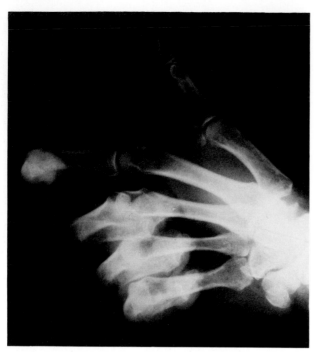

Fig. 7.1 Anatomy of the hand.

touch the lower part of the forehead when the object is tilted to its fullest point for drinking. If the vessel is less than the above dimension, it may feel awkward to both the lips and nose at the same time.

FINGERS, HANDS, WRISTS, ELBOWS, AND SHOULDERS

The joints of the arms are pivot points, which come into action whenever an object is lifted or tilted. The shoulder and elbow basically work like ball and socket joints, with only a limited amount of flexibility. The wrist is like a universal joint and can go in a variety of directions. The knuckles are like small ball and socket joints, limited in movement by the web of skin between the fingers. The finger joints are like small hinges. The combination of differently engineered joints gives the arm a wonderfully complex range of possible movements.

If everybody conformed to a set pattern, and the width and length of fingers were constant, it would be easy to design objects which served the needs of all. It would also be very boring! Part of

Fig. 7.2 Finger/mug fit.

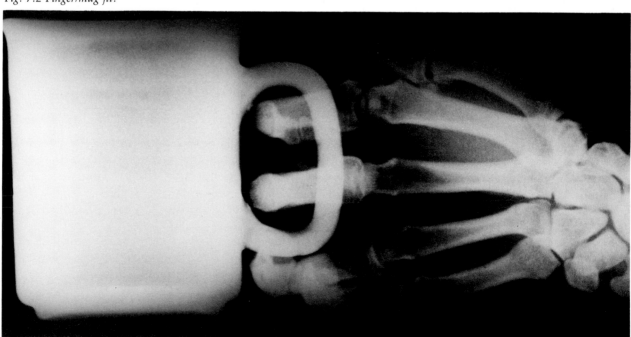

the great challenge of making pottery for use is to make things which can satisfy either the individual, or the masses.

The way that hands are used in the lifting and holding of objects varies from person to person, depending on the length and thickness of the fingers, the strength of both fingers and wrist and, to some extent, the cultural background of the user. The finger is made of three parts, with two joints within its length from the knuckle. The thumb has two parts, and one joint within its length. When the fingers or thumb are bent, the muscles on the inner part of the finger are compressed to half, or less, of their normal length. In many fine-quality, generally industrially produced cups, the handle is made in such a way as to make it impossible to get a finger through, necessitating a pinching action between the forefinger and thumb, with the middle finger supporting beneath. Most potters usually make handles where at least one finger goes through the aperture between handle and pot. The thickness of the thickest part of an average forefinger is approximately 1 inch. For a cup or mug to contain hot liquid, and not burn the finger holding the handle, the space between the finger and the body of the pot need be no more than $\frac{1}{4}''$, or a total space of $1\frac{1}{4}''$ from the inside of the handle to the body of the vessel. Although this might change slightly depending on the shape of the object, it won't change much. An excessively large handle is likely to feel awkward in use, as there will probably be too much lateral movement to feel totally secure. The forefinger is used most often for picking up and holding cups and mugs. Since the finger is in a crooked or bent state, a handle that is excessively wide or thick will also feel awkward.

For objects larger than drinking vessels, the placement and spacing of handles is equally crucial, since it also concerns leverage (see Forms and Forces). The human wrist is one of the more fragile parts of our anatomy, being made up of a number of interlocking, moveable bones. The angles that it has to operate at, and the weights it has to carry or move, make it quite vulnerable in use, and comparatively easy to damage. Pots, becoming excessively heavy with their contents, should be carefully balanced so that they can be made as easy as possible to pick up or to pour from. A liter of water

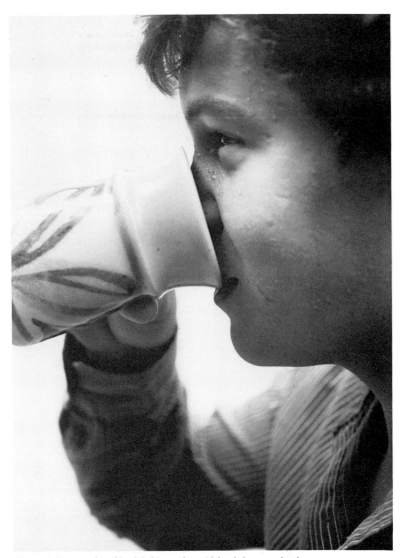

Fig. 7.3 For comfortable drinking, the width of the mouth of a drinking vessel should be no more than the distance from the lips to the bridge of the nose.

weighs 2 pounds, 2 ounces, or 1000 grams. An average pitcher with enough capacity to contain a liter of water will itself weigh about the same as the liquid. The total combined weight of pitcher and water will therefore be a minimum of 4 pounds, 4 ounces, or 2000 grams. If the handle of the pitcher juts out at an excessive distance from the center of gravity, the apparent weight will be considerably more than the actual weight, as discussed in the leverage test, page 63. This could cause a severe strain to the wrist, and be very uncomfortable in use.

Fig. 7.4 *Varying hand positions in holding a goblet. The form is designed with comfortable variations in mind.*

Elbows and shoulders act as pivot points, raising and lowering the wrist to a point where it can most efficiently do the job required. In the lifting of some heavy weights, both arms, as well as the pectoral and stomach muscles, may come into use. This is often the case when lifting a large family casserole from a hot oven. The more easily the user can grip the object, the less strain is put on the individual parts of the anatomy. It is particularly important with hot kitchen utensils, since, in addition to the heat and weight factors, there is also a likelihood of the pot being somewhat greasy and slippery.

EARS

One might not think of the ears as having much of a role in the function of pottery. However, sound is quite important to many people. We can all remember the sound of a teacher screeching chalk or fingernails down a chalkboard to get our attention. It is a sound which, even in memory, sends shivers down the spine. There are many sounds which can do this, and some of them are found in pottery.

The type and surface of glazes or clay bodies that might be selected for use may bring about abrasive sounds. Some pots have pleasant ringing sounds and some have dull thuds. The oriental user of a pot often flicks it before use to hear its voice. Sometimes it sings, sometimes it whispers, and sometimes it moans. When one cuts food on some surfaces there is often an unpleasant sound, and the same is true of some unglazed surfaces in contact with each other.

All of these things may seem excessively fastidious, but they are questions which concern a great number of pottery buyers and users to some extent. Any concern that a buyer may have is likely to be a legitimate one, and listening to these concerns might just help us to make better pots.

1 Are the top rims and the edges of the handles sharp to the touch for either lips or fingers?
2 Is the curvature at the top of a drinking vessel suitable for drinking from? Does it curve in, or out, or is it straight up?
3 Is the shape of the object suitable to be held or drunk from?

4 Does the handle have sufficient room for fingers?

5 Does the handle fit the hand, or do the fingers have to conform to the handle?

6 Is it balanced?

7 Does the shape of the pot need handles to fulfill its intended use?

8 Does the sound or texture of the surface aggravate the user?

9 Does the object as designed get too hot to hold?

10 Could it work better and be more comfortable to use than it is?

Lidded Forms:
An Historical Collection

Honey jar with lid; stoneware. Yi dynasty,
19th century A.D.*, Korea. Height, 8¼". Cour-*
tesy of the Brooklyn Museum: lent by
Robert T. Anderson.

Hes vase with cover; Faience. 2500 B.C., Tomb of Tutankhamen, Egypt. Height, 20.5 cm. Courtesy of the Brooklyn Museum: Charles Edwin Wilbour Fund.

Pyxis (cosmetic box). Attic, 465–460 B.C., Greece. Courtesy of the Metropolitan Museum of Art: Rogers Fund, 1907 (07.286.36).

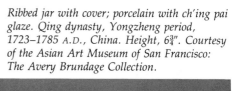

Ribbed jar with cover; porcelain with ch'ing pai glaze. Qing dynasty, Yongzheng period, 1723–1785 A.D., China. Height, 6¾". Courtesy of the Asian Art Museum of San Francisco: The Avery Brundage Collection.

Ribbed covered jar; porcelain, celadon glazed. Longquan, 14th century A.D., China. Height, 8.2 cm. Private collection.

Deep bowl with cover; porcellanous stoneware. 14th century A.D., Vietnam. Height, 14 cm. Private collection.

Lidded jar with lotus knob; earthenware with blue lead glaze. Tang dynasty, 8th century A.D., China. Height, 25.9 cm. Courtesy of the Montreal Museum of Fine Arts: gift of F. Cleveland Morgan.

Covered urn with miniature stupa knob; stoneware. Great Silla dynasty, 8th–9th century A.D., Korea. Height, 10". Courtesy of the Asian Art Museum of San Francisco: The Avery Brundage Collection.

Large, deep bowl with cover. Ming dynasty, 16th–17th century A.D., China. Height, 20 cm. Private collection.

Ewer with knob in the form of a peony or lotus; stoneware. Koryo dynasty, 918–1392 A.D., Korea. Height, 17.6 cm. Courtesy of the Brooklyn Museum: gift of Mrs. Darwin R. James III.

Vase with four looped handles; porcelain inlaid, with celadon glaze over. Koryo dynasty, 12th–13th century A.D., Korea. Height, 8". Courtesy of the Asian Art Museum of San Francisco: The Avery Brundage Collection.

Opposite: Altar jar; porcelain. Song dynasty, ca. 11th century A.D., China. Height, 9½" Courtesy of the Asian Art Museum of San Francisco.

Tripod vessel with cover; knob decorated with a head wearing an elaborate headdress. Mayan, 400–600 A.D., probably Quatemala. Height, 24.5 cm. Courtesy of the Brooklyn Museum: The Francis Pratt Fund.

Lidded bowl with bird's head knob; burnished earthenware. Mixtec, 250–550 A.D., Mexico. Courtesy of the George R. Gardiner Museum of Ceramic Art.

Bowl with cover in the form of a tower; tin-glazed earthenware with luster. Venice, late 15th century, Italy. Courtesy of the George R. Gardiner Museum of Ceramic Art.

8

Roots, Growth, Rhythm, and Balance

ROOTS

Roots are the part of a plant that lie unseen, holding it in position, drawing nourishment from the soil, and storing it. Roots are also ancestors, those who have gone before. For most potters both of these meanings have great validity. As artists and craftsmen, we have all grown from somewhere, and the combined experiences that have emotionally moved us in some way become part of the structural network that supports, nourishes, and makes us do the things we do.

In the last few essays, I have tried to put together some of the aspects which have concerned many cultures about the making of pottery, art, and architecture. In Part One, I outlined some of the growth and development that has occurred in worldwide pottery since it was first developed. Now comes the delicate task of trying to draw together from this mass of possible visual stimulus the way that one finds one's own direction in this incredibly complex discipline.

One of the first things to realize is that making pottery is a rigorous discipline, demanding constant and continuous effort to grow and develop. There are few short cuts. Development goes on through life, sometimes in major strides, sometimes with almost imperceptible movement. It is probably the most frustrating of the art disciplines, being an amalgam of art and science, sculpture and

painting, and form and surface. To survive as a potter, one needs to be an artist, craftsman, businessperson, carpenter, laborer, chemist, technician, pyromaniac, fireman, artisan and innovator—in all, a thoroughly practical person. Pottery making is a discipline that, once one is thoroughly hooked on, is like an addiction and almost impossible to separate from. At the same time, it can be seductive, sensuous, and so hedonistically satisfying as to occasionally make one feel pangs of guilt. The joy of making useful objects that please the senses out of seemingly formless and inert clay is hard to adequately describe. Those who do it well are seldom financially successful in the way that "success" is usually measured in a money-oriented society. But looking at the overall quality of life, they are rich beyond measure. However one evaluates success, there is really nothing that I have found in life that gives me as much satisfaction as the practice of being a potter. Most potters that I know from various countries around the world wouldn't voluntarily change their vocation for anything else.

Relatively "new" countries, such as Canada, Australia, South Africa, New Zealand and the United States, have few long-term indigenous pottery traditions beyond a small number of aboriginal ones. The societal makeup of these countries is an amalgamation of different cultural and ethnic groups from many parts of the world. During the pioneer-

Fig. 8.1 Unity.

ing period, little time was available for the niceties of life, such as the arts. Life itself was a process of survival, and in this process the arts took a place of little immediate importance. The net result of many generations with a very limited experience of the arts tends to be cultural starvation, and a resultant quest for individual identity. How different this is from many countries of the Orient, Europe, the Middle East and Islam, where ongoing ceramic traditions have developed over hundreds, if not thousands, of years. It is like a huge tap root of steady growth and intermittent flowering.

The contemporary potter in "new" countries often feels rootless and at a loss for a source of meaningful inspiration and personal growth. We are bombarded with visual stimuli through books, magazines, television, and so on, to the point that excessive confusion of the senses tends to obliterate clear vision of the directions we should take. The net result of this bombardment is often immersion into alien or exotic cultures for sources of stimulation, as an alternative to the natural growth coming from things of the potter's immediate environment, experience, and local needs, which it always did in the past. In some ways this rootlessness is healthy, forcing the potter to evaluate the self, and to make decisions based on his or her own indi-

vidual aesthetic, while developing it at the same time. This is particularly the case with people having a strong individual identity. For others, rootlessness may lead to a dependence on eclecticism, picking little bits from various places and sandwiching them together with little knowledge of or consideration for their origins or their relevance.

GROWTH

The development of a personal statement in any form of pottery making usually comes with a long and thorough immersion in the mechanics of the craft, and a tightly selective view of those stimuli that spiritually move one. Thorough discipline gives the skills needed to enable freedom of expression, so that one is not bound up with the "how-to," and can concern oneself with the "why-to." It is like the musician who practices endless scales and arpeggios, without which he cannot make music. If we are to "make music" in our clay works, an understanding of form, functions, details, and variations is our equivalent of the musician's scales and arpeggios. Without them, our compositions are amorphous and limp.

Discipline can be its own form of stimulus, through the gradual control that is gained from experience. It encourages a natural security, much as a child progresses from lying to walking, through a series of known and expected learning processes. For the potter, it is not until the equivalent of the child's running stage that one begins to feel the confidence that one is not going to fall over, and make a fool of oneself. As with a child running, the concern usually tends to be not with the likelihood of taking a fall, but with getting somewhere fast. It usually takes a child two-and-a-half to three years of constant daily effort, through every waking moment, to become confident enough to run. If the child wants to become an athlete, or a dancer, it takes many more years of rigorous training and practice to reach a peak. There are parallels here, since the time and effort needed to reach any peak as an artist is much the same as the period from infancy to athlete—approximately fifteen years. There are a few precocious developers, but not many. For most it is a hard slog to get to the point of being able to dance.

Part of the path to understanding oneself, and to developing a strong personal root structure, lies in learning how to discern and use visual stimuli. This can come from any source: natural forms, mathematics, architecture, periods in history, tin cans, engineering, or anything else. The important thing is that the stimulus sparks the imagination in such a way as to open new doors to making objects. One can call it inspiration or whatever one wishes, but it boils down to the same equation: stimulus and response. Without stimulus of some kind, the work is likely to be either stagnant or plagiaristic.

Many potters who have developed particularly strong visions of design or new concepts in work, suffer through the slavish plagiarism which seems rampant in potting circles. What usually happens is this: A potter studies and works for years to develop something which is his or her own personal statement. No matter what the original stimulus, the response is to develop a personal idiom based on an individual search. The new vision is most likely an amalgamation of various stimuli which fuse together in the maker's brain and, through a period of considerable gestation, emerges in its new metamorphosed state. This new state will probably have taken that maker months if not years to arrive at. Much of this growth and development occurs unconsciously, but the final statement is a very personal digestion of whatever stimuli has affected him. Through exposure in books, magazines, and often in workshops and demonstrations, the potter's work becomes widely known, and often the source of stimulus for others. If the original work has a strong personal style, this can unfortunately lead to many feeble and insipid copies. The copiers understand neither the full growth of the original, nor the potter's digestion of the stimulus that is the basis of his work.

Copying the styles of well-known clayworkers brings about a sort of ceramic kleptomania, which inevitably leads to debasement. If one is influenced or inspired by any contemporary artist, to the point of wishing to emulate that person's work, it is best to find out what the stimulus was that gave that person his or her new vision. If one looks back to the source material, whatever it may be, one is less likely to become a clone and to develop in a parallel yet different way. No person is the same as another, yet there is a vast sameness about much of the pottery being produced today. If one is cognizant of the work being done around the world, it becomes obvious that there are few originals but many clones.

Not only is the work of well-known individuals copied, but also well-known styles from other countries and cultures. Throughout the western and southern hemispheres, for about fifty years, there has been a heavy concentration of Orientalia—slavish imitation of the work done in various cultures of Asian countries. More often than not, the perpetrators of these imitations are aware of neither the qualities of the objects that they imitate, nor of the cultural significance behind them. Real oriental pots can be wonderful and valuable, but the copies, most often, are insipid and valueless. How out-of-place are the quasi-oriental country pottery objects produced by caucasian urban-living clayworkers. The originals relate to their environment, have strength, power, and an inner beauty: the copies are merely a pastiche with little or no meaning.

The contemporary studio potter who delves into his own inner feelings to find out what it is that excites his visual imagination will likely produce work which has honesty and integrity. True style cannot be forced. It is the result of an intense searching and personal analysis, much of which will probably be intuitive. When fully developed it will have harmony, rhythm, and balance.

RHYTHM

All organisms have rhythm, whether it be the cycle of birth to death, or any movements and heartbeats along the way. Once a potter's root structure is established, he or she goes through a series of growth and flowering cycles, which are themselves influenced or controlled by other rhythms. These are cycles of nature, life itself, personal biological rhythms, and rhythms of work, from preparing clay, shaping it, firing, glazing, decorating, glaze firing, to the eventual selling. Each has a rhythm and cycle of its own.

Part of being a potter lies in balancing the purely practical with the purely aesthetic. Our concerns on one hand are form, function, technique, and economic survival. These are constants. On the other hand, surface, color, vision, and intent are variables. Many of these aspects flow from the rhythm of various phases of the work, each of which plays an important role. It would be good if we could ignore some of the cycles, such as the economic ebb and flow, but it too has its effect on what we do, and how and why we do it. The degree to which any potter subjugates himself to that particular rhythm is an individual concern. Many concern themselves heavily with the financial aspects of making, usually to the detriment of the work itself. To work to the extent of one's capability and at the same time grow and flourish, one has to adapt one's own rhythm in order to strike one's own balance.

BALANCE

Balance is the point of equilibrium where stimulus, analysis, and concern is matched by skill, imagination, and understanding. It is the Yin and Yang principle applied to clay works, and perhaps can best be summed up with a series of antonyms:

> *freedom* or *limitation*
> *continuity* or *change*
> *design* or *accident*
> *subjectivity* or *objectivity*
> *tradition* or *innovation*
> *conservative* or *radical*
> *prudence* or *abandonment*
> *harmony* or *discord*

With an art form as old as pottery making, nothing much is new, and most of what is done is a variation on a theme from another time and place. The contemporary studio potter has more liberty in pursuing new directions than any potter of the past. He can be as expressive and expansive as he likes. He can make objects of beauty or ugliness, of whimsy or classicism, of coarseness or refinement. The confines in which he has to work are often more economic than artistic. With today's eclectic society, almost anything goes in the form of art and craft works. What makes something beautiful or good is continually questioned but rarely answered.

For most studio potters, a balance also vacillates between life and work, to the point that they become totally integrated with each other. It is different for each person. The striking of some kind of balance is crucial to the stability and growth of the individual, as it forms the foundation that allows for personal exploration in whichever direction seems valid to that person. Balance, more than anything else, is the springboard which we can use to grow in our own ways. It is the state of being from which we can then become what we choose. We are an amalgamation of whatever we have ever seen, heard, eaten, drunk, felt, or loved. We are individuals searching for meaning and growth in existence. When we can achieve a balance the world is wide open for further exploration.

Making utilitarian pottery inevitably involves compromise to fulfill the needs required of a given object. The balance comes from the question, "What is most important to the maker—self-satisfaction or satisfying needs?" There is no reason on earth why one can't do both at the same time. From my experience, the nature of the functional potter is usually such that he or she wishes to produce objects that give pleasure to the user through their use, things designed with people in mind, and made with love, conviction, honesty, and integrity. If one can do this, whatever one's personal aesthetic likes may be, one will probably produce objects that not only reflect their maker, but through their honesty, receive notice and bring pleasure to others.

Handled Forms:
An Historical Collection

Vase with high handle (probably a ladle); polished red earthenware. Early Bronze Age, Cyprus. Courtesy of the Metropolitan Museum of Art: The Cesnola Collection, purchased by subscription, 1874–76 (74.51.1168).

Water container; stoneware. Iga ware, early Edo period, 17th century A.D., Japan. Height, 7¾". Courtesy of the Asian Art Museum of San Francisco: The Avery Brundage Collection.

Storage jar. Northern Qi, late 6th century A.D., China. Height, 9". Courtesy of the Asian Art Museum of San Francisco: The Avery Brundage Collection.

Aryballos with panther and bird; earthenware. Proto-Corinthian, ca. 600 B.C., Greece. Height, 27 cm. Courtesy of the Brooklyn Museum: loaned by Nasli and Alice Heermanneck Collection.

Long-necked jar; stoneware. Kuangtung type, western Han dynasty (2nd–1st century B.C., China. Height, 9". Courtesy of the Asian Art Museum of San Francisco: The Avery Brundage Collection.

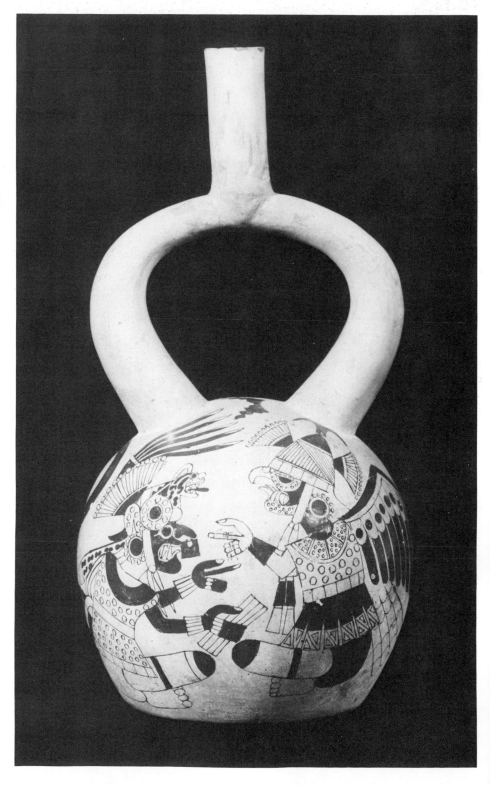

Stirrup jar with two squatting figures; burnished earthenware. Mochica culture, 300–500 A.D., Peru. Height, 9 cm. Courtesy of the Brooklyn Museum: gift of the Eugene Schaefer Collection.

114

Gourd-shaped water jug. Congo, late 19th century, Africa. Courtesy of the Royal Ontario Museum.

Ceramic bowl with handle. Ogata Kenzan, 1663–1743, Japan. Height, 5⅞". Courtesy of the Asian Art Museum of San Francisco: The Avery Brundage Collection, gift of Ney Wolfskill Fund.

Spouted jar with lion handles. Minai ware, early 13th century A.D., Persia. Height, 16 cm. Courtesy of the Montreal Museum of Fine Arts: gift of Harry A. Norton.

Coffee pot with twisted handle; soft paste porcelain. Worcester, ca. 1770, England. Height, 20.9 cm. Courtesy of the Art Gallery of Greater Victoria.

Kyathos (ladle) with finial; earthenware. Bucchero ware, 6th–5th century B.C., Etruscan. Height, 16.8 cm. Courtesy of the Brooklyn Museum: loaned by Miss Iris C. Love.

Large, handbuilt bowl with integrated handles; earthenware. Emily Carr, 1871–1945. Height, 6.8 cm. Courtesy of the Art Gallery of Greater Victoria: gift of Commander and Mrs. A. J. Tullis.

Teapot; thrown form, press-molded handle and spout. Contemporary Japan. Collection of Judi Dyelle.

Ewer; glazed stoneware. Tang dynasty, 8th century A.D., China. Height, 5½″. Courtesy of the Asian Art Museum of San Francisco: The Avery Brundage Collection.

Cup with dragon handles; porcelain. Qingbai ware, Song dynasty, 960–1279 A.D., China. Height, 2⅞″. Courtesy of the Asian Art Museum of San Francisco: The Avery Brundage Collection, gift of the Asian Art Foundation of San Francisco.

Spouted vessel; earthenware. Southern Apulian, ca. 550 B.C., Italy. Height, 3.8 cm. Courtesy, Museum of Fine Arts, Boston: Pierce Fund.

Cylindrical ewer, with dragon spout and handles. Dehua ware, 17th–18th century A.D., China. Height, 11". Courtesy of the Asian Art Museum of San Francisco: The Avery Brundage Collection.

Amphora. Sui or early Tang dynasty, 6th–7th century A.D., China. Height, 13". Courtesy of the Asian Art Museum of San Francisco: The Avery Brundage Collection.

Amphora with dragon handles; stoneware. Tang dynasty, 618–906 A.D., China. Height, 40 cm. Courtesy of the Montreal Museum of Fine Arts.

Red figured oinochoe; earthenware. Taliscan, 4th century B.C., Etruscan. Height, 15.8 cm. Courtesy of the Brooklyn Museum: anonymous gift.

119

Opposite: Tankard; tin-glazed earthenware. London, ca. 1690, England. Courtesy of the George R. Gardiner Museum of Ceramic Art.

Fuddling cup; tin-glazed earthenware. London, 1639, England. Courtesy of the George R. Gardiner Museum of Ceramic Art.

Double-handled urn; tin-glazed earthenware. London, ca. 1660, England. Courtesy of the George R. Gardiner Museum of Ceramic Art.

Jug; hard paste porcelain. Vienna, Du Paquier factory ca. 1725–1735, Austria. Courtesy of the George R. Gardiner Museum of Ceramic Art.

Teapot, copied from a Chinese original; hard paste porcelain. Meissen, ca. 1740, Germany. Courtesy of the George R. Gardiner Museum of Ceramic Art.

Opposite, top: Covered bowl; hard paste porcelain. Meissen, ca. 1725–30 A.D., Germany. Courtesy of the George R. Gardiner Museum of Ceramic Art.

Opposite, bottom: Chocolate cup and saucer; soft paste porcelain. Derby, ca. 1795, England. Courtesy of the George R. Gardiner Museum of Ceramic Art.

Butter dish; hard paste porcelain. Plymouth, ca. 1768–70 A.D., England. Courtesy of the George R. Gardiner Museum of Ceramic Art.

Teapot. Meissen, ca. 1730, Germany. Courtesy of the George R. Gardiner Museum of Ceramic Art.

Covered jar; hard paste porcelain. Vienna, Du Paquier factory ca. 1720–25, Austria. Courtesy of the George R. Gardiner Museum of Ceramic Art.

Lemon tureen; hard paste porcelain. Meissen, ca. 1745 A.D., Germany. Courtesy of the George R. Gardiner Museum of Ceramic Art.

Stoneware crock; saltglazed. Brantford, 19th century A.D., Canada. Courtesy of the Royal Ontario Museum: gift of the McGills, Brantford.

Watercooler with lion head handles; saltglazed stoneware. Brantford, 19th century A.D., Canada. Courtesy of the Royal Ontario Museum.

Part Three

Mechanics:
Analysis, Practice, Considerations

INTRODUCTION

The basic process of composition in pottery as in any other art appears to depend upon an intuitive perception of the way in which similar and dissimilar elements can be coordinated into a new whole.

—*Bernard Leach,* A Potter's Portfolio

The first part of this book has been a brief survey of the development of functional pottery, an analysis of its forms, and details of those forms. Part Two was concerned with the roots of those forms, be they organic or mathematical, and their validity for use by contemporary craftsmen and artists producing functional pottery. This part is a down-to-earth section dealing with the pragmatic approach to the production of functional pottery by the use of the potter's wheel. I have chosen to focus on wheel-made pottery since the wheel is still the most efficient and most widely used tool for the production of most styles of handmade, or limited run, pottery throughout the world. Although functional studio pottery can be, and often is, made by methods other than using a wheel, as outlined in Chapter 2, the great majority of studio pottery is made on the wheel. For those who prefer to make things by other hand methods, much of what is stated here in terms of design analysis and attention to detail is just as relevant. All methods have their good points, and it is a purely personal matter how one approaches their development. To make a living at any form of pottery making requires a high degree of efficiency and discipline, as well as a sound personal vision.

The potter's wheel is a simple mechanical device, little changed in principle and use since its origins somewhere in the Middle East about 5000 years ago. Although it is now powered by various methods in addition to the human hand and foot, its basic form is the same, namely a flat surface made to revolve at either constant or variable speed. It is a deceptively simple tool, requiring great skill to manipulate. Learning to guide the spinning mass of soft clay into myriad limitless forms of space confined within a clay skin, generally takes many years to master. The process of gaining control is full of great frustration, and mastery of this simple tool and material does not come easily.

This book is not designed to teach anyone to throw. This, I feel, can't be done through words and pictures, although some pictures can serve to clarify the finger positions which the demonstrator uses to achieve certain ends. Learning to throw is like learning to write: one starts with a basic discipline and personal style develops naturally through experience. Since we are all built slightly different from each other, and since we all use our fingers with slight variations from one another, it follows that photographs of the process in action leave much to be desired in such a sensitive, tactile, and fluid art form. Even a teacher is limited to expressing the need of "a little more or less pressure" at this point or that. The art of throwing clay on the wheel involves an intimacy with the manipulated mass which incorporates both strength and sensitivity in an unusual balance. Although heavy muscle power can be beneficial in the early stages of throwing, such as centering and opening up, it is the sensitivity which the potter uses that gives finesse to the objects being formed. The refinements of the form and its details are achieved with the slightest of pressures, using a variety of movements with both fingers and tools. No pictures, words, or vicarious actions can convey this sensitivity, nor can they give any inkling of the time and concentrated effort needed to master this exceptionally difficult discipline.

More than showing multiple variations of the throwing process in picture form, I feel that it is better to discuss and illustrate the reasons why certain objects and details do or do not work. As the process of throwing is more or less a mechanical one, I therefore call this part of the book *Mechanics*. In the way I choose to explore it, mechanics incorporates the actions of design analysis, and the practicality of production. Design analysis deals with the considerations required to make an object function properly according to both desire and need; what it is that makes one object function more efficiently than another. Practicality is the concrete approach to making objects which work. It is the concern for the details of functional objects and considerations in the manipulation of clay that achieve the desired ends. Utilitarian pottery needs a great deal of thought in design, and skill in making, before satisfactory works are likely to emerge.

In the hope of simplifying the process of design, the next stage is to take a number of regularly produced functional objects such as cooking pots, pouring and drinking vessels, pots for eating from, for storing things in, for rituals, and for putting flowers in, and to analyze their intended function. Perhaps the easiest way for a potter to begin is to develop a good understanding of the needs which any potential purchaser sees as priorities before a purchase is made. Just what is it that is required in an object? Can the maker match the requirements within a satisfactory degree of compromise? This can be developed in what I call a "mini-market-research" approach, accomplished by getting a group of potential buyers and users together and asking their opinions on what they might be looking for in a specific object. If a dozen or so people are questioned, there will undoubtedly be a good variation in perceived priorities. I call these *considerations*, and they can be made up in a graph form, similar to the accompanying sample I made for casseroles. While I am not suggesting that the potter should kowtow to the whims of the buying public, he can at least have a fair idea of needs to be concerned with and which may be incorporated in the final object. For example, if you ask a dozen or so people just what they might look for in purchasing a mug, you will probably find at least five variations, not counting shape or volume, related to the size and placement of a handle alone. There are the one-finger people, two-finger people, whole fist people, people who put their thumb through the handle and hold the mug from below, not to mention those who turn the handle away and hold the mug by the handleless side, like an oriental teabowl. It is obviously impossible to satisfy every single person's desires and in so doing produce the *ultimate mug*, but one can at least see the logic behind the analytical process. The more of these perceived priorities that can be accommodated, the more likely the objects are to sell. It is an interesting exercise to question potential buyers in this way, as they often have clearcut views about what they will put out money for. Bearing the perceived needs in mind, the potter can then superimpose his own aesthetic view, and the resulting object should most likely look good, work efficiently, satisfy the desires of both maker and buyer, whilst simultaneously sell well. Each of the previously mentioned groups of functional objects is analyzed in this way from criteria which I have found by experience to work well.

Many potters seem to feel that they can impose ill-conceived and badly made objects on the public, with the result that they receive limited success in the marketplace. There will always be compromise. Even the most basic of needs causes the potter to effect change on what might be a pure art aesthetic. However, an analytical approach coupled with a meticulous attention to detail is usually the most satisfactory way to develop a viable product for either short or long-term production. In the following chapters, each type of functional form is considered and analyzed, along with relevant mechanical requirements. Throughout Part Three, *analysis* refers to what the object is intended to do, and also includes some discussion on aesthetics. *Practice* refers to technicalities which one should be aware of, such as spouts and handles which twist, forms that alter in firing, and lids which seem to change in size. *Considerations* refers to a list of priorities gained from group discussions, put in question form. These three concerns, *analysis*, *practice*, and *considerations*, in concert with the potter's own aesthetic and intuitive sensitivity, should help in the development and production of well-designed and well-made objects for use.

Sample Graph for Casseroles

FORM AND DETAILS	JONES	SMITH	BROWN	COLES	GRAY	HIGGINS	GREEN	DOYLE	DIXON
SPHERICAL FORM	x		x	x			x		
CYLINDER FORM		x			x	x		x	x
DEEP AND TALL	x			x		x			
SHALLOW AND WIDE		x	x		x		x	x	x
HIGH LID AND KNOB	x		x			x			x
LOW LID AND HANDLE		x		x	x		x	x	
STEAM VENT IN LID	x			x				x	
POURING SPOUT		x		x		x			x
NO HANDLES	x				x				
GENEROUS HANDLES		x	x	x		x	x	x	x

Along with these considerations of form and details come some technical concerns, such as clay bodies and glazes, and their attendant problems; storage concerns with smaller houses; and hygiene.

There are certain generalities which many pots have in common. I refer to these as *details*, and they may be applicable to many different types of functional object. Details include such things as lips; galleries or flanges; lids and covers; spouts and pouring lips; handles, lugs, and knobs; and feet. To a large extent the basic form of a functional object looks after itself once design considerations have been analyzed and a suitable shape decided upon. Details are much more difficult to deal with, not only in technique, but also in aesthetics. It is the attention to detail, how they look, how they feel, and how they work, which marks the work of a master and separates it from the rest of the crowd.

The making of pots is an intensely private affair. Doing battle with apparently lifeless chunks of prepared mud, in the process extracting some form of aesthetic satisfaction, is, at the same time, both masochistic and stimulating. If and when beauty is achieved, it is a personal triumph. On the other hand, the making of pots designed to function is a very public affair. They are used, eaten from, drunk from, and poured from in the presence of company. When their inadequacies come to light it is usually in the public arena. In the hope of minimizing the number of inadequacies, I offer these observations from thirty years of making pots with a purpose.

Attention to Details

Quite a lot of concern is required to balance the functional with the aesthetic considerations of any object. To function properly the needs may be one thing, whereas to be visually satisfying they may be another. Although this is a difficult balance to achieve, any measure of imbalance should most likely be geared more toward making the object do what it is intended to do, rather than making it look a little more enticing. I am not suggesting that making ugly pots that work is any more commendable than making beautiful pots which don't work. Rather, that one should do all that is in one's power to make the balance between function and looks as equitable as possible, without the one compromising the other.

Unless they are done for a special effect, the use of oversize appendages and details of any kind, be they lids, spouts, knobs, or handles, is usually visually destructive to the total aesthetic quality of the pot, while at the same time not necessarily helping it to function. There is a right size for all appendages to work properly, both functionally and visually, on any object. However, achieving this balance and finding the right size only comes with considerable experience, coupled with astute observation. In this section, I am more concerned with the practical aspects in both the design and in the making, but I would like to make it clear that no matter how much attention is paid to the details, if the form or basic intention of the object

is weak, the final object will be a dud. If the form is strong and satisfying, the attachment of weak details will likely also render this piece a dud. If both form and details are well related, the piece is likely to be good. If the form and details are good, and the object functions as desired, then it should be a winner.

Unless a pot is a complete sphere, or some other totally enclosed form, it will have a beginning and an end. In the usual method of anthropomorphic association, we normally name these parts *lip* or *mouth*, and *bottom* or *foot*. In between, we are likely to find some or all of the following: neck, throat, collar, shoulder, belly, and waist, depending on the form of the object. We talk about forms being masculine or feminine, their relative strength or sensuousness, and of how they sit or stand. We also give them other human characteristics. They are sometimes called weak, mean, thin, slight, tight, loose, robust, rotund, vigorous, sensuous, virile and many others.

Simple (meaning made in one piece) thrown forms grow from the base upward, moving in a sometimes fluid line, often called feminine; sometimes in an interrupted line with angular changes in direction, often called masculine. These points of movement or change in linear profile from one part of a form to another are known as *articulation*.

Forms that are made on the potter's wheel do not necessarily have to be round and symmetrical.

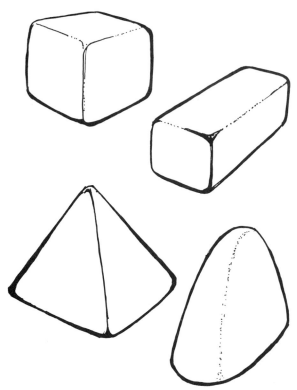

Fig. 9.1 *Simple forms that can easily be beaten from round thrown forms.*

The wheel may be used as the basic tool for forming almost any shape. Pots can be adjusted to the potter's desire by the use of a paddle when the pot has stiffened to some degree. Cube-shaped thrown forms are best developed from a totally enclosed sphere. Pyramidal and parabolic forms are best made from a cone shape made without a base, and a slab base attached later. Any sort of free asymmetrical forms can be developed quite simply through gentle beating with a variety of paddles. Paddles may be made of wood, and may have patterns carved in them to create surface variation while altering the form. Any development of asymmetrical form allows great freedom for the potter, freedom which can easily lead one into the trap of novelty for novelty's sake. If one is not careful to impose some parameters to the forms to be explored, things may easily get out of hand.

Of all the possible variations of altered thrown forms, perhaps the one most commonly asked for is the oval form. Oval forms can be made in various ways using the potter's wheel. Figure 9.3 shows three. First, the most traditional way of making oval dishes is to cut an elliptical or long leaf-shaped piece from the base of a stiffened but not yet leather-hard dish. The sides are then squashed together so the long sides of the ellipse meet and can be joined. The cut-out ellipse is often placed across the join, and pressed in to complete and strengthen the base. If they are not carefully compressed in

Fig. 9.2 *A variety of wooden paddles with patterns cut into the surface.*

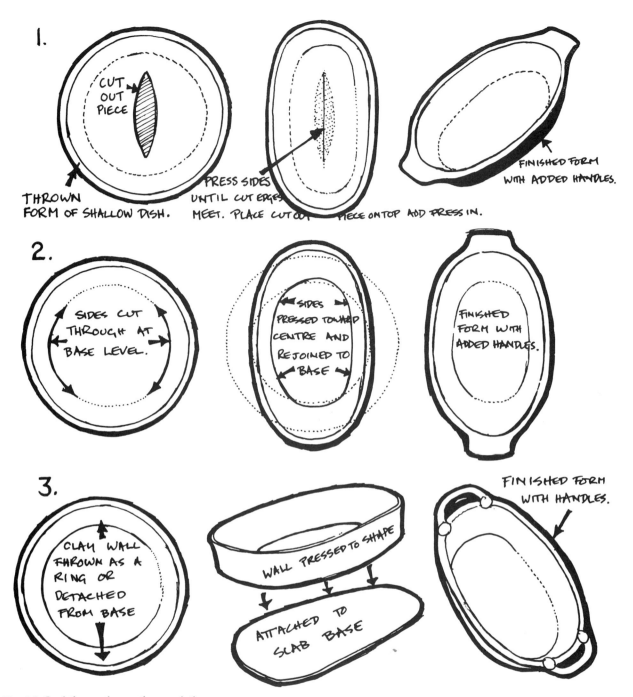

Fig. 9.3 Oval thrown forms, three variations.

the base, dishes made in this way are prone to cracking. The second method takes a thrown form at the same stage of stiffness as the first. A thin knife, or cutting wire, is inserted through the walls at the level of the inside base, and a horizontal cut made for what will become the length of the side. This is done on both sides. After cutting, the surface is coated with a light slip or water, and the walls may be slid across to form an oval shape. When the shape is satisfactory, the walls are stuck down in their new position, and any excess clay trimmed away. The third method uses a thrown clay wall, made without a base. If it is thrown on a batt, the walls should be able to be slid into any form after first undercutting with a wire. Once the altered form has stiffened to leather hard, it can be attached to a slab base to make the oval dish. Method three is widely adaptable to make freeform shapes.

For any pot to be aesthetically satisfying, the basic form has to be well considered. The development of form was explored in Parts One and Two. Here, I am mainly considering details, either the beginnings and ends of pots themselves, or appendages, such as lids, spouts, and handles. In the historical review of Part One, I attempted to outline the general growth, implementation, and change of these details as they appear to have developed through the ages. Now they are considered in a more analytical vein in how they function, a more practical vein of how they are made, and what are the relevant considerations which should be looked at in their production. Since there are many ways to achieve the different ends employed in making pots on a wheel, I will try to show as many variations as space will allow. There will undoubtedly be some omissions in the complexities of clayworking, and individuals reading this book will almost certainly have their own variations to just about everything which I might mention. However, without somewhere to start, one can't imagine getting anywhere at the finish. In order to start on firm ground, we will start with base terminations, namely bottoms or feet.

BASE TERMINATIONS: BOTTOMS AND FEET

One tends to think of the bottom as the part of a form which is heavy, rotund, and gets sat upon. Feet are the foundations from which a form grows and develops. They can have many diverse qualities from heavy, solid, and earthbound as in military, to light, ethereal, and dancing, as in ballet. Feet, in pots as in people, create the stability needed to stand properly. Are they on duty, or may they dance?

Decisions in shape and size of feet demand aesthetic, structural, and practical consideration. Small feet reflect elegant, delicate, and refined forms, more suited to contemplation and display, whereas large bottoms and large feet suggest stolidity, sta-

bility, and an ability to deal with the stresses and strains of daily family living. The relationship of foot size to the rest of the form, as well as to its efficiency as a stabilizer, is partially controlled by the type of use which will be made of the object. For instance, a small elegant foot, well suited to a purely decorative bowl, is unlikely to satisfy the needs of a soup bowl where stability on a flat surface is paramount, or where moving volumes of liquid make them vulnerable. The foot is also important structurally, as it supports the object in the drying and firing processes. If it is made too narrow, it may well cause the pot to slump due to the weight above. If it is made too wide, then the inner part of the foot might sag and deform the interior. The outside of a form must relate to the inside, otherwise not only will sagging and slumping likely occur, but cracking from uneven wall thickness might also develop. Practicality can refer both to the practical nature of the foot itself, and also the trimming of a shape that makes later gripping easier during the glazing process.

It is not always necessary to finish a piece with a trimmed, turned, applied, or cut foot. Depending on what the object is to do, combined with the aesthetic considerations which go with that object, pots are often cut from the wheel with a wire, and left with little or no further working. Profiles can be used to give the bottom edge a range of interesting linear effects (Fig. 9.5). A slight cleaning or softening of the bottom edge, by rolling it on a hard surface or rubbing with a moistened finger, is often all that is needed to satisfy the needs of function. Slight indenting of the whole base, by a gentle pressure of the palm, assists in alleviating the problem of bases warping into a convex and wobbly, and thus unstable, state: a recurrent problem with untrimmed bases. A further alternative to, or even addition to, wire-cut bases can be small buttons of clay or modeled feet. If this is done, indenting of the base is not necessary.

Cutting wires of different types, from twine and smooth nylon filament fishing line, to thin stretched springs or curtain wires, can be used to create differing decorative effects. The most usual wire-cut effect is commonly found on untrimmed wares from Romano-Britain to modern peasant wares from Europe, although it is most associated

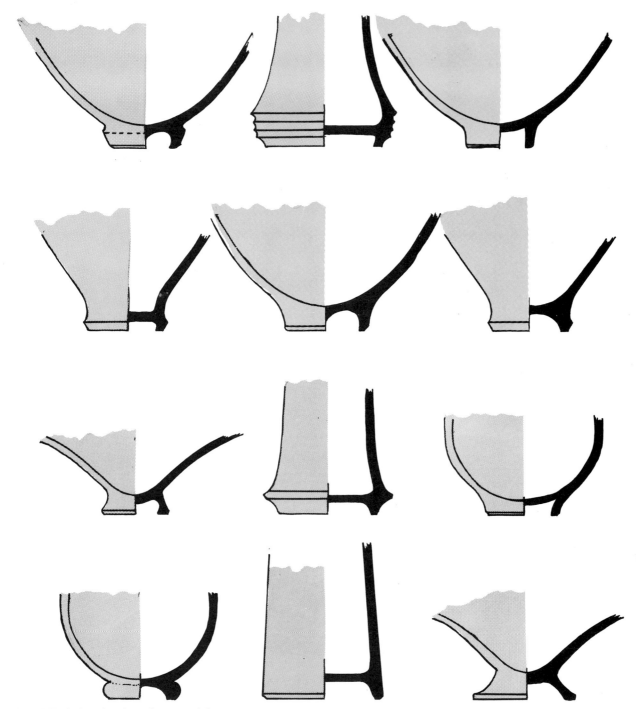

Fig. 9.4 Variations in trimmed or turned feet.

with the Far East. A fine twisted metal, or cord, cutting wire is pulled through the soft clay while the wheel is slowly revolved to create a shell-like pattern (Fig. 9.6). By using various forms of twisted wire, many variations of cut can be made. Other patterned bases can be made by pressing the medium-soft clay on textured surfaces, such as basket weave, burlap, or even corduroy fabrics. Textured bases, like most feet, are only noticed when the pot is lifted and the base exposed. As such, they

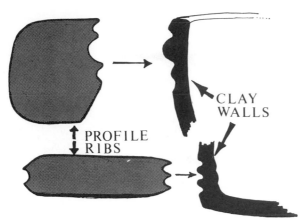

CLAY
WALLS

PROFILE
RIBS

Fig. 9.5 Profile ribs can be made with wood, metal, or plastic, depending on the size and flexibility required. For small ribs, old credit cards work well. For larger ones, samples of formica or arborite sheet are good, and can easily be cut with fret saw and files.

Fig. 9.6 Shell-like pattern produced from cutting cord or wire.

can become an important decorative adjunct to the rest of the form. In parts of the Orient, the first part of an object to receive the close scrutiny of collectors and users is often the foot. To connoisseurs, the foot tells a great deal about the person who made it, quite apart from it being the most usual place where a piece might be signed. The way a potter finishes the base is read like a signature, knowledgeable people often being able to tell the identity of the maker from the foot alone. The suitability of the base is an important concern of the overall form, and although it is underneath the piece and seldom seen, nevertheless needs careful consideration. Good houses need good foundations. So do pots!

Once a decision on the final desired form is made, the inverted piece can be centered on the

wheelhead, over a chuck or in a chum for trimming or turning (Fig. 9.8). The consistency of the clay at this point is critical. If too soft, it will deform; too hard, and it won't cut properly, and may well crack in the process. The clay should be what is called *leather hard*, a consistency similar to cheddar cheese in the way that it cuts, able to be pared away cleanly without clogging the tools or dragging on the surface of the clay. The clay should be evenly dried to the cheese or leather-hard state throughout the object for even trimming to take place. Unevenly thrown or dried, or off-center pieces, or pieces being trimmed with blunt tools, will all be harder to trim efficiently. Tools should be kept sharp to eliminate the likelihood of chattering, where the tool bounces

Fig. 9.7 Trimmed feet on Korean (left) and Japanese tea bowls. Collection of the author.

Fig. 9.8 Chucks or chums should be contoured to support the object at its most vulnerable point.

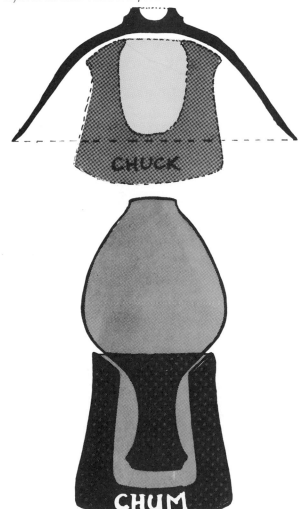

on the clay, forming slight ridges and depressions and giving a corrugated effect. There may be times when this effect is desirable for a decorative treatment, as in a number of oriental surface effects where chattering is encouraged by the use of extra long and springy metal tools called *kanna.* This technique has the Japanese name *kasuri-mon.* For the most part, however, chattering is an annoying fault, which can be easily rectified by sharpening the tools and possibly holding them a little tighter, in a different way, or at a different angle. Tools for trimming can be of several kinds (Fig. 9.9), and their efficiency for different uses can only be felt by experience. The great majority of potters make their own tools, suited to their own needs or to the needs of the pieces being made.

In trimming, the relationship between the shape of the inside to that of the outside is vital. (Different styles of trimming are shown in Fig. 9.4.) Foot trimming for production work is most easily accomplished when the objects are placed on a chuck contoured to fit the inside of the object (Fig. 9.8). Quick, efficient trimming of small numbers of low forms such as bowls and plates is often best done on the flat wheelhead. By dampening the head and the edge of the piece to be trimmed, and applying slight downward pressure once the piece is centered, it can be trimmed without the need for small dots or coils of clay being used to hold the pot in place. This results in a clear view of the total exterior of the piece, and the slight pressure exudes a small amount of air from beneath, holding the object in place by means of a vacuum. If the trimming is done quickly, the vacuum will hold firm

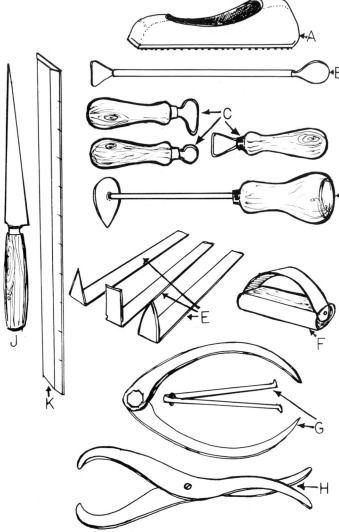

objects which are low and wide, as taller, slimmer pieces can sometimes detach themselves from the wheel, due to side and lifting pressures. After trimming, feet may be further adapted and altered by cutting or modelling. These practices can also be the basic way of foot development as is often found in Japanese teabowls, where the entire foot is cut with a tool while the bowl is rotated in the hands. Feet can also be thrown with soft clay directly onto the trimmed leather-hard form, or be thrown separately and joined at the leather-hard stage.

Single feet are the most obvious and most used forms, although it is, of course, possible to make an infinite variety of feet in ways other than throwing. Thrown feet can also be made separately and added either individually or in multiples. The most common multiple foot is the tripod, which has been used throughout history (see Footed Forms in Part One). A tripod is a good stable form if the legs are the same length and applied with the same angle and vertical thrust. The applications of feet in functional pottery discussed in this book refer mainly to the single foot, since it would be quite impossible to cover all possible variations.

The foot is an important aesthetic and functional detail that is often made in ways which reflect the individual maker. It plays an integral part in the form of a pot, whether one views it as the beginning or the end of the piece. Since the ends of the line are so important, the one being where it springs from and the other being where it terminates, it follows that these points should receive prime consideration in both the design and the making stages.

TOP TERMINATIONS: RIMS, MOUTHS, AND LIPS

The most quickly noticed detail, after the eye takes in the general form of any pot, is usually the lip, mouth, or edge. Strangely, it is the part which so often betrays the potter, showing weakness, by looking as though the clay ran out just before it got to where it was supposed to go. Lips and edges often have a starved or pinched look, which not only is aesthetically displeasing, but also leaves the thin edge vulnerable to easy chipping and break-

Fig. 9.9 Tools used in throwing and trimming: A. surform plane, a rasp for removing heavy excesses of clay, particularly on altered forms; B. Wire-ended modeling tools; C. Metal loop tools; D. Solid paint scraper for heavy work; E. Flat strip metal tools, ends made to a variety of shapes; F. Heavy duty hand grip tool for preliminary trimming of large forms. G. Calipers; H. Double-ended calipers; J. Knife; K. Ruler.

for several minutes, at least long enough to easily trim most forms. To break the vacuum and remove the piece, all that is needed is a light tap on the side. The pot can then be removed easily. One may lose a few pieces in learning the exact dampness required, and the right consistency of the clay; but, once learned, this method of trimming saves a considerable amount of time with no compromise to the quality. Vacuum trimming is most useful for age. If anything, edges of functional ware need to be slightly thicker than the rest of the piece as a protection. There are, of course, exceptions to this, such as in drinking vessels, where extra thickness is uncomfortable, but in the main edges should be strengthened. This is usually done by a controlled downward pressure being applied to the rim in a compressive action, as one of the very last movements in the throwing stage. With some clays, such as porcelain, which are often finely thrown, late compression might lead to deformation of the form, so the answer here is to keep the edge fairly compressed throughout the throwing process. The range of lip variations made possible by slight pressures and finger positions is great, and it is often a stimulating process for the developing potter to spend a good deal of time practicing them on simple cylindrical forms. Such continuous practice forms the basic discipline necessary to gaining some mastery in the making of any pottery. A fine edge, or a refined piece of pottery, can often demand a more reverent approach by the user. It can, and perhaps should, affect the way that the object is used.

In the making of any object which is designed to pour liquids from the top edge of the basic form, rather than through a spout, special notice should be made that the inner surface of the form be very smooth for the top two or three inches. It is also preferable that there be a sharp edge at the top of that inside surface (Fig. 9.10). This ensures that when a pouring lip is pulled out from the basic form, it has a sharp edge to pour over when the form is tilted. When the form is returned to its upright state the sharpness of the edge makes sure of cutting the flow of liquid, resulting in less likelihood of dripping. Pots that pour are like miniature waterfalls, and those with sharp pouring edges will normally function best. Extended pouring lips, which can also improve the pouring ability, can be made by pinching the clay to a thinner wall at the point determined to be the site of the lip. This is best done with a pressure between thumb and forefinger, gently pulling the clay up before attempting to pull it out from the form (Fig. 9.11). When the clay has been pulled up adequately, it is then teased out to complement the vessel, and at the same time create a good throat to direct the liquid in its path. There are a number of other ways which can be

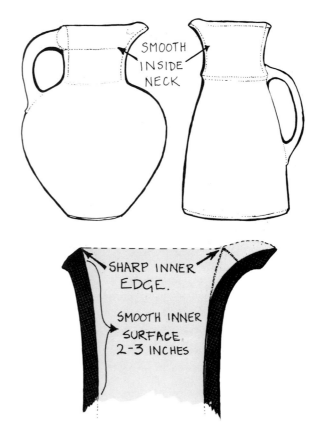

Fig. 9.10 Interior of vessels designed for pouring liquids.

used to form pouring lips. These will be explored in the section, Spouts, later in this chapter.

One form of top termination that is sometimes found, and could be much more developed than it has been, is that of cutting the top of thrown forms. It is often used for pitchers and jugs, but could easily be incorporated in a wide range of other ways. The clay is usually cut when leather hard, and can be softened by misting with a water spray, with a damp sponge, or being wrapped with wet newspaper, to re-form the shapes of the cut areas. The flat side of a knife can be used to compress the newly cut areas. Any rough edges can easily be sponged to make them smooth (Fig. 9.12).

A common form of top termination is that requiring the seating for a lid or cover. For some lids this will be a simple termination of the pot's wall. For others it may be in the formation of an inner gallery, or in a seating on the exterior below the pot's top edge. The latter may only need a variation in curvature of the form, combined with accurate lid measurement, to suffice. As a general

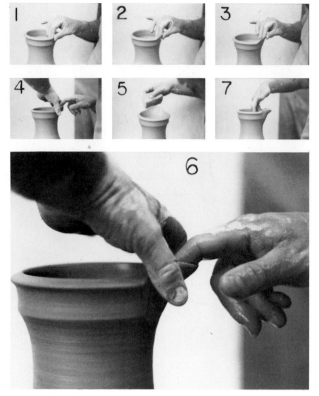

Fig. 9.11 Pulling a spout: 1–3. Pinching out the thickened lip to thin the edge; 4. Starting a pouring lip; 5. Sponging the curve of the lip; 6. Pulling the pouring lip; 7. Easing out the throat to give a good inner pouring surface.

rule in the making stages, the simpler top terminations require the more complicated lid forms. For pots which have a gallery on the inside, or a support form on the outside, the simpler lid forms are more often appropriate (Fig. 9.13). The inner gallery needs to be made very carefully to avoid deforming the pot in the process of applying pressure at or near the termination point. The best way to make sure that the form beneath the gallery is not weakened is to put an embryonic gallery thickness in place fairly early on in the throwing process. This not only allows greater pressure to be applied later, but also ensures that there is, in fact, enough clay to be able to make the flange. Running out of clay is a common fault in inadequately made lid seatings, resulting in a thin to almost nonexistent flange. Should the lid also be badly made, there is a strong likelihood of it warping into the pot during the firing process, due to a lack of support when the maturing clay is softened. It is possible to use tools for the entire formation of the gallery, or to do the main formation with the fingers, followed

Fig. 9.13 Top terminations with internal flange (A), or simple support for more complex lid fittings. (B and C).

Fig. 9.12 Cut rims.

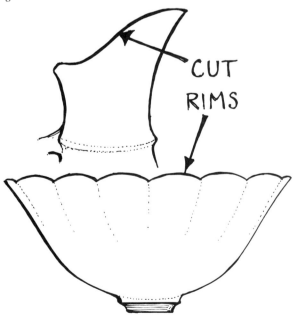

CUT RIMS

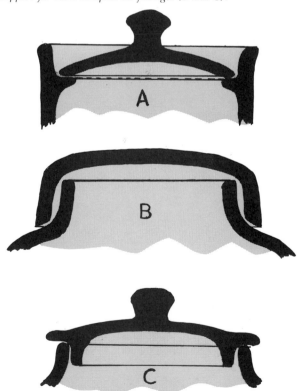

with a cleaning and finishing operation with a flat-edged tool, such as the end of a flat metal trimming tool. The actual finishing of the gallery should be almost the last thing done in the throwing of a form designed to take a lid. Only a little base trimming should follow, in order not to disturb or deform the lid seating. It is easy to push the form into an oval shape at this time, making proper lid fitting nearly impossible.

LIDS AND COVERS

Lids and covers might seem to be the simplest part of the pots for which they are made. Nothing could be further from the truth! They are perhaps the most demanding and frustrating of the pot's details to deal with and, once again, quickly show the degree of skill which the potter may have. First, they should fit properly. Second, they should be carefully related proportionately to the pot which carries them. Third, they should seem to belong to that piece by the extending fluidity of the line from the base through to the top, so that they don't look as incongruous as either a top hat on an elephant or, alternatively, on a mouse. There are, of course, times when an extra small or extra large lid might be desirable for the form being made, usually for special effect or aesthetic concern. Fourth, they should fulfill the intended function; select from the different lid types that which is most suitable for a specific use.

As I explained earlier, lids fit on three different types of top termination (see Fig. 9.13). Generally, simple terminations require a more complicated lid, and the more complex, galleried termination receives the simpler lid. No matter which combination is used, if the piece is intended to function, the lid should fit properly. Proper fitting is usually achieved by a combination of careful measurement and observation of what the lid has to fit onto. Measurement can be done quite simply with a ruler, a piece of bent stiff wire, a pair of simple calipers, or sophisticated double-ended calipers which give the dimension of both inside the form and outside the lid. It is also possible to use an oriental T-shaped bamboo measure which can measure both width and depth at the same time or, for some lids, a measure attached to the wheel

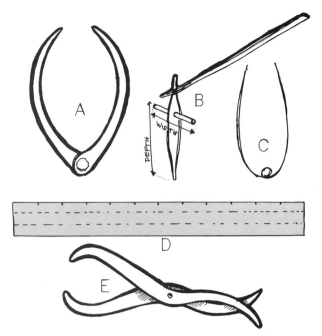

Fig. 9.14 Tools used for taking lid measurements. A. Calipers; B. Japanese "Tombo" measures height and depth of form at the same time; C. Bent wire; D. Double-ended calipers.

tray or surround. Tools for measuring are shown in Fig. 9.14. Simple calipers can be used in two ways, either by measuring the gap between the points, or across the closed caliper to the two points (Fig. 9.15). No matter how one takes the measurement, the prime concern is that it be accurate. It

Fig. 9.15 Caliper measurements may be taken across the gap for outside measure (A), or between the points for inside measure (B).

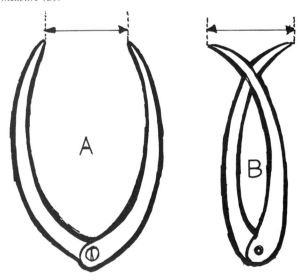

takes far more time to try to rectify a bad fitting than it does to measure and make it right in the first place.

If a lid is required to fit onto a pot which has an internal gallery, and at the same time has a pulled pouring lip, the part of the gallery where the lip is going to be can be cut away with a pin-tool or simple wire tool, as in Fig. 9.16. This should be done straight after the piece is thrown, to allow for easier pulling of the lip. After the gallery section is removed, the pouring lip can be pulled as normal, taking care not to deform the rest of the top edge and gallery of the pot. Once the piece is stiffened, drying the lid on the form usually helps to minimize potential warping.

There are some instances when lids may shrink more than the body of the pot. If this happens, it is usually due to the degree of stretching which the clay undergoes during the throwing process, in comparison to that which the basic form undergoes. Clay is formed from myriads of microscopic platelike crystals, sliding over each other with water as the lubricant surrounding each platelet. In the process of throwing and stretching clay, the lubrication between platelets becomes extended, depending on the degree to which the clay has been pulled. Since there are only a certain number of platelets available in a given piece of clay, the excessive extending process of the throwing will cause a small increase in the shrinkage, due to the evaporation of water used to assist in pulling the clay to its extreme. In the drying stage, where the clay usually shrinks significantly, the platelets return again to close contact. This process is somewhat elastic in nature, and has given rise to what is sometimes termed *clay memory*, or elastic or plastic mem-

ory. It is particularly prevalent in some clays, and some forms, notably lids, necks, and spouts (see Spouts). However, it is not a consistent problem. Different people throwing the same forms with the same clays will likely experience different degrees of change, depending on the speed and strength of the throwing. It should be looked at as a difficulty of making which is relative to the individual, and therefore it is up to the individual to accommodate it in his own work.

There are approximately eleven different types of lid, with countless variations. Some varieties of lid forms are made the right way up, more or less as they would appear when sitting in place on the pot. It is, of course, much easier to visualize the completed object in this way. Most, however, are made upside-down. The reasons for this are the ease of measurement, accuracy in making some lids, and the fact that some can't be thrown in any other way. Once the required type of lid to suit the form is decided upon, and relevant measurements taken, the piece is thrown. Some lids are easily thrown from a hump of clay, others with weighed-out amounts are thrown directly on the wheelhead or on a batt. The illustrations show the lids in section form, as they would usually be thrown, and as they would probably be after trimming. Average weights for weighed-out lids are included in the list of Weights and Measures for production ware, page 157.

Trimming lids, like trimming feet, is accomplished by using a wide variety of possible tools. Lids needn't be trimmed on a wheel, although this might be the quickest way. They can be cut with different wires, wire-ended tools, or knives, to achieve variety. It is often a wise precaution to leave the edge of lids with a slight thickness to make them more resistant to the chipping and abrasion which occurs with the wear and tear of normal use.

Fig. 9.16 Tools for removing sections of flange or tops of forms. A. Homemade tool with taut metal wire; B, C. Pin tools.

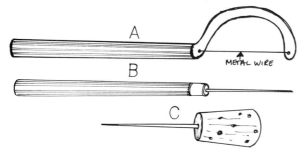

Lids Thrown Upside-Down

1. This is one of the simplest lids, usually thrown off the hump, and made like a small shallow bowl sitting on a short stalk (Fig. 9.17). The stalk should have enough height and volume of

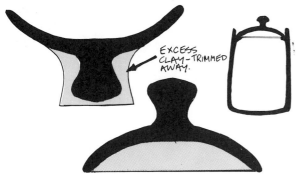

Fig. 9.17 Lid type 1.

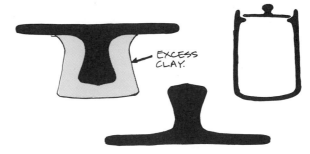

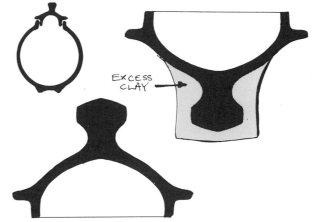

Fig. 9.18 Lid type 2.

Fig. 9.19 Lid type 3.

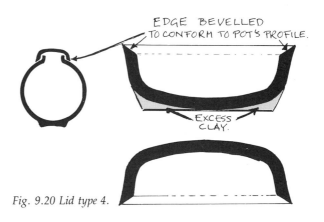

Fig. 9.20 Lid type 4.

clay to allow later trimming of the knob. It needs to sit on a gallery inside the pot.

2. This lid is thrown in the same way as Type 1, except that it is pulled out as a flat disc, in order to make a flat lid (Fig. 9.18). This lid also has to sit on a gallery. Depending on its size, it might be more difficult than Type 1 because of the difficulty of maintaining a flat disc unsupported on a horizontal plane.

3. This type of lid (Fig. 9.19) is probably the most commonly seen, and is made with a flange, therefore not necessarily needing a gallery on the pot. It can be thrown off the hump, with enough excess clay for a knob to be trimmed, or may be thrown on a batt, with weighed-out clay. For larger lids, the latter is probably the best method. This lid type is useful for most lid applications. In sizes larger than 6″ diameter, it is probably best to throw a knob on after trimming has been done.

4. Type 4 (Fig. 9.20) is like those used on Chinese ginger jars. Owing to the difficulty of lifting it cleanly from a hump, this lid is often best thrown on a batt. It is thrown like a small bowl, usually with short, straight sides. It has to fit over the top of a pot, or into a recessed gallery, to make sure that it doesn't fall off. Angling the inside top edge to the reciprocal angle of the top of the pot helps to give a clean profile to the finished object.

5. This lid is a more complicated version of Type 4, being made as a double-walled piece (Fig. 9.21). The top termination of the pot fits between the two walls of the lid. It requires two sets of measurements to fit properly. It is used to seal in either the aroma or moisture of the pot's contents. It is also best made with an angled edge on the outside wall, to fit the shoulder of the pot.

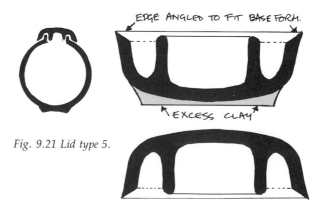

Fig. 9.21 Lid type 5.

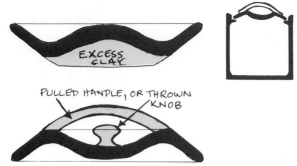

Fig. 9.22 Lid type 6.

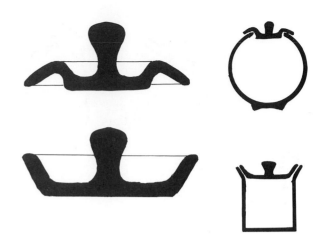

Fig. 9.24 Lid type 8.

6. This lid is made like a small, shallow bowl thrown with a flattened dome in the center (Fig. 9.22). It is best thrown on a batt with weighed-out clay. In trimming, the dome is hollowed out, leaving a recess which may be bridged with a pulled handle or decorative recessed knob. It usually fits on an internal gallery.

Lids Thrown Right Way Up

7. To make large lids similar to the finished Type 2 lid, the simplest way is to throw a flat disc on a batt, measured to fit, and leave enough clay in the center to throw a knob if desired (Fig. 9.23). It is basically finished in one operation, save for a little cleaning up when the lid is leather hard.

8. This is perhaps the fastest lid to make. It can be done off the hump, or with weighed-out clay. It has its own built-in flange so therefore fits onto the simple pot termination (Fig. 9.24). After centering, the knob is formed first, followed by pulling up a small cylinder around it. The outside width of the cylinder is measured to fit the opening of the pot and, when accurate, the top half-inch or so is bent to conform with the top of the pot. It

generally needs a little cleaning to finish it. A common variation of this is where the walls of the lid are only pressed out at a slight angle, to conform to the inside of the pot's top section, which is similarly angled. In this way the lid forms a friction fit, rather like a wedge. This fitting is often used on storage jars or kitchen containers.

9. Another lid that is thrown off the hump is Type 9 (Fig. 9.25). In process, it looks a little like a mushroom. After centering, the lump of clay is pressed into two directions, one becoming the knob, and the other a flange which is initially pulled out straight and, when the knob is finished, pulled to its full measured width, and either left flat or curved down. When leather hard, it is inverted on the pot, or a small chuck, and the "stalk" of the mushroom is trimmed away.

10. This lid (Fig. 9.26) is very tricky to throw, but is quite useful for certain objects. It is often used on large crocks, or places where a hollow lid might be beneficial. It is thrown as a shaped pot,

Fig. 9.23 Lid type 7.

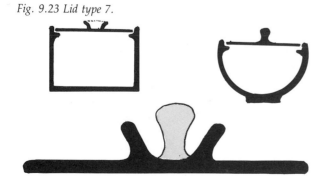

Fig. 9.25 Lid type 9.

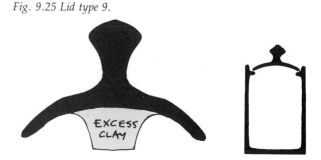

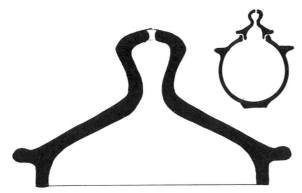

Fig. 9.26 Lid type 10.

by establishing the necessary width first and then collaring, or narrowing, the top to the form required. It is usually trimmed to fit the opening, by inverting it on the top of the pot. It can either fit a gallery or a simple termination. Hollow lids can also be made by cutting a hole through the center of a solid knob, or by using lid Type 3, throwing a small hollow knob onto the trimmed form, and boring a hole through afterward.

11. This is an example of throwing the pot and lid as a complete, enclosed form (Fig. 9.27). When the throwing is finished, a small, straight-edged tool is pressed against the rotating pot to form an indentation almost the thickness of the clay wall. When the clay has stiffened to leather hard,

a needle tool, scalpel, or sharp knife is used to cut the narrow joining part. A small amount of trimming is usually necessary to clean up the edges and get a good fit. Many variations of this form can be made, with a wavy line cut at an angle replacing the tool indentation. This form of cutting should be done when the piece is leather hard, and deformation is less likely. With any of these forms, it is necessary to make a small pin prick somewhere in the form to allow air to escape while drying to leather-hard takes place; otherwise, the piece will crack or deform at the weakest point.

These are the basic variations of lid types. When one adds the variety of knobs, handles, and modeled finials which may be attached to this group of lid types, one realizes that this part of the pot alone allows an infinity of interpretations.

Locking Lids

If lids are made properly, and are made to fit, rarely will they fall off—or into the pot which carries them. However, there are some occasions when locking devices may be incorporated into the design of a lid, form, or both, so the lid can't easily be knocked off. Most lids can be made to lock by adding a small tongue of clay at a point where it will inhibit movement. Figure 9.28 shows how these tongues may look. Sometimes it may be necessary to cut out a

Fig. 9.27 Lid type 11.

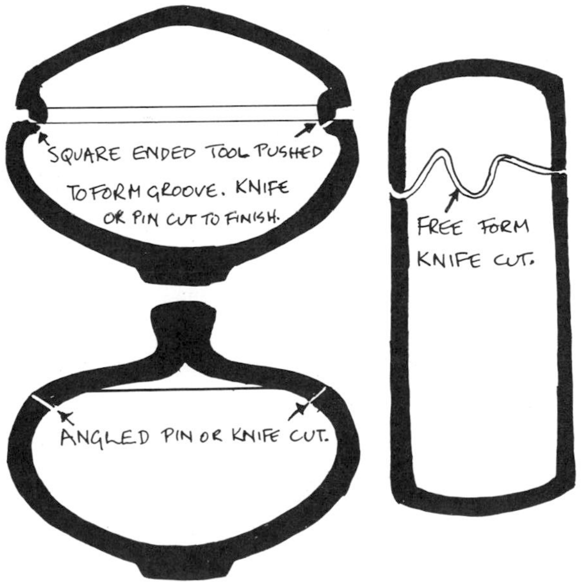

Fig. 9.28 Lid locking devices.

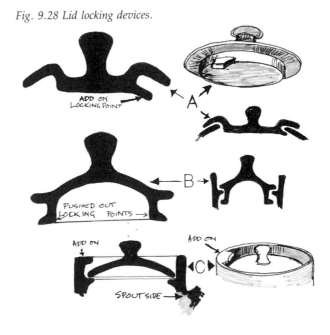

small section of the inner gallery to accommodate the tongue. On lid Type 3, a small pressure can be made like small pulled spouts on each side of the lid flange. These will hook under the inner gallery, and are particularly useful on such objects as coffee pots and teapots. If one bores the vent hole on the same side of the lid as the tongue, it is easy to remember where the tongue is situated. This is particularly useful in the dry stage, where lifting the lid might inadvertently break off the tongue. For inset lids with no built-in flange, it may be necessary to add a small piece of clay to the rim of the pot. If it is a pot for pouring from, it should be located on the opposite side from the spout or pouring lip, usually, but not always, on the same side as the handles (Fig. 9.28C).

It is possible to make lids which fit with a screw thread, either as an internally threaded neck which receives a stopper, or externally, like a standard jam jar lid. Either way, it is necessary to develop a tap and die system to cut the matching threads. This is an involved process which usually requires the cooperation of a small engineering company, unless one is a competent technician oneself. Since a description of the process of making screw thread lids, and the accoutrements required to make them, is likely to take longer than it warrants here, I would suggest that any reader who may wish to explore this form of locking device look at Michael Cardew's excellent book, *Pioneer Pottery*, published by Longmans, 1969. This has the best description that I have seen. It is often difficult to tell whether the end result achieved by the process is worth the time spent mastering it, or whether it is just an engineering conundrum. Interestingly enough, after using screw lids for quite a time, Michael Cardew confided that he had come to regard it as a time-consuming gimmick.

SPOUTS

Spouts can be press-molded, slip-cast, pinched, coiled, slab-built, or thrown. There are some practical advantages to making spouts by ways other than throwing. These are mainly in the consistent quality of the finished article, in producing a spout that is not likely to twist in the firing stages, and

Fig. 9.29 Swan or goose neck spout with multiple curves.

in a spout which has multiple curves (Fig. 9.29). The main uses of spouts are in lidded jugs, coffee pots, teapots, pitchers, and a few other items. The main consideration in their function is that they pour properly, preferably in an even flow, without dripping or clogging. As with pouring lips, the sharpness of the edge is an important factor in whether spouts function well or not. As long as the final edge which the liquid has to go over is sharp, the flow should cut off without dripping. The edges of spouts which are rounded are almost always prone to dripping. Many potters clean the glaze off the very end of the spout to assist in the flow-cutting action. There is no foolproof way of making spouts that don't drip, as there is a combination of factors which come into play, such as length, angle of attachment, width of aperture, and complexity of curves. Factors which assist in clean flow are a sharp edge, good angle, and smoothness of the inside of the spout.

Thrown Spouts

Throwing spouts is usually done off the hump, as it is easier to get one's hands around a larger piece of clay. Spouts are made like a funnel, with the fat end at the bottom. In the process of throwing, the clay is often constricted into a small, tight form, with a narrow aperture in the middle. It is important to remember just what sort of liquids may be flowing through the spout. If the aperture is too tight, it may become clogged by a coagulation of viscous liquid. Even milk, and certainly any thicker liquid, can possibly cause this to happen.

Thrown spouts often have a tendency to twist in the firing, due to the previously mentioned phenomenon known as elastic memory. If the clay is compressed into a small space while spinning, the alignment of particles is stretched as the torque of the clay goes in the opposite direction to the rotation of the wheel. The tension that is put into the movement often continues the direction during the drying and firing stages. This creates an annoying problem, where the cut end of the spout is sometimes twisted to the point where it is almost impossible to pour the liquid cleanly. One solution to this is in having a narrow spout, and not cutting the end. With a narrow spout more pressure is able to build inside the pot, which can result in a clean flow. With a larger aperture spout, a cut end aids in the pouring action, allowing a passage of air from the vent to the pouring edge. For a clean flow it is often best to smooth the inside of the spout, to eliminate the vortex action of the liquid, which would otherwise be caught up in the throwing ridges inside the spout, making the liquid pour from the spout in a spiraling movement. The problem of the twisting spout is one of an individual nature, and can only be correctly solved by the individual. As with lids that sometimes shrink excessively, the torque developed in the same clay used for the same forms will vary considerably from one thrower to another. It will also vary with different clays thrown by the same thrower. The usual solution,

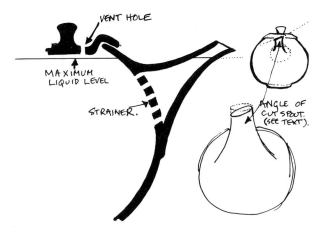

Fig. 9.31 The placement of spouts and angle of cut.

if the problem is a consistent one, is to apply the cut end of the spout at an angle slightly down to the left as one looks at it end-on (Fig. 9.31). It generally takes some time to gauge the right degree of slant, and it is never totally foolproof.

Spouts may also be made from ordinary thrown spouts cut in half lengthwise, or sections cut from bowllike forms and applied to the outside lip of the main form. Both of these spouts should perform well, particularly for thicker and more viscous liquids (Fig. 9.32).

Press-Molded and Slip-Cast Spouts

Many potters use the processes of press-molding and casting spouts to eliminate the aggravating habit of spout twisting. Casting, particularly, can also be extremely useful in making spouts in shapes not suitable for the wheel, or which may be needed in quantity. Press-molding is a slower process, but can also be very useful for asymetrical shapes not

Fig. 9.30 The torque or twisting action of clay in spouts.

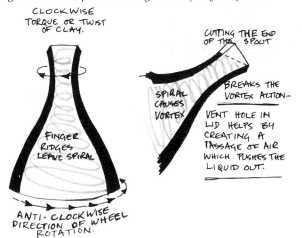

Fig. 9.32 Thrown and cut spouts.

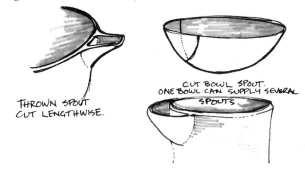

suitable for wheel making. In either case, plaster or bisque molds need to be made from a model. Molds for press molding can be less carefully prepared than for casting, since press-molding doesn't pick up as much detail, and imperfections can be cleaned up later. Molds for casting need to be more carefully made in order to cast properly, and also as the liquid slip shows every mark. A well-finished model saves a lot of cleanup time in removing unwanted seams and marks.

The process for making molds shown in Fig. 9.33 is as follows. First, a model must be made as accurately as possible, with a small amount of excess at each end to facilitate cutting to fit the body of the pot at one end, and for developing a good pouring edge at the other. For the simple conical type of spout, made by pressing, a simple one-piece mold is all that is necessary. The model is made as a solid cone-shaped form, which can be made on the wheel. When leather hard, the end which attaches to the pot is cut to the required angle. The individual press-molded spout can be altered easily to exactly fit each body after pressing. Once the model is complete, a wall of clay or linoleum cottle is made to surround it, in order to contain the setting plaster. Plaster is mixed and poured into the mold, to a line penciled on the model giving the length needed. Once the plaster is completely set, the model is removed, and the edges of the mold cleaned to make sure that pieces

of plaster can't chip off into the clay, causing problems later in the firing. The mold is then ready for use. A small cone of clay is pressed into the mold, and a modeling tool or sharpened piece of dowel or a pencil is used to both make the hollow and compress the clay against the side of the mold. Any excess is removed with a knife. When the clay has stiffened, it can be removed from the mold and fitted to the pot.

For pressing or casting more complicated forms, a two-or-more-piece mold is necessary. The process starts with making a model, with a small amount of excess at each end. The model is then marked with a seam line, along the most logical point, making sure there are no undercuts. This usually cuts the spout into two equal parts. A mold is made by first placing the model in soft clay up to the drawn seam line, with a retaining wall, or cottle, placed around it. Plaster is then poured over the model to cast half of the mold. When the plaster is set, the cottle is removed, the plaster part is turned over, leaving the model in place. The excess soft clay bed that the model was set in is removed, and the first half of the mold is cleaned. Indentations called keys are cut into the plaster to enable the two halves of the finished mold to fit back together in use. Keys can be cut by rotating the end of a knife in the plaster, or plastic keys can be purchased and cast into the mold. The plaster is then cleaned, and given four to six coatings of soft soap, to allow easy separation. The soap should be burnished between coatings or the two halves of the mold might stick together or have a rough surface. The second half of the mold is made by forming a cottle around the first part, and then pouring the liquid plaster to the depth necessary, and allowing it to set. After setting, the cottle is removed, the mold separated, and the model removed. All that is needed now is for the mold to be cleaned and left to dry out. The drying should be done with the two halves of the mold held in place with casting straps, usually made from old automobile inner tubes. This process produces a rough mold, sometimes called a wastemold, which is suitable for taking a limited number (150 maximum) of casts. For greater numbers, working molds need to be made. This is done by taking a solid plaster cast of the model and then repeating the procedure above

Fig. 9.33 Simple spout molds.

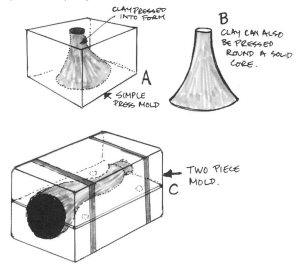

to create a working mold. The advantage of this is that there is always the plaster model to make another working mold. Casting slip can usually be made from the same body as the basic pot form, with deflocculants added to produce a smooth liquid. For large numbers of spouts, battery molds for producing several at the same time might be considered. For further information on mold making, I recommend that you select one of the more specialized books in the Bibliography.

Both casting and press-molding are good alternatives to throwing for spouts, particularly where non-round or modeled spouts are required. Since there is no throwing required, there is no problem with twisting or other distortion. Although sometimes questionable from the aesthetic viewpoint, spouts are often made by either slab or coil methods. It is extremely difficult to effect a happy marriage of thrown body with handbuilt additions. If handbuilt spouts are preferred, since they also do not twist, it is often a good idea to make small templates, so that the slabs can be cut, with ease and accuracy, for rolling and sticking (Fig. 9.34). A small cone of plaster or fired clay or a tapered dowel can be useful for wrapping the spout around, so that some pressure can be applied for sticking the ends together. Another method consists of pinching a small ball of clay flat to create an oval lip or overlapping spout. No matter how one makes the spout, its need to function properly remains the same, and hints given earlier for clean pouring should also be kept in mind here. However, if all else fails, one can always stick a piece of angle-cut plastic tube on the end! It may not be aesthetically pleasing, but it usually does the trick! In Japan, a great many teapots are sold with the plastic tubes

in place. It not only helps with the pouring action, but also protects the vulnerable end of the spout. One must admit, however, that there is really no aesthetic comparison between the beautiful, well-made teapot with a spout that pours properly, and a teapot which may be just as beautiful to look at, but which needs a prophylactic in order to function properly!

KNOBS AND FINIALS

The knob or finial, finishing point of a lid, is a point of the form where the potter has great license for play, giving a flourish to the top termination of the piece. Likewise, the lugs and handles which are required to function properly, may also be an avenue for freedom and inventiveness. They are all points of definition, where the attention of the viewer is likely to be caught, and sometimes captivated. Sometimes the knob is used to make or show some kind of sculptural statement, which is of greater importance and artistic concern than the function required of the pot.

There are, of course, a few qualifying requirements to these handling details which should be borne in mind, such as the ability to efficiently pick the object up, particularly if its function is generally in kitchen use. Greasy fingers, or residual grease which may be found on the surface, can cause potentially dangerous situations to develop in the preparation and cooking of hot food or liquids, or even in their storage. If cooking pots or storage containers are not easy to pick up, even with slippery fingers, the user may drop them, and lose both pot and contents, burning themselves at the same time. Potters who make pots such as these should perhaps consider product liability insurance!

Knobs are the top finials of lids, although not all lids necessarily have them. To function fully, the knob should be easy to pick up, without risk of it sliding or dropping from the user's fingers. If a lid is smaller than the span of a hand, or can be picked up easily because of its shape, a knob may not be necessary. Knobs can also be replaced by handles of many types, or by modeled details, like miniature sculptures. Not only is the knob the fin-

Fig. 9.34 Template model for a handbuilt spout and placement.

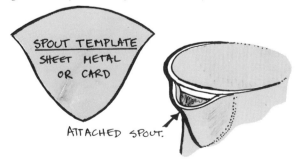

SPOUT TEMPLATE
SHEET METAL
OR CARD

ATTACHED SPOUT.

ishing point of the lid, but usually it is the finishing point of the pot which carries that lid. Its size should be considered carefully, as a point of emphasis, or as a point of quietude. It can be trimmed from the mass of clay specifically left in throwing, or can be thrown or modeled onto the leather-hard, partially finished lid. No matter how it is made, it should relate to the overall form. Some of the ways of achieving this can be through an echo of the form itself in miniature, repetition of part of the form, of a movement or line within the form, or of an inversion of any of these. The interplay between form, lid, and knob can become a compulsive exercise where the form may stay constant, and the details change, creating a vast series of variations, in a similar vein to musicians creating improvisations on a theme. It is a form of intellectual play, which usually leads to exciting results, as well as to an acute awareness of the effect that can be achieved by subtle variation, not only in shape, but also in scale. A small knob on a large form emphasizes its monumentality.

Trimming Knobs from Existing Clay

Perhaps the most important point of concern here is that the clay be of the right consistency throughout the form to be trimmed. This is usually done with leather-hard clay, to allow for proper cutting. It is also important that there is enough clay left, in the throwing stage, to enable the trimming to be done without the final knob being starved. It usually takes a good deal of experience to be able to judge this amount, but as a general rule it is better to err on the side of excess. Unless an off-center knob is required, the lid should be centered on the wheelhead, batt, or a stiffened clay pad. It is sometimes useful to place a small ball of clay underneath the lid to support the downward pressure during trimming. The clay is trimmed away to leave a lid having much the same thickness as the pot it is to fit.

Throwing or Modeling
Knobs onto Trimmed Lids

In throwing small pieces of clay onto the trimmed lid to develop a knob, the clay of the lid should be sufficiently moist to allow the knob to stick without

Fig. 9.35 Dual-purpose lid-plate.

later cracking, but not so moist that it might cause the lid to deform with the pressure and weight. Once the lid is sufficiently trimmed, a small scratched area in the center can be dampened either with slip or water. A small piece of clay is then pressed on, centered, and formed quickly to make the knob. It is often better to use slightly softened clay for this, as it allows easier forming with less pressure. As little water as possible should be used so that the danger of deforming the lid is lessened.

Thrown knobs or finials can also include the throwing on of coils, or short walls of clay, to give the knob a dual function. It can be both the handle for the lid and, when inverted, the foot of a shallow bowl for serving, or for holding serving tools (Fig. 9.35). Trimming can also accomplish a similar result.

Modeled and thrown knobs can be made separately and applied by scoring and slipping, or may be modeled directly onto the lid, preferably when it is placed on the form. This makes it easier to relate the scale of the modeling to the rest of the form, and facilitates determining the relevant importance of each part.

In place of knobs, lids may also be fitted with handles which may be pulled, coiled, slabbed, wire-cut, press-molded, extruded, or slipcast. There is an incredible potential variety for finishing the top of forms, and it is up to the potter to explore wherever he can, to satisfy his own aesthetics, and to create interesting details.

HANDLES

The word *handle* suggests something which is to fit or, at least be used, in the hand. This seems to be an element often forgotten by people making pots, where little consideration is given to how the handle is related to the natural shapes of the hand. (See Chapter 7, Pots and Anatomy.) Different people find different types of handles comfortable to hold as the handle either fits, or doesn't fit, their hand. There are many different ways to hold pots, and the same type of handle will not always suit everyone who may wish to use the object. There are also different wrist actions being used, from that of pouring from a pitcher, to that of tipping a cup for drinking. As long as the potter is aware of the principles behind these variations, it becomes easier to accommodate them into the work. Aesthetic and practical questions of the relative size and flow of the handle in relation to the pot are, to some extent, resolved by the intended use of the object. The use of an extra large handle on a large form such as a pitcher tends to diminish the visual impact that a smaller hand-sized handle would give. One often sees handles that fly out from the pot, exaggerated in size, and unrelated to the form or its function. For lifting and pouring hot liquid, for instance, all the space that is actually needed between the knuckles of the user and the body of the pot is in fact a maximum of a quarter of an inch, or half a centimeter. Even when the object is at its hottest, the small air space from knuckles to pot acts as an adequate insulator from the heat. A large flowing handle generally gives a sense of insecurity when pouring liquids, since it is much easier for the slopping movement of liquid inside to disturb the balance of the pouring action.

Handles are difficult things to make well, and particularly difficult to fit to the variety of forms that may call for them. As with knobs, there are many ways in which they can be made. They may be thrown, pulled, wire-cut, pinched, coiled, coiled

Fig. 9.36 Pitchers with excessive handles.

and braided, slabbed, extruded, press-molded or slipcast. For many forms they may also be made from other materials, such as bamboo, rattan, wood, metal, leather, bone, or many materials in combination. The decision on which method of handle-making is best, or which material might be used for any one piece is a very personal one, coming from a combination of aesthetics and experience. A badly made handle is a very detrimental detail to any pot, as it is the one part of that pot that is continually in contact with the hand of the user. If it feels inadequate it will be a constant reminder of its inadequacies. Other details don't have such an intimacy about them except, perhaps, for knobs on lids and lips on vessels we drink from. It is hard to feel any joy in using something that is continually uncomfortable, and holding hands with either a flaccid or bony, pinched handle can quickly quench the desire for further contact.

Another problem encountered in making pots with handles lies in the decision of where to place the handle. Much of Part Two was related to form and its relationships, as well as to the physics of lifting, leverage, gravity, and structure. In the design of forms which require a handle, the shape should be considered with this in mind, and not as an afterthought. Whether one makes an articulation change in the form, or simply makes a groove or raised linear emphasis, that emphasis is best placed where it marks a suitable point for handle attachment. The placement of a handle should be at the point where the maximum efficiency in use is found, or where, because of the shape concerned, efficient leverage is found.

Attachment of Handles

Handles, and indeed any additions, may be attached to the basic form by various methods. Essentially what usually happens is that the basic form is scored with a knife point, an old fork, or similar sharp tool, at the points where the handle, or other attachment, is to be fixed. The area is then dampened with water or slip made from the same clay, and the attachment firmly pressed into place. Some potters don't bother to roughen the surface, but it usually does help in gaining a secure fastening of one piece of clay to another. Some clays stick together easily, with little or no scoring, slip, or water, and some require a lot before they will stick without cracking off. Only firsthand experience with any given clay will tell what that particular clay requires.

It is important that the ends of handles carefully and effectively adhere to the vessel, and here is yet another point for inventiveness by the potter. Handles can be pressed into place leaving finger or thumb marks, they can be smoothed into the form leaving no marks, or they can be pressed with stamps, seals, or have sprigs or other modeled details attached.

Having decided what the handle is to look like, how it is to be made, where and how it is to fit, the next stage is in making it.

Thrown Handles

Thrown handles are mainly used as an attachment on side-handled casseroles, some soup bowls, oriental sauce pots, teapots, and coffee pots. They can also be made as a circular form, which may be used as lugs. When full of liquid, larger pots require a strong wrist to lift and pour, so the thrown side-handle is generally used on smaller pieces. They may also have a small lug on the opposite side. Thrown handles should be shaped with the inner shape of the half-closed hand in mind to make gripping easier, either as a tapering tube, or a contoured tube (Fig. 9.37). If the end of the handle can be completely sealed, it saves the annoyance of filling with water during washing. A small pinhole underneath, allowing steam to escape, makes sure that the handle will not explode during firing. In use, this small hole will allow any dishwashing water that may have inadvertently got in, to drain out. The lower end of the handle is cut to fit the contour of the pot, and attached.

Pulled Handles

Pulling handles is probably the most widely employed method of handle forming used by potters. It is quick and efficient, and when done well, is a joy to make, to hold, and to look at. It is done by gently applying pressure, and water or slip for lubrication, to a pear-shaped piece of clay, and pull-

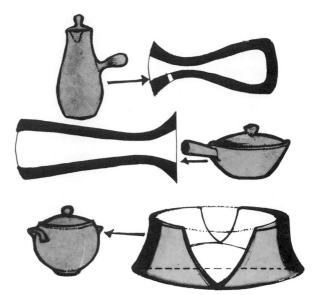

Fig. 9.37 Thrown handles.

ing from the narrow end into a long tapering sausage. Depending on the required size of the handle, the clay can be cut or torn from the basic clay lump, trimmed of any excess, and applied to the pot. If the clay is too soft, the freshly applied handle may tend to droop. This is usually rectified by placing the pieces upside-down, until they have stiffened. Once the clay has stiffened slightly, adjustments to its form can easily be made by exerting slight pressures wherever needed. The way in which the hands and fingers are manipulated will make wide variety in the cross-section. Different placements of the thumb or first two fingers can form ridges or grooves down the length of the handle. Some people prefer to attach pieces of clay, or partially pulled sections of handle, directly onto the pot, and then pull that into the finished handle form. Others prefer to pull the handles separate from the object. After they are pulled, they are formed into the required curve and laid on a smooth flat surface to stiffen before attachment. When they have stiffened sufficiently, they are trimmed to fit and attached. From my experience, there seems to be no particular benefit to any one method, except perhaps that the handle pulled directly from the pot may be a little more integrated with the form, than those pulled separately and then attached. The quality of a good handle of any scale is in its invitation to be held. A good pulled handle usually has a form which tapers slightly from the top end to the middle, and thickens again slightly at the bottom. The tapering effect is found in both its thickness and its width, and conforms to the normal thickness variations of the fingers, where the first and baby fingers are usually slimmer than the middle two. Some potters prefer to make the heavier attachment at the lower end, on such forms as pitchers and mugs, pulling toward the top and thinning at the upper end. For comfort in use, the inner surface should be convex rather than concave. It should seem to grow out of the form rather than being merely stuck on, giving the feeling that the form would be incomplete without its presence. There should be a satisfying and related negative space between the handle and the form of the pot, a fluidity of curve, and a strength at the joins. Above all, it needs to feel good to hold and have a built-in sense of security.

On forms which in use might be excessively weightly, a thumb-stop is often used. This is usually a small piece of clay, either a compressed ball or preformed wedge-shaped piece. It is attached to the handle at a point where its incorporation will help the user to get a better grip. They are particularly useful on larger pots such as pitchers and teapots, but largely redundant on small objects such as mugs, except as a decorative detail.

Wire-Cut Handles

Wire-cutting of handles is done with shaped wire-ended tools. The shape of the aperture in the wire is what makes the cross-section of the handle (Fig. 9.39). Handles made in this way are even in section throughout their length. The process is done by cutting through a block of clay, with the tool either held upright, or at an angle, as long as the angle of cut is constant. After cutting, the length of contoured clay is lifted from the block, and curved as desired. It is better to let the handle strips stiffen slightly before attachment, particularly if the contour shaping is complex, with ridges. When the clay has stiffened, the handle is then cut to fit and attached to the pot. Any ragged edges along the ridges may be smoothed off with a sponge at the time of attachment.

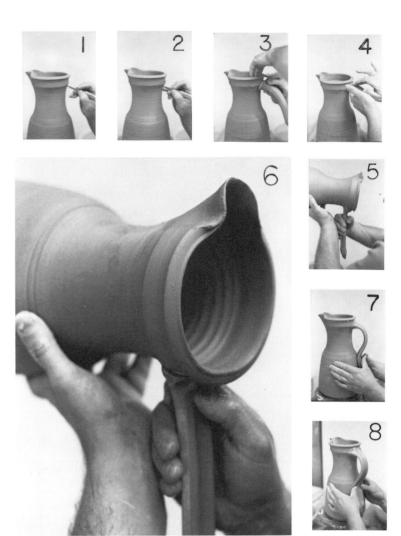

Fig. 9.38 Pulling and attaching handles: 1, 2. Scoring the surface for handle placement; 3, 4. Attaching partially pulled handle; 5. Pulling the handle from the pot; 6. Creating a center groove; 7, 8. Attaching the lower end.

Pinched Handles

The total freedom of expression in handbuilding techniques gives rise to many variations in handle-making. Freely shaped handles can easily be pinched either from the basic form itself, or from small balls of clay. When formed into suitable handles they can be attached in the usual way.

Coiled Handles

Coils, or rolled sausages of clay, can also make interesting handles. They may be rolled with an even thickness throughout their length, or with

Fig. 9.39 Tools for wire-cut handles and cross-sections of shaped handles.

Coiled and Braided Handles

Once rolled, coils can be joined together and braided in a variety of ways. Two, three, or five-strand braiding can be done in exactly the same way as with hair, cord, or rope. Any more than five strands will become very difficult to control. In order to do braiding without too much difficulty, the clay should be reasonably soft, and long enough lengths prepared to allow for interlacement. The clay is braided without the use of slip. If it should seem necessary to use slip to fill gaps, or to stick coils together, this is best done with a brush after the handle is attached. Braided coils may be flattened by a light pressure from the hand, or with a rolling pin. This not only flattens them, but can make extremely interesting free patterns develop from the intertwined coils.

Slabbed Handles

The slab allows all manner of possibilities in handle-making, from the hard architectural aspects suggested by stiff clay, to maleable pillowlike possibilities of soft clay. Differing degrees in the dryness of the clay offer a wealth of potential.

Extruded Handles

Extruded handles are made with a small machine or hand-press tool which pushes clay through a shaped die into a continuous length. The die can be cut to form almost any cross section, and the clay pushed through it can be either used in its length, or as a cross-cut (Fig. 9.41). The final result

variations in thickness built in, either accidentally or by design. The process is simply done by rolling the clay between the hands and a solid surface, until the desired thickness is achieved. Short lengths of over-thick clay can be cut off, and then further rolled to thin out sections such as the middle or ends. When the handle is formed, it is often left to stiffen before being applied to the base form. Coiled handles can easily be modified using short lengths of wood, either longitudinally or across the length to produce a concertinalike effect (Fig. 9.40).

Fig. 9.40 How one can modify coiled handles to create added interest.

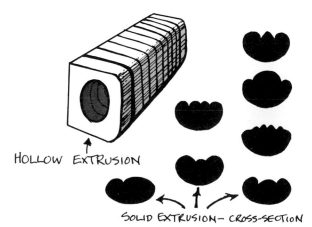

HOLLOW EXTRUSION

SOLID EXTRUSION — CROSS-SECTION

Fig. 9.41 Extruded shapes used for handles.

of an extruded length is visually similar to a simple wire-cut handle. Cross-cut extrusions are done by making the extrusion, and then slicing it across to make handles like small slabs, sometimes with finger holes already in place. A small amount of trimming of rough edges is all that is needed before the handle may be attached. Pug mills used in clay preparation can easily be adapted to make die extrusions, although there are currently many different makes of small extruder available in the marketplace.

Press-Molded Handles

The basic method of making press molds was explained earlier in this section, as related to spouts. They are quite simple to make, and particularly useful for handles which might have simple modeling included in the design of the handle. Molded impressions make it possible for numerous copies to be made of an original, and thus cut down on the time which may be required for each one. Press molding is limited to fairly simple impressions, but does allow considerable freedom for expression in repetitive work.

Slip-Cast Handles

Slip-casting was also discussed earlier, in the section on spouts. Cast handles can be made in single molds, or in battery molds when a great number are needed. Battery molds usually make twelve to eighteen handles at a single pouring of slip and consequently save much time. The technique is basically an industrial one, although it can easily be put to good use by the studio potter. Depending on the skill of the mold-maker, almost any form of handle can be made by slip casting. Extremely detailed forms might need complex molds. In volume production, the use of slip casting can offer a viable alternative as it can be done with semiskilled labor, thus freeing the potter's time for something else. Once slip-cast pieces are removed from the mold, they should be trimmed of any seam lines, and are then ready to attach. Provided that the basic form is leather hard, only water or the smallest drop of slip is needed to effect a good bond.

LUGS

The word *lug* comes from Old Scandinavia and means to pull or lift. In Old Scots, it means an ear. In pottery, the term means a small handle or earlike projection. Originally these small handles were intended to tie lids or skin covers down to, or to sling cords through to hang or carry objects. The term is usually applied to any small handle which may be used for lifting or carrying, particularly on kitchen wares, casseroles, and on teapots as a base to attach a handle of some other material. Now, they are often used in a purely decorative way, as an emphasis to the basic form.

Lugs on kitchen and cooking wares are usually applied horizontally, and may be attached to the basic form either at the ends, or throughout the length of one side of the lug. The placement and method of attachment is usually dependent on the function to be served. On teapots, the lug is the attachment point for handles which may be made in bamboo, rattan, wood, metal, or leather. Lugs may be made in the same way as any other form of handle, and attached by simply using slip or water. Where lugs are used on cooking pots, they should be substantial enough for the user to hold and carry while probably wearing oven mitts. Also on cooking ware, it is often useful to press a soft clay coil into the crevice which usually occurs where the lug joins the form. This not only strengthens the join, but also makes sure that cleaning of any burned-on foods or liquids is easier.

Other lugs may be made by cutting away part of the rim on some types of bowl, or casserole, where the handle is in fact the clay remaining (Fig. 9.42). Coils of soft clay can be wrapped around a form requiring handles, attached, and thrown on in a wedge-shaped flange, with the thick end stuck to the pot. When this flange is pressed down, handles are formed directly, and the excess flange can be cut away either completely or partially. The partial cutting leaves a wide soft ribbon between the handles on each side. This soft area can be used in a variety of decorative ways, such as fluting or stamping, or just left as it is.

Details of pots are very important parts. They certainly tell very quickly the degree of mastery

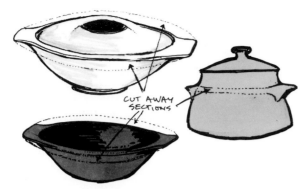

Fig. 9.42 Handles that are formed when sections from the thrown form are cut away.

which any potter has over his medium. Sadly, however, details are often neglected in the degree of consideration which is given to them, and many a potentially good pot suffers needlessly as a result. Pots which are designed to function should do just that. There is really no excuse for objects to function badly just because they are made by hand. In fact, they should really function better than the industrial model because they have the caring close attention to detail which the industry cannot closely control. The potter has a responsibility to thoroughly think out the object he makes, and to make it as well as it can be made.

The buying public is often badly underestimated by potters, and all manner of functional inadequacies are lavished upon them. There is no limit to the expression which an individual potter can put into his functional pottery, but it should be done with great concern for the real requirements of that object. Certainly this represents a great and often frustrating challenge to the maker, as it makes the need to compromise a major factor in production. Objects made to function can also be works of art, as the past has so often shown us. One only has to see tomb objects from almost any period to realize this. There is nothing mundane about making functional pottery for use by people; it is a demanding process, requiring all of the artistry and skill that can be mustered to solve the problems which the design and making of any given object deserves. Making good functional pottery is not making art for art's sake, it is making art for people's sake.

WEIGHTS AND MEASURES

If one is doing a great deal of repetitious throwing, it is convenient to keep a chart of weights and measures, giving the amounts of clay needed and sizes of objects at the throwing stage. Following is a list of weights and measures of standard items produced in my studio. These are for an average throwing thickness of $\frac{3}{16}$ inch (5 mm) for smaller objects, and $\frac{3}{8}$ inch (1 cm) for larger objects. If you throw either thinner or thicker than this, you will have to adjust accordingly.

Weights and Measures for Basic Production Items

ITEM	WEIGHT		HEIGHT		WIDTH	
	Grams	lb./oz.	Inches	cm	Inches	cm
Drinking Vessels						
6-oz. coffee mug	275	10 oz.	3	7.5	3	7.5
8-oz. coffee mug	400	14 oz.	5	12.5	3	7.5
14-oz. beer mug	600	1 lb. 5 oz.	7	17.5	3½	8.5
chalice (cup only)	500	1 lb. 2 oz.	4	10.0	4	10.0
goblet (cup only)	340	12 oz.	5	12.5	3	7.5
cup	300	11 oz.	2¾	7.0	3¾	9.5
saucer	350	13 oz.	1	2.5	5½	13.5

Weights and Measures for Basic Production Items

ITEM	WEIGHT		HEIGHT		WIDTH	
	Grams	lb./oz.	Inches	cm	Inches	cm
Plates						
large dinner plate	1800	4 lb.	1¼	3.0	11½	29.0
medium dinner plate	1350	3 lb.	1	2.5	10	25.0
side plate	1000	2 lb. 3 oz.	1	2.5	8	20.0
bread and butter	600	1 lb. 5 oz.	¾	2.0	6½	16.0
glutton plate	2300	5 lb. 2 oz.	1¼	3.0	14	35.0
Bowls						
large, general purpose	2600	5 lb. 12 oz.	6	15.0	12	30.0
medium, general purpose	1800	4 lb.	4½	11.0	10	25.0
small, general purpose	600	1 lb. 6 oz.	3	7.5	6	15.0
onion soup	600	1 lb. 5 oz.	3	7.5	6	15.0
large mixing bowl	1800	4 lb.	4½	11	10	25.0
Casseroles						
4-quart	2600	5 lb. 12 oz.	8	20	12	30.0
lid	1600	3 lb. 8 oz.	—	—	—	—
2-quart	1800	4 lb.	4½	11	8½	21.0
lid	1000	2 lb. 3 oz.	—	—	—	—
1-quart	1000	2 lb. 3 oz.	4	10	6½	16.0
lid	750	1 lb. 12 oz.	—	—	—	—
individual	600	1 lb. 6 oz.	3	7.5	5½	13.5
lid	450	16 oz.	—	—	—	—
Pots for Pouring						
cream pitcher	400	14 oz.	5	12.5	3	7.5
1-pint pitcher	675	1 lb. 8 oz.	6½	16.5	4	10.0
4-pint pitcher	2600	5 lb. 12 oz.	14	35	6	15.0
coffee pot	1800	4 lb.	11	27.5	4½	11.0
lid	400	14 oz.	—	—	—	—
large teapot	2000	4 lb. 6 oz.	8	20	8	20.0
lid	250	9 oz.				
medium teapot	1500	3 lb. 6 oz.	6	15	6	15.0
lid	200	7 oz.	—	—	—	—
small teapot	1000	2 lb. 3 oz.	4½	11	5	12.5
lid	150	5 oz.	—	—	—	—
1-liter decanter	2000	4 lb. 6 oz.	12	30	6	20.0
small decanter	1200	2 lb. 11 oz.	8	20	5	12.5
liqueur or sake bottle	1000	2 lb. 3 oz.	—	—	—	—

Weights and Measures for Basic Production Items

ITEM	WEIGHT		HEIGHT		WIDTH	
	Grams	lb./oz.	Inches	cm	Inches	cm
Storage Containers						
large storage jar	2250	5 lb.	12	30	5	12.5
medium storage jar	1500	3 lb. 6 oz.	10	25	4	10.0
small storage jar	800	1 lb. 12 oz.	7	17.5	3	7.5
jam or honey pot	450	16 oz.	3½	8.5	4	10.0
Serving Dishes						
large cooking/serving dish	2500	5 lb. 8 oz.	3½	8.5	15	37.5
small cooking/serving dish	1350	3 lb.	2¼	6	10	25.0
cheese bell	2000	4 lb. 6 oz.	6	15	10	25.0
base	1500	3 lb. 6 oz.				
butter dish	600	1 lb. 5 oz.	3	7.5	5½	13.5
base	600	1 lb. 5 oz.				
salt and pepper shakers	400	14 oz.	4½	11	3	7.5
egg bakers	400	14 oz.	1¼	3	3½	8.5

Pots for Eating From

Eating must be one of the most pleasant rituals of human existence, whether it be in the simple process of daily nourishment, or as a major celebration, such as a banquet or even a dinner party. Quite apart from its role of giving sustenance, the breaking of bread with members of one's family, friends or acquaintances becomes a time of special significance. It is a time of discussion, compassion, contentment, and contemplation. Food and drink act as lubricants to tongues and stimulate the flow of speech. The whole ambience of the dining room, from the warmth and lighting, to the table and its accessories, can serve to make the mundane into the memorable. With visually satisfying objects to eat and drink from, even the simplest of meals can feel like a special occasion. It always amazes me just how much better food can seem to taste just because one is eating from aesthetically pleasing ware, normally bowls and plates. The interaction between the senses seems at its most profound when contemplating food, from the obvious of smell, taste, and sight, to the less obvious of touch and sound. Apart from certain cacophonous cereal products, which go snap, crackle, and pop, various sounds made in cooking, chewing and slurping, and some esoteric sounds made during various ethnic food and drink rituals, sound plays little part in the process of eating and drinking. Eating is a mute enjoyment.

Touch, however, is often very important. In various parts of the world, foods are eaten in different ways. Over large tracts of the globe, people sit on the ground and eat with their fingers, usually with their right hand, pinching food from the surface of leaves, plates, or bowls held in the left hand. Sometimes the serving vessel is cradled between the thighs or knees, depending on the sitting position. There is an intimacy, and immediate contact with both the food and its container. Eating in this way, one feels close to the core of life, which is part of the joy of outdoor life, camping, and picnics.

In most so-called civilized countries, in what is termed "polite society," it is considered normal to elevate oneself above the ground, and sit on a chair at a table. The food is served on or in an object that one doesn't touch or seldom touches, and it is eaten, at a proper distance from barbaric finger contact, by the use of knives, forks, and spoons. Granted there are a few foods that are socially acceptable to eat with the fingers but, in the main, we have lost contact with much of our tactile sense. Now, it is somewhere between these two extremes of eating style that the most usual, and most socially acceptable, form of eating is found. People often hold bowls in their hands, drinking from their edges. In today's less formal society, it is also quite common to hold plates in one hand, while holding a fork or spoon in the other. At this point one is again in close contact with the vessels of daily use. Pots made for eating from are probably the main, if not only, pots with which we come into daily physical contact. It follows that pottery makers should carefully explore the visual and tactile qualities of them. In the culinary arts of Japan, for example, this sensitivity to these qualities seems to be unquestioned, and yet, in the western hemisphere, they are looked at with suspicion. We tend to look for shapes that are machine-pure, with perfect surfaces. Machine-pure shapes are, more often than not, made for the convenience of the machine, while the slick perfect surface is made for the sake of hygiene. Perhaps in a society where the dishwashing machine is in common use, cleaning with water that is much hotter than hands can bear, there is a place for using glazes of varying surface qualities, including pitted and crazed ones. Surface quality serves to satisfy both visual and tactile senses, and adds to the pleasure of the eating ritual.

BOWLS

Bowls come in many forms and have many uses. Their sizes vary from those small enough to be held in a cupped hand to large communal serving bowls. Many have multiple uses. Specialized bowls, such as mortars, may be made for grinding foods. Colanders and sieves may be used for straining and steaming. Bowls may come with spouts and lids depending on their potential use. Perhaps bowls are the most useful of household objects, as their functions are so numerous. The considerations in making bowls are mainly related to their generally determined function. Their shapes may vary from shallow and wide, to deep and tall. Since the bottom of the form is normally curved, they usually have a foot of some kind. They may have a rim at their top edge either for decorative or functional purposes.

Soup Bowls

Bowls for serving soup are usually of two basic forms, either shallow with an almost flat base, or deeper with a noticeably rounded base. Differing preferences among users, as well as the considerations of the type of soup being served, account for the two basic shapes. Occasionally, even the time of year and the climate influence the style of bowl preferred. A wide, shallow bowl with an outward-flaring rim is often used in summer, or for cold soups, whereas the deeper bowl, often with an inward-turning edge, is more often used for hot soups, and in winter, when it can also be used for warming the hands. Soup bowls occasionally have lids and handles.

Rice Bowls

In the Orient, rice bowls are often lidded. They are usually shaped in a convenient way for holding comfortably. Rice bowls and bowls for Asian foods sometimes have a slight depression in the top rim, as a convenient place to lay the chopsticks. This depression can be cut into the rim, or pressed with chopsticks into the soft clay rim to get the right fit. In many lidded rice bowls, the lid acts as a secondary container for pickles or condiments, giving dual purpose. The way that the lid is to be used will determine its style.

Dessert Bowls

Dessert bowls are usually of the wide, shallow type, often with a rim. This can be a convenient place to put unwanted cherry or grape pits, or for serving biscuits or wafers. In making sets of dinnerware, which also contain cups or mugs with saucers, matching the foot of the bowls to fit the saucer depression is often worth considering.

Salad Bowls

Individual bowls for salad can be just about any shape, as long as they are wide enough to conveniently use with the eating utensils. Salad serving bowls need to be big enough to allow for the salad, and also the movement of the salad servers or tongs used in the tossing process. Salad serving bowls and individual bowls are often made in sets.

Mixing Bowls

Mixing bowls need to be both solid and stable for the functions they perform. The pressures of beating tools and whisks make any fragility a liability. Many mixing bowls have a flattened side which may be used as a second foot for tilting the bowl while beating. Mixing bowls often have a pouring lip, or short half-spout. They can be made as nesting sets for the convenience of space.

Serving Bowls

Serving bowls can be just about anything, and there are few restrictions, if any, in their form. Whether they do the intended job or not is the question and, since there is such a variety of things which may be served, almost any bowl will fulfill the needs of serving something.

Grinding Bowls

Mortars for grinding of foods are usually low, with a very stable foot. They should be solidly made as they are likely to take considerable hard wear. The inside of the bowl is usually unglazed, and may have a serrated surface to assist in the crushing and grinding action of the pestle.

Colanders and Sieves

Colanders and sieves are basically bowls with holes cut through them for washing and straining foods. Pottery sieves can also be used for steaming foods by placing them with the food contents in a saucepan with a little water, and boiling until cooked. The placement of holes can be random, or carefully controlled as a part of pattern making.

Practice

Bowls are deceptively simple things to make. In the earliest learning stages of throwing, they happen almost by accident, especially when one is aiming to make cylinders! The control of the inner curve of the form and, subsequently, the outside form, takes considerable practice. The best way to develop this is by continual repetitive practice of similar forms, using a constant weight of clay. Potters often throw bowls and other smaller items "off the hump" (see Fig. 10.1). A large lump of clay is attached to the wheel, and roughly centered. A small part of the lump is centered and thrown, the initial size being gauged by the volume of clay in the

Fig. 10.1 Throwing off the hump: If the bases of hump-thrown pieces are not adequately compressed, an "S" crack may result.

hand. This process continues until the lump is totally consumed. In throwing off the hump, compression of the base is very important to alleviate possible problems of "S" cracks occurring.

PLATES

Plates are made in a variety of sizes to serve various functions, including eating from and serving on, as well as for pure contemplation. Their form and structure need careful consideration, particularly in relation to the placement of the foot; see Fig. 10.2 A and B. Depending upon the clay which is being used, and also on the temperature to which it is fired, plates may be subject to various problems. If any clay is fired to its maturity, it will soften at the top end of its temperature range. At this temperature, the rims are liable to slump slightly if there is not adequate support from a foot, fairly

Fig. 10.2 Trimming and placement of foot rim.

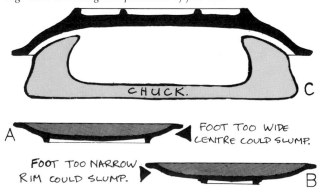

close to the edge. Unfortunately, if the foot is placed close to the edge, then the middle of the plate might slump. To cover these eventualities, it is quite common to have two foot-rings, an outer one which supports the rim, and an inner one which supports the center of the plate. On extra large plates, even a third foot or center point might be considered.

Practice

Depending on the size of the plate, throwing requires a heavy downward pressure as the clay is squeezed outward to form the flat interior. This can be done with the full palm of the hand, with the side of the hand, or with a rib. This compression minimizes the likelihood of "S" cracks in the base. When the full desired width is arrived at, the rim is usually pulled up and out to its final form. Trimming plates is most easily done over a chuck, which is made to support as wide as possible a section of the inner surface. Figure 10.2C shows the supportive fitting of a chuck. If the chuck is thrown at the same time as the plates, it will probably have stiffened to the same degree, giving support to a substantial part of the plate's interior, especially where pressure may be applied during the trimming. It also relieves pressure on the rim of finely thrown plates.

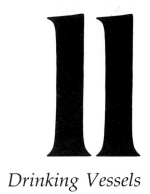

11

Drinking Vessels

Drinking is the natural companion to eating. There is a wide and varied group of objects that are used for drinking from, including beakers, mugs, cups and saucers, teabowls, goblets, and chalices. My concerns here are with fairly standard drinking vessels, which are in common use around the world.

Drinking vessels are invariably held in the hands, some by means of a handle, and others by directly holding the body of the pot. Some generally hold hot liquids, and others cold. The design of drinking vessels should take into account the shape of hands and fingers, the shape of mouths (see Pots and Anatomy, Chapter 7), the type and temperature of liquid generally being used, and the volume of that liquid which may be desirable.

BEAKERS, TUMBLERS, AND HANDLELESS CUPS

These are the simplest form of drinking vessel, usually used for cold drinks. A beaker is basically derived from the earliest forms of pottery, being a simple cup. Its form is either cylindrical, slightly barrel-shaped, or lightly flaring from the base to the top.

MUGS

The one object which potters in the western and southern hemispheres probably make more of than any other is the simple mug. It would seem that there is an inexhaustible need for them, although there seem to be amazingly few really well-thought-out ones. Although a mug is a simple object, it is a very intimate pot which often becomes cherished by its owner. Because of this intimacy, the composition of a satisfying form, with handles which fit the hands, and rims which fit the mouth, poses a number of problems for the potter. After ten years of trying all manner of variation in the shape of a mug, I finally settled on one. This was a composite, based on requirements which I had, related to the space I required for decoration and pattern making, in conjunction with what I had observed were the priorities of several other people. When asked about form, the major concern seemed to be with the handle, and whether it could accommodate the required number of fingers! Shape, it seems, is quite secondary to many people. Yet, the space for various numbers of fingers is a vital concern.

A great variety of forms can be suitable for a mug, somewhat depending on the size required.

Although mugs may vary in size for different beverages, demitasse, coffee, and beer, for example, it is not always possible to scale one suitable form up to a larger version of the same form, and retain the satisfaction that the smaller form gives. This is in part due to the way that the design, size, and placement of the handle has been solved. Simply enlarging the form of a small coffee mug, where the handle was designed to accommodate one finger, to a large beer mug where a whole fist may be needed to securely hold the mug plus contents, usually ends in an unsatisfactory solution. The reason for this is that the shape of handle required for one finger on the small mug will be out of proportion in the enlarged form. Instead of being easily held, it will most likely pinch the edges of the hand, while sticking out like an ear away from the form. In the large mug, one needs a quite different shape of handle to fit the clenched fist.

CUPS AND SAUCERS

The cup and saucer is the western equivalent of the teabowl. The most important difference is that the teabowl has to be held in the hands, whereas the cup is usually held by a handle. The form therefore has to be considered with this addition in mind. Most of the time the cup is used to hold hot liquids, therefore the design of cup and handle shapes and the handle placement need to be well thought out. As with the teabowl and the soup bowl, there are two basic common forms, wide and squat, and tall and deep. In between there are a lot of slight variations.

Handles for cups vary from the florid, ornate, or sinuous appendages which we see on most of the industrially produced cups in common use, to the simple, pulled, no-nonsense variety made by most potters. The former are derived from the eighteenth and nineteenth centuries and are a throwback to the days of elegance, where this type of handle forced the fingers into unnatural contortions, ending with the baby finger pointing outward (Fig. 11.1). They are difficult to hold with any sense of security, since most have no space to actually place a finger. The alternative is to grip the handle hard between the thumb and forefinger.

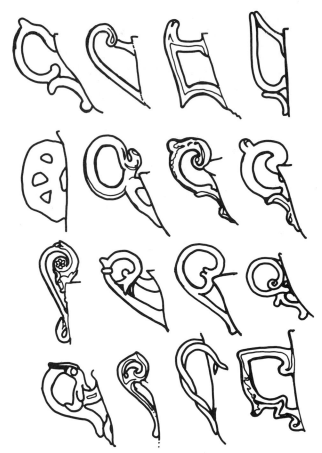

Fig. 11.1 Cup handles from 18th and 19th century European pottery and porcelain.

Fortunately, current industrial design trends usually consider anatomy, and recent pottery often reflects this.

Practice

Cups are like small bowls and mugs are usually variations of a cylinder. Both can be either thrown off a hump of clay, or with weighed-out amounts. Special consideration in any drinking vessel should be given to the rim which touches the mouth. The lips are very sensitive, and an overly thick edge usually feels most uncomfortable in use. A slight thickening of the clay just beneath the rim helps to make a thin edge less vulnerable. Saucers made for cups and mugs may often serve a dual function as a saucer for soup or dessert bowls. The way that saucers stack together is also a question of concern for some people. If the foot is too narrow, the stack will be prone to tipping over. For the best stacking,

A SLIGHT THICKENING BELOW THE RIM MAKES IT COMFORTABLE FOR THE LIPS AND STRENGTHENS FOR HANDLE JOINTS.

STACKING SAUCERS NEED WIDE FEET FOR STABILITY.

Fig. 11.2 The placement of a cup in a saucer and the stacking of saucers.

width of the foot should be double the width of the cup depression (Fig. 11.2).

TEABOWLS

Bowls have become more widely used in the last few years for everyday tea drinking. The most famous type of teabowl is used in variations of the Japanese tea ceremony, *Cha-no-yu.* These bowls have their aesthetic roots mainly in the peasant rice bowls of Korea. As a bowl of exquisite simplicity, it had the qualities deemed desirable as a meditative bowl for an extremely formalized and spiritual ceremony. All of the senses are brought into contact with a good teabowl, or *Cha-wan.* Perhaps the most obvious are the senses of sight and touch, where both are satisfied through the processes of looking, both at the form and the surface, and the tactile experience which reinforces the visual one. There are different forms for different times of the year, the winter bowl being a somewhat closed form, and the summer bowl being generally more flared and open. The tea ceremony formalities require the bowl to be held in a special way, with the left hand held flat beneath the bowl, while the right hand is placed lightly cupping the top edge of the bowl.

Although both winter and summer bowls are designed to be cupped in the hands, the shape of the winter bowl is more conducive to close contact, giving warmth to the body as well as the soul. The sound of the bowl is also considered, as the movement of the teawhisk, or *Cha-sen,* in stirring the green tea against the side of the bowl gives a particular pitch. Lower tones, such as those found in a raku bowl, are likened to the pleasant gurgling sounds of mountain streams running fast over stones. In comparison, the teawhisk used in a porcelain bowl will produce high-pitched sounds, reminiscent of a buzz-saw or a cicada, and not too conducive to meditation and contemplation. The shape of the winter teabowl assists in the dispersal of the aroma, much as a brandy glass does, where the confluence of imaginary lines extending from the bowl itself intensifies the perfume. Other points of consideration in the teabowl include the depression, either naturally formed by the movement of the fingers, or induced by later cutting, at the bottom of the bowl's interior. The way that the residue of the tea sticks to the walls of the bowl, and runs to a small pool at the bottom, is said to be evocative of small pools of water found in wooded areas. The faiths of both Zen and Shinto are deeply concerned with nature, and the esoteric qualities that are looked for in a fine teabowl are appreciated by few but the Japanese. Enthusiastic aficionados of the tea ceremony and collectors of tea ceremony wares will pay many thousands of dollars for a choice bowl made by a famous potter.

The second type of bowl is more commonly used for the everyday drinking of tea. It is not concerned with the formalities and subtle qualities attached to *Cha-no-yu.* In Japan, these bowls are called *yuonomi.* They are often made in pairs, for the male and female, with the male bowl being slightly larger than the female. They are usually taller than they are wide, somewhat barrel shaped, and have a deeply cut foot. This facilitates holding between the first two fingers placed beneath the foot, and the thumb placed on the rim. In Japan, *yuonomi* teabowls are usually served on a saucer made from wood, bronze, or lacquer.

The special qualities of both types of oriental teabowl have, to a large extent, been overlooked in the western hemisphere. The teabowl as a spe-

Fig. 11.3 Bowls for Japanese tea ceremony, cha-no-yu: (A) Korean summer bowl; (B) Japanese summer bowl; (C) Japanese winter bowl; (D) Japanese red raku winter bowl.

cial object, venerated in Japan for some 350 years, has, in many parts of the world, become debased by many pretentious potters' productions of it. More often than not, it seems, these teabowls are little more than clumsy, badly made parodies, with little understanding of the original aesthetic that they try to emulate.

Practice

Most oriental-type tea bowls are thrown off a hump or mound of clay. If they are made to any measure, it is usually a cross-shaped piece of bamboo which measures both the depth and width of the interior at the same time. Many oriental teabowl makers

concern themselves primarily with the interior of the bowl. For them, this is where one finds the soul, while the outside is mainly cosmetic.

GOBLETS AND CHALICES

Goblets and chalices are essentially cups placed on an elevated foot, often in a form similar to a wine glass. Although the chalice is usually larger and wider, they are similar objects, and therefore can be considered to have much the same problems. The physical nature of clay makes it unsuitable for very fine stems to be made without considerable vulnerability. In the firing stages, fine-stemmed goblets are likely to deform easily. The clay softens, and the weight of the cup is likely to cause the stem to bend toward the heat source. Depending on the sort of form one decides to make, the foot or stem needs careful consideration. Goblets and chalices are usually used for water, beer, or wine, as well as for hot drinks such as Irish coffee or rum toddies. These beverages are most often served in glasses. There is often a built-in reluctance amongst purchasers to use pottery vessels for these liquids, since part of the quality of the liquid may also be judged by its color. There may be good reason for this reluctance, but it might not all be related to the desire for transparency. Many goblets which are found in the market place are badly designed in various ways. Common problems are: too-small feet, making it easy to knock over the goblet and contents; too-tall stem, causing instability: too-narrow cup for comfortable drinking: too-thick rim for comfortable drinking: too-short stem for comfortable handling; and weight too much to feel comfortable.

In order to make pottery goblets which will satisfy a good segment of the market, various considerations must be made. There will always be those people who prefer glass; however, a well-made and well-balanced goblet or chalice can give a great deal of user satisfaction quite different from that given by the use of glass. There is usually a weight to clay goblets which imparts a feeling of well-being and stability. The fact that they are opaque gives mystery to their contents. The conductive quality of clay assures that pottery drinking vessels keep their contents at the desired temperature longer than glass.

Practice

Depending on size and design, goblets and chalices can be made in one piece. However, it is more usual to make them in two parts, which are joined together when leather-hard. Sometimes a foot is thrown onto the trimmed base of the leather-hard cup, using soft clay to minimize deformation of the cup. To ensure equality in the portions of liquid they contain, cups are often best made to a measure with weighed-out pieces of clay. Stems may be

Fig. 11.4 Japanese yuonomi *tea bowls by Tatsuzo Shimaoka. Private collection.*

Fig. 11.5 *Trimming chucks for goblets and chalices.*

thrown off the hump, and later attached when both they and the cup are leather-hard. Trimming of taller goblet forms is easiest when the cup is fitted over a chuck. This minimizes the likelihood of movement, and gives stability during the trimming. The chuck is best made at the same time as the cups, and should be shaped to accurately fit the interior of the cup.

12

Pots for Storage

Throughout the last 8000 or so years, pots have been used for storing things in. In the last forty years, plastics have probably superceded clay as the most universally used material for the making of storage containers. Since the inception of the plastics industry, there has always been some reticence against the inherent qualities of the various materials. For quite a long time, a large volume of plastic objects were made to represent another material, basketry and pottery being the most obvious. The design end of the plastics industry has, in recent years, produced a much more satisfying product which recognizes those special qualities that plastics do possess—clean, crisp, machine-efficient objects. There are undoubtedly some jobs which plastics can do better than clay, but clay still has some qualities which make it preferable for many uses.

Clay is abundant and comparatively inexpensive, and is a constantly renewing resource. It is a good conductor of both heat and cold. In many countries, clay pots are made from low-temperature red clays purposely left porous for cooking purposes. The pot doesn't crack on the open flame due to its conduction properties. They are used for water storage, where the evaporation or conden-sation on the outside of the container keeps the liquid cool inside; and for food storage, where the ability of the clay to "breathe" allows stored organic materials to be kept safely for long periods of time.

Most studio potters making functional ware work with clays fired at high temperatures, where the clay is more or less vitrified. Vitrified clay is generally unsuitable for some of the jobs that porous clay is used for, particularly open flame cooking, and evaporation cooling. However, its conductive qualities combined with its incredible decorative potential, make it a far more valuable material for many other uses. It can be frozen, heated, used in a microwave or regular oven and, if the clay body is specially prepared for thermal shock, may even be used for cooking on a direct flame. Its surfaces can be as smooth and sanitary as plastic, impregnable to even the strongest acids.

Our main concern here is with its use in making pots for storing things in. The above digression serves mainly to show that clay is alive and well, and not surpassed by plastics, for many necessary jobs around the home. It is a serviceable alternative to plastics for most things, and far superior for others.

Storage refers to anything that may need to be kept in a container, for reasons of tidyness, freshness, odor, aroma, dryness, wetness, stickiness, oiliness, and cleanliness. Differently designed storage containers can do all of these jobs.

KITCHEN CANISTERS

Commonly used to hold such things as flour, tea, coffee, rice, nuts, pasta, biscuits, and dried foods of many kinds, kitchen containers are subject to a strong possibility of slight residual grease from cooking to be on the surface. The user's hands are often wet from food preparation, and the combination of wet hands and this slippery coating on the container can make picking them up hazardous. The design of the jars should be such that they are as easy to hold as possible. This can be done by making indentations or ridges in the form, by various types of surface decoration, or by including a handle or lugs. Most containers need lids, and the type of material being stored is the deciding factor on which type of lid is best. Some lids can be loose fitting, while others need to be tight to keep moisture in or out. Considerations of space should also be made, since spherical forms take up much more space than cylindrical ones.

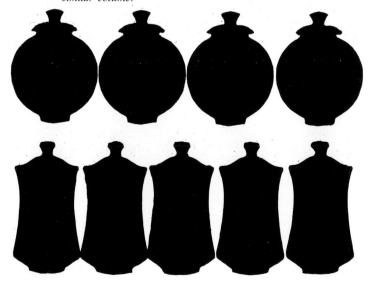

Fig. 12.1 *The difference in space taken by pots of a similar volume.*

TEA CADDIES AND TOBACCO JARS

These are similar pots, one for keeping its contents moist, and the other for sealing in an aroma. The tea caddy is usually smaller than the tobacco jar. Tobacco needs to be kept in a container which is as airtight as possible to prevent the escape of moisture, and the resultant drying out of the tobacco. Obviously the fit of the lid is critical for optimum efficiency to take place. There are various ways of achieving this, either through the design of lid being made, the use of two ceramic lids, or one ceramic lid and a cork interior cover, or the addition of cork linings to the lid, and/or container. The choice is up to the potter, and the efficiency of the pot is really dependent upon his skills.

BISCUIT OR COOKIE JARS

For a lot of parents, the ultimate jar for this use is one that the children can't get into! Short of putting some sort of locking device on the lid, or a series of three interlocking loops, one on the lid and two on the body, secured with a padlock, a totally impregnable, childproof lid is just about impossible! Since most cookies are highly susceptible to humidity, it follows that a container be as airtight as possible. It should also have an opening that allows access to a hand, and space for the added cookie on the way out. If it is too big, it might encourage the user to take the cookies by the handful!

JAM AND HONEY POTS

Jam and honey pots often perform a dual function of storing and serving. The fact that their contents are always sticky should have some bearing on their design. They can be simple forms with simple lids, which usually have a cutout section to accommodate a small spoon. The cutout need only be quite small, since the thickness and width of a spoon's shaft is usually a maximum of 2mm × 8mm ($\frac{3}{32}''$ × $\frac{3}{8}''$). The wooden or plastic servers for liquid honey are usually a maximum of 8mm in diameter. Any excessively large aperture will possibly allow the contents to dry out, or insects to get in.

BREADCROCKS

Breadcrocks are large lidded pots, usually used for storing homemade bread. In today's society, with freezers and refrigerators, breadcrocks are largely redundant, however, they are still used in many country areas. For the potter who enjoys the challenge of larger forms, they are satisfying objects to make, allowing free rein for self expression. The bread has to be protected from excess humidity, or it will mold. Since the bread normally has quite a high moisture content, some escape for condensation is necessary either in the lid, or in the body. Sometimes this might be done simply with small holes, and sometimes with a larger hole covered with a net fabric, glued into place.

RUM POTS

Rum pots are generally straight-sided containers used for submerging soft fruits in alcohol. They are relatively common in Europe. Soft fruits are gathered as they ripen, prepared and layered, covered with sugar, and submerged under rum or brandy.

Fig. 12.2 A rum pot with weight.

ALCOHOL LEVEL.

WEIGHT.

SUBMERGED FRUITS.

The fruit needs a weight to keep it below the alcohol syrup level or it may ferment. This can be done either with a plate, or a flat lidlike cover with a tall knob. The form is best as a cylinder, to enable the weight to work efficiently.

PICKLING JARS

Jars for pickling need to be robust, and should have a strong rim for securing an airtight film. They are often cylindrical, allowing a weight to be placed on whatever food is submerged beneath the pickling solution, so that fermentation doesn't occur.

BUTTER OR MARGARINE DISHES

Butter comes in a variety of packaged shapes. Maybe it is an anomaly to make circular butter dishes! However, people seem to be quite content putting square butter into a round pot. Margarine is often purchased in round plastic containers, and many people look for a suitably sized covered dish to hold the plastic one. Butter dishes are generally one of two basic types: the French type, where the butter has often been whipped, and is kept in what initially looks like the lid, inverted and submerged in water held inside a cylindrical or barrel form; or the dish with dome cover which is probably more common (Fig. 12.3). Both types work well, with the benefit of keeping the butter at room temperature, and thus easier to spread. The dish and dome system usually needs a wall to be integrated in the dish, so that the butter is less likely to get on the bottom of the cover, and be later transferred to the table whenever the lid is removed and set down. Dishes without some kind of retaining wall usually end up being very messy, particularly if one has children.

CHEESE BELLS

For short-term storage, most cheeses are better kept out of the refrigerator, under a domed lid. The usual form of cheese bell is a dish and dome affair, similar to, but larger than, the second form of but-

FRENCH BUTTER DISH

BUTTER

WATER.

DOME
AND
DISH
TYPE

Fig. 12.3 Butter dish types.

ter dish, above. The dish may have a raised wall to contain the cheese or, alternatively, the lid might be kept in place by providing a slight trough for it to sit in. If the preference is for runny cheeses, the former fitting is more suitable. For some specialty cheeses, such as stilton or gorgonzola, a lid with straight sides is generally preferred. Keeping cheese at room temperature allows it to mature properly, particularly if the cheese is a whole one where the skin surface is uncut.

Practice

Perhaps the most important point with storage containers is their need for lids that fit. If an object demands to have a lid to fulfill a specific function, then the potter should see that its type is suitable, and that it fits accurately.

CONTAINERS FOR LIQUIDS

Pots for containing and storing liquids need to be carefully considered. Spill-proof and watertight containers usually need a lid or stopper made of cork, or at least with some liner made of cork. Cork swells slightly when wet, and effects a watertight bond between the stopper and the body. If one ceramic surface is in contact with another ceramic surface, the granular nature of the two surfaces will allow air or liquid to get through, unless the clay is sufficiently dense for an impervious surface to be ground. This would probably require a fine porcelain body. Grinding may be done by placing a small amount of fine silicon carbide mixed with water in the neck or on the stopper, and twisting until there is a snug fit. For liquids which might evaporate, a cork is probably the best solution, since even the tightest of ceramic lids usually allows some evaporation.

13

Pots for Pouring

The historical development of spouts for pouring vessels went all the way from none to exaggerated long beaks (see Pouring Forms). For purely practical purposes, the most efficient spouts or pouring lips lie somewhere between the two. The types of liquids that are used to some extent control the type of spout which is most applicable to a given pot, as well as possibly influencing the shape of that pot. The fluidity of liquids varies from as thin as water, to as thick as whipped cream or porridge. Some particularly viscous liquids will quickly clog a spout which is too narrow.

If pouring vessels are designed and made well, they are a joy to use. If they continually drip, they can be very aggravating.

PITCHERS

Pitchers or jugs are made in a great variety of forms and sizes. They are pouring vessels which normally have a pouring lip, or spout, a handle, and occasionally a lid. Small pitchers often do not need a handle, and the form is made in such a way that it affords a good grip for the user. Perhaps the main considerations in the design of any pouring vessel are to do with leverage, balance (see Chapter 5), and weight. Where one decides to put the handle

to help the wrist movement used in pouring, is critical to making a pitcher comfortable to use. In a fairly large pitcher, perhaps containing a gallon of liquid, there are two points of easy movement. If the handle is placed high up, it is easy to carry but hard to pour from, because the weight of both pot and liquid are below the placement of the hand. If the handle is placed low down, it is usually more difficult to carry, because of strain on the wrist, but far easier to pour, because of leverage. These variations are due to weight displacement. In a case such as this, it is worth considering two handles, one to aid in lifting, and the other to aid in pouring. What one really needs is to find the ideal point of balance in a form, and to place the handle there for the best leverage. Unfortunately, the best place for physical movement is not necessarily the best visual solution. A compromise has then to be made.

Forms for pitchers may be immensely varied and are a challenge to make well. Since they need to be stable, the bases usually function better if they are wide rather than narrow. Bulbous forms have a homely curvaceous quality. If their feet are too small in relation to the bulk of the form, they are quite easy to knock over. Rotund forms are also difficult to fit aesthetically pleasing handles to, since the already fat form causes the handle to be thrust even further out. Bulbous forms are often more

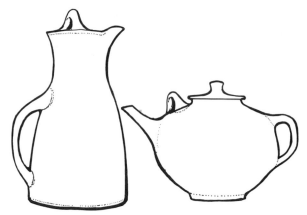

Fig. 13.1 Double handle placement for extra large or heavy objects.

difficult to pour from, usually requiring to be totally inverted before all the contents of the pitcher are removed. Simple cylindrical forms make it easier to decide where the handle should go, and easier to empty.

DECANTERS

Pottery decanters are subject to the same prejudice that sometimes accompanies goblets and chalices, namely, that they are not transparent and therefore it is impossible to see the contents. Obviously, this is a valid complaint, but decanters made of clay can have benefits. The conductive quality of pottery allows it to be preheated for any liquids that are to be served hot, such as sake, and chilled for anything served cold. It will retain both heat and cold for longer periods than glass. Decanters are used for serving drinks such as wine and sherry, or for storing and serving spirits. For serving, the decanter doesn't necessarily require a lid or stopper. However, for storing spirits it will need a stopper which is airtight; otherwise, the alcohol will evaporate (see Containers for Liquids). Some consideration should be given to whether the decanter needs a handle or not. If it doesn't need a handle, the form should be designed so that there is no risk of it slipping through the fingers. This can easily be done through designing a suitable form, or having some surface ridging or raised pattern on the neck.

TEAPOTS

Probably the most difficult single article that a potter is required to make, a teapot has all of the details, and takes a great deal of discipline, skill, and patience to solve all the problems of design and making. On the face of it, it sounds simple: a pot to carry and pour hot liquids, without spilling them, without dripping from the spout after pouring, with a lid that doesn't fall out, and a handle that is not so close that one might burn one's knuckles, yet, at the same time, not so distant that the pot feels awkward to use, and with both spout and handle invulnerable to breakage from contact with the kitchen plumbing fittings—all this, and to be aesthetically pleasing and affordable too! A teapot is a nightmare of composition, with a body and odd-shaped appendages jutting out at various angles and places. Not only is the basic visual composition complex, but to add to that problem, one has technical considerations also: spouts that may twist or droop, strainers that may clog with glaze, handles that may twist, lugs that may be too thin to take the combined weight of pot plus contents, or too fat to fit a cane handle on, and lids which need to be held in place while pouring.

In the western hemisphere, tea makers pour boiling water over the tea leaves, or teabag, and the resulting beverage is allowed to steep or brew until it has reached a satisfactory strength. There are some conflicting ideals in the making of tea which possibly affect the optimum position of the teapot spout. In England, tea is generally consumed as a stronger brew than in North America. For this reason, the majority of English teapots have a spout which starts from quite low down. This is where the strongest brew is found, floating just above the leaves or bag. In other parts of the world, tea is drunk more as a weak solution where the leaves or bag can be removed from the brew by means of an infuser of some kind. The base of the teapot spout in these areas is more often placed quite high, at or near the shoulder of the pot.

Whether one likes tea or not, if one calls oneself a potter, someday one is likely to get the urge to make a teapot. The production of a good teapot represents, perhaps, the ultimate challenge for the maker of domestic pottery.

Fig. 13.2 Typical low-spout placement on 19th century English teapots.

COFFEE POTS

Coffee is prepared in a number of ways, many of which do not utilize the standard types of ceramic coffee pot. Many coffee aficionados swear by using glass, while others use high-pressure aluminum containers or stainless steel.

The ceramic coffee pot can be used for making coffee in, or merely as a serving pitcher. Making methods include placing coffee in paper filters in a funnel-shaped holder, or just pouring the boiling water over the coffee grounds in the bottom of the jug and waiting for the grounds to settle. The way that the coffee is made, coupled with the buyer's needs, will largely determine the form that is preferred. Unlike most tea leaves, coffee grounds are small enough to go through most strainers made of clay, and metal infusers can affect the taste of good coffee. For this reason, the spouts of coffee pots are placed high up on the form, and the forms themselves are quite tall to allow any grounds to settle to the bottom. There is often a slight belly low on the pot, just below the spout, to catch the grounds when the pot is tipped to its extreme. With so many other coffee pots currently available, the ceramic coffee pot has lost favor in the last few years, but it still has its following of fans.

SAUCE BOATS

Sauces and gravies are generally served in a boat-shaped vessel, hence the name. The boat form is a very elegant one, but not particularly suited to wheel-made pots, unless they are squashed into an oval form after throwing or trimming. However, a wide variety of other forms that are perfectly serviceable for sauce containers can be easily made on the wheel.

Gravies and sauces may have a variety of different thicknesses from thin and watery to thick and gluey. Some sauces also separate, with the thick part rising to the top while the thin stays below. This floating is dependent on the fat content. For sauces like this, where some people prefer the thick and some the thin, a dual pouring method is sometimes incorporated: one spout is set low on the container, while a pouring lip pours off the thicker sauce on the opposite side of the pot. The pot may need a lid to keep the contents hot and uncongealed.

Pots for Cooking

Perhaps the largest variations of form are in pots made for cooking. As we have already seen in Part One, the historical and ethnic variations cover the globe, and current approaches to cooking do the same. Partly because of easy travel to far-off places, and the resultant tasting of exotic foods, dishes which until comparatively recently were little known, are now being cooked in ordinary household kitchens.

Cooking pots are made for steaming, poaching, baking, roasting, frying, and serving. They get used in all manner of ovens, from wood-fired to microwave. Their design has to concern itself with optimum performance, both in the conduction of heat and cooking, and in the handling ability of hot containers. So often one finds handles and knobs which are next to impossible to pick up when cold, let alone when they are hot and the user is wearing oven mitts! Kitchen accidents are among the most common, and although there are no statistics that I have been able to find, I feel sure that a good number must be caused by inadequacies in the pots being used.

Attention to details, although important at any time, is particularly important in cooking pots, where the user's sense of touch is often masked through thick layers of fabric. Any of the various types of handles, knobs, and lids need to be able to be picked up easily, with a total sense of security. If anything,

these details need to be overstated rather than understated.

CLOSED COOKING POTS

The list of closed cooking pots includes casseroles, beanpots, steamers, stewpots, chicken bakers and fish bricks, and there are many common generalities. These pots are mainly used for stews and casseroles, where the ingredients simmer in their own juices for a comparatively long period of time. Depending on what the casserole is used for, it might be deep, or wide and shallow. Deep casseroles are most useful for cooking ingredients which have been coarsely chopped. Wide, flat casseroles are better when used for cuts of meat such as pork or lamb chops, steaks, or veal escallops. They are also good for cooking whole fish.

In a good casserole, the food is constantly basted by condensation dripping off the inside of the lid and back into the pot. The type and shape of lid that is used is therefore important (Fig. 14.1). If the food is not basted it will dry out and the meat will be tough. Different cooks have strong ideas about cooking pots, and what will be one person's favorite may well be another's throwout.

The width of the base is an area of concern for the casserole user. If the base is narrow it might

Fig. 14.1 Domed lids keep contents of casserole well basted by condensation.

cause the casserole to tip in an oven that has wire sliding racks. The spaces between the wires varies from one manufacturer to another, but it is usually 1–2 inches (2.5–5 cm). If the casserole base is smaller than the span of three wires, it will be prone to tipping.

Chicken and fish bakers are porous pots often made to represent a chicken or fish. The pot is soaked in water before use for about 15 minutes. The bird or fish is lightly greased, seasoned, and placed with vegetables into the baker. The baker is then tied together so that no steam can escape from inside, and the meat is cooked by a combination of steaming from the water-soaked baker and basting from the juices inside (Fig. 14.2).

Steamers are made in two types. The pot is like a standard casserole with many holes in the base, and is placed over a saucepan of boiling water

Fig. 14.2 Chicken and fish bakers (bricks) made from thrown forms, laid on one side and then cut to form a lid and base. They are sometimes elaborately decorated; others are left plain. They are unglazed and porous.

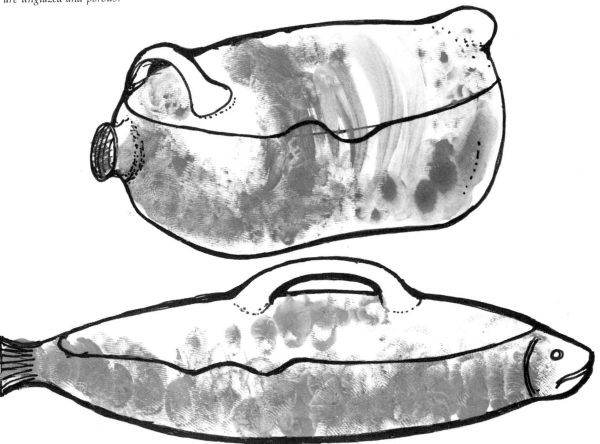

Fig. 14.3 Steamers, both made to sit on top of a saucepan of boiling water. Type A allows the contents to steam from below, but doesn't allow them to cook in their own juices. Type B bastes from above and cooks the contents in their own juices.

to cook the ingredients; or, instead of holes, it has a tube inside shaped like an inverted funnel joined to the base and level with the top of the steamer's sides (Fig. 14.3). The shape of the lid is also designed to drop condensation onto the contents. In the first type, the liquids formed in cooking are lost into the saucepan. In the second, the contents will cook in their own juices, along with the condensed water.

OPEN COOKING POTS

There are many variations of open-topped cooking pots for different foods. Most of the pots have handles of some kind, and are variations of a wide, shallow cylinder. Foods cooked in them include terrines and patés; fish, pasta, and rice dishes; many Mexican, Greek, Italian, and Oriental foods; soufflés, fricassees, pies, and baked eggs. The type of pot does vary, but not to the degree that casseroles

do. The two main concerns for many of these pots are that there is enough depth for the food to be able to cook without bubbling over, and that there is space on the top for the melting and browning of "au gratin" crusts.

Pots for cooking terrines, patés, and soufflés are usually straight-sided and 3–5 inches (7.5–12.5 cm) in depth. Soufflé dishes require a smooth, straight internal surface to allow for upward expansion. For other foods, flaring shapes are more suitable. Small individual baking dishes, called ramekins, are useful for individual portions of a great variety of foods. These are straight-sided or slightly flared, and sometimes have a small handle like a frying pan. A smaller version is for baked eggs, where an egg is broken into the previously buttered baker, covered with sour cream or grated cheese, seasoned to taste with garlic, chives, and pepper, and then cooked in the oven for 15–20 minutes, or for 2 minutes in a microwave oven.

Flameware open pots are designed to be used on the open flame or burner surface. Clays either have to be quite porous to absorb thermal shock, or made from a specially formulated body. Such bodies are usually made with materials containing a relatively high quantity of lithium, which is resistant to thermal shock. Lithium is found in spodumene, petalite, and lepidolite, and a clay body for flameware may be made including these materials. The costs of producing lithium-bearing clays is considerable, and there is no guarantee that they will work. I know of one potter who had to replace $6000 worth of flameware because of a fault in the body makeup. Most potters can't afford that kind of costly mistake, so it is probably best to leave flameware to companies like Pyrex or Corning, and concentrate on other cooking wares.

POTS FOR MICROWAVE COOKING

Cooking in microwave ovens has become a major method of food preparation in the last few years, but potters generally seem to have paid little attention to the challenge of making vessels specially for them (see Microwave Ovens, Chapter 17). Some materials (glass and paper) are virtually transparent to microwave energy, while they are readily absorbed by others (food and water), and reflected by metals. Most standard types of nonmetallic cooking pots can be used in the microwave oven, and almost any shape is applicable, depending both on the food being cooked and its volume. Most pots for microwave cooking are shallow open dishes, seldom having a depth of more than 2–3 inches. This is plenty of depth for most foods, and allows easy access to the bombardment of low-frequency radiant energy waves that cause molecules to vibrate and heat, and thus cook the food. For some foods, a deep pot allows better penetration of the microwave energy. The foot size is not critical here, as it is in standard ovens, since the container normally stands on a solid base. In some ovens, the microwaves come from all sides and a relatively narrow foot is often an aid to even cooking. Since it is the food which gets hot, and the dish only by conducted heat coming from the food, the need for handles is lessened, but they are still a good idea. Pottery used in microwave cooking is often the container for serving the food at the table.

Clays and glazes for microwave use must have little or no metal content, as metal may cause the waves to arc, and possibly cause a fire by overheating. Clay bodies, such as porcelain, which are relatively free from iron or other coloring materials, are preferable to stoneware or earthenware clays, where the iron may not be evenly dispersed. Similarly, glazes with high colorant content should also be avoided, as should any form of metallic luster, such as gold, platinum, palladium, or copper. To determine if an article is suitable one should do the following test: Measure 1 cup of water in a glass measuring cup. Place in the oven on or beside the object being tested. Microwave for 1 minute at the "high" setting. If the water becomes hot without the dish heating, the dish is microwave safe. If the dish becomes hot as well as the water, it should not be used for microwave cooking.

POTS FOR SERVING IN

The way food is presented can add immeasurably to its flavor. Many of the abovementioned cooking pots may also be used for serving at the table. The marriage of function and aesthetics is complete here,

Fig. 14.4 Open cooking pots. A. Terrine or paté; B. Soufflé or fricassee; C. Lasagna or risotto; D. Egg baker; E. Ramekin; F. Fish dish.

since the pots have done their first job in preparing the food, and now they receive part of the culinary glory for a job well done. They and their contents are on display, albeit fleetingly. For a good cook, a major part of food preparation is in the presentation. If the utensils are as good looking as the food, it makes the whole ritual of the table that much more enjoyable.

There are all kinds of different ceramic forms which are used for serving, and it would be both foolish and time-consuming to try to discuss them all individually. Some of the general types are bowls, plates, lidded containers, vegetable dishes, and tureens. Of these, perhaps the only ones which haven't been discussed elsewhere to some extent are vegetable dishes and tureens.

VEGETABLE DISHES

Although they are sometimes used for direct cooking, they are more often used for serving vegetables which have been cooked in some other vessel. They may be of a wide variety of shape, as long as they can satisfactorily contain what they are supposed to. They generally are lidded forms, to keep the contents hot. Specific considerations are few.

TUREENS

Tureens are large lidded containers, usually in a bowl form, made for serving soups or stews. The use of a ladle usually requires that the lid has a cut-out section for its placement. Since the pot will likely be carried containing hot liquid, it needs good handles and a stable foot. Many types of lid are suitable, as are many variations of handle.

15

Pots for Rituals

POTS FOR FLOWERS

Flowers are associated with rituals of many kinds, both sacramental and secular. The love of flowers is integral to most of humanity and the inclusion of floral display central to most of the major rituals of life and death. Flowers are a symbol to the glorification of love, both divine and hedonistic. They are also symbols of birth, growth, life, death, regeneration, and metamorphosis.

The floral container, or vase, is essentially anything that will hold water to sustain temporary life in the plants chosen for sacrifice. Flowers are either plunked randomly or artfully arranged in whatever vessel is chosen for the honor. For a considerable period of time there have been two basic concepts of floral arts, the western way and the eastern way. In the last three decades there has been a gradual merging of styles, as the cultures of the world intermix and the customs migrate from one continent to another, with the inevitable blurring of distinguishing identities. The use of flowers in rituals probably goes back to prehistoric times throughout the world, and they were certainly in great use by the Egyptians, Greeks, Romans, the countries of Islam, the Orient and of Central and South America.

The origins of studied floral arrangement in the Orient come from the Buddhist faith in China, initially as altar decoration. They often used the lotus as the symbol of purity and life, with its roots in water and mud, and its head in the heavens. In the west, floral arrangement most likely comes from either the precious nature of special flowers, such as tulips in seventeenth-century Holland, or from the use of personal pomanders to disguise body odors in less hygienic times. Developing from the Chinese beginnings, floral art became a major preoccupation with the Zen priests of Japan and, in a different approach, with the scholars. The arrangement of flowers and natural objects in Japanese floral art encompasses a great deal of philosophy and symbolism in the relationships among man, heaven, and earth. There is a carefully considered subjugation of the arranger to the material being arranged, and there is always space for the viewer to involve himself or herself in the arrangement. At this point, they are made to provoke thought and contemplation. Different plants and colors suggest seasonal variations, at the same time soliciting emotional reaction. It is often difficult to comprehend oriental arrangements, since there is so much more to them than meets the average untrained eye.

Floral arrangement in the western hemisphere hasn't, until recently, concerned itself with deep philosophical meaning, but has been more an exposure of flowers as specimen, or as a color group. A bunch of wildflowers placed lovingly in a jam jar often gives as much uplift to the occidental viewer as the mannered ikebana does to the oriental. Where spiritual significance doesn't exist, or is not part of the conscious rules of arrangement, intuitive pattern making or juxtaposition of mass, line, and color takes over a free and unconfined way.

Flower containers can be just about anything, depending on the visualization of the arranger. Pots are often made for flowers with little regard to the sense of completeness which comes with the arrangement. Of all pots made to fulfill a functional role, the vase is the most incomplete until it is in use. Paradoxically, it is also the object which allows the potter the most freedom. The form, surface, texture, and color of the container reacts in the totality of the composition no matter how structured or unstructured the flower placement may be.

In upright forms of traditional Japanese vases, there is often a scratching of the inner surface of the top inch or two to allow wooden or twig crosspieces to be wedged in to hold the flowers. On flat trays for open arrangements, concern is often for stability of the kenzan or pinholder. For any container, the form, surface texture, color, and size are what are considered. So there can be no *ultimate* vase, merely that which satisfies the need of the user.

POTS FOR THE ASHES OF THE DEAD

Throughout history, pots have been used as containers for the remains of the dead, either in a cremated or interred state. The production of these cinerary urns brought forth many wonderful objects, full of compassion, often humor and joy, as seen in Chapter 2.

In recent years, there has been a steady growth in the number of people who wish their remains to be cremated. Without wishing to seem unduly mercenary or macabre, this is an area which could be developed by the functional potter. Many bereaved people must look for urns for the ashes of their loved ones, either to bury or to keep above ground. As part of their social service in the community, potters could well perform a humanitarian function in making urns which celebrate a life which has passed.

After cremation, human remains are about 6 pounds (2.5 kg approx) in weight and fit into a box measuring approximately $9'' \times 6'' \times 3''$ deep ($22.2 \times 15 \times 7.5$ cm). An urn to contain the remains has to be made after a fair amount of discussion with the family of the deceased to know their wishes.

My first experience with such a project came when a distraught young man asked me to make an urn for his wife's remains. She had been killed in an automobile accident. Before her death she had been a collector of my work, and her husband felt that he could give no greater tribute to her than to have her remains placed and sealed in a specially commissioned pot. I felt honored to do that commission.

16
Considerations

Throughout the range of utilitarian pottery there are a number of generalizations which can be applied to almost every functional object. These concern the development of *form, foot* or *base,* and *rim.* Most pots have all of these. Depending on the nature of the object and its intended function it may also have a *lid, spout* or *pouring lip,* and *handles.* The last few chapters have tried to analyze the jobs that a variety of functional objects are expected to do. This chapter is a summary of these needs, in question form, and can be used as a quick reference guide. The questions relate only to form and intent, and do not concern the many other questions which may be in the potter's mind, such as clay, glaze, surface, color, decoration, and so on.

FORM

1 What is the object to be used for?
2 Is its size and weight suitable for its intended use?
3 What degree of control should the function have over the shape of the object?
4 If the object is to be used in the hand, e.g., goblet or decanter, how does its form relate to the shape of the hand? Is it easy to lift, pour, drink, or serve from?
5 If the object is designed to pour from, where is the center of gravity, and how will this leverage affect use?
6 Can it be easily cleaned?

FOOT OR BASE

1 Does it need a trimmed foot?
2 Is the foot positioned correctly to support the curve of the form?
3 Is it wide enough to be stable?
4 Is it small enough to be elegant if that is desired?
5 Does it stand evenly?
6 Does it complete and complement the form?
7 Would a tripod or quadruped of small feet give better stability?
8 Should the foot be wheel trimmed, or finished by hand cutting?
9 Would a trimmed double or multiple foot help support sagging parts, e.g., on plates?

10 Is the base rough and likely to scratch surfaces?

RIM

1 What type of rim best suits the needs of function? Is it to carry a lid?

2 Is it likely to be drunk from?

3 If it is to be drunk from, how does it fit the shape of the mouth?

4 Is it substantial enough to withstand the general wear and tear of use?

5 How wide does it need to be for easy cleaning?

6 Does it complete and complement the form?

7 If it is for storage, is it wide enough to easily get hands, spoons, and scoops in and out?

LID

1 What type of top termination is needed on the pot?

2 What kind of lid is most suitable for the function?

3 What type of lid best suits the form?

4 Is the function of the object such that a double lid might be better?

5 If the object has both lid and pouring spout, how does this affect the lid seating?

6 Is it to have a knob or other form of handle?

7 Is it made in such a way that it won't fall off or out?

8 Does it fit?

9 Is it an effective sealer?

10 Would a lid of another material be more suitable?

11 Does the lid need a hole in it to either facilitate pouring, or to allow evaporation and prevent condensation?

12 Is the edge of the lid substantial enough to take everyday use?

13 Does it need a locking device?

14 If it is on a casserole, can it be easily picked up when hot?

SPOUT OR POURING LIP

1 Would the form be better with a spout or a pouring lip? What type of spout is most suitable?

2 Does it pour without dripping?

3 Does it drip without pouring?

4 Does it complement the form?

5 Is it placed so that the pouring end is higher than the highest likely point of liquid inside the container?

6 Where on the pot should a spout spring from?

7 Is the end to be cut to break the vortex spiral?

8 Will it twist in firing?

9 Is it wide enough to allow the liquid through easily?

10 Does it need a strainer?

11 How big should the strainer be?

HANDLES, KNOBS, AND LUGS

1 Does the object need a handle or handles? Do the handles complement the form?

2 How do they feel in the hand? Do they feel comfortable, secure?

3 Are they substantial enough to take the weight of the pot plus its contents?

4 Are they for decorative effect only?

5 If they are on cooking pots, are they able to be picked up when wearing oven mitts?

6 How many fingers need to be accommodated?

7 Are they too large or too small?

8 What is the thickness and width of the handle?

9 Does it contribute to easy lifting and leverage?

10 Where should handles be placed?

11 Would another material, such as wood, metal, rattan, bone, etc., be suitable or better than clay handles?

12 If a teapot has a bale handle going over the form, is it vulnerable to easy breakage?

13 Does the handle need a thumb-stop?

14 Are the edges excessively sharp?

17

Technical Requirements

Technical requirements, in the way they are considered here, refer to two distinctly different aspects of producing pottery for human use. First, some concerns which buyers have in the purchase of pottery; and second, some concerns regarding the technology behind producing pots which are technically sound.

CAVEAT EMPTOR

References were made occasionally to dishwashers, microwave ovens, regular ovens, refrigerators, and freezers, but little specific information has been given about these common appliances. About 95 percent of all domestic functional pottery is in some way connected with the kitchen. The previous chapters will give some idea how close that connection is. Yet, how many potters ever give much thought to the appliances which accommodate the wares that we make? Do we look at the interiors of ovens or dishwashers to see how wide the spaces between the racks are, for instance? How do these racks support the pots which are placed on them? Even simple draining stands for hand-washed dishes have a measurable space for the dishes to fit into. Do we ever think about these dimensions when

we are wrapped up in the process of making? Judging by the pottery which one finds in volume in the marketplaces of the western hemisphere, the most likely answer is: not much!

I would like to devote closer attention to some of these things, as I feel sure that they have a direct bearing on how one fares as a craftsman producing utilitarian work. The concerns are not my concerns, but those of many of the people who buy my work. I have already said that the making of functional pottery is a compromise with certain limitations to one's artistic freedom. Limitation demands greater artistry and a more specific form of concentration than does total freedom. Dealing with many of these specifics is anathema for some potters, while others relish them. Problems need solutions. The potters of history had a different set of needs to deal with, and we see their solutions to those needs in our museums and art galleries. Even with the compromises which we may have to make, we bask in much more freedom than they ever had. The work they made served the people's needs. Perhaps we can take a lesson from them.

The pottery that we make should live in harmony with the gadgetry of the kitchen. Freezers and refrigerators chill the raw materials of meals, ovens warm and cook the preparations our pots contain, and dishwashers cleanse the dishes after use. So what are some of the things we should know about them?

Freezers and Refrigerators

Pottery may be used in both appliances. However, there are some concerns about pottery use in the freezer, and particularly taking food in a frozen pottery container and putting it straight into a regular oven. Few clays, either naturally occurring or prepared bodies, will stand the thermal punishment of freezer to standard oven use. However, most vitrified clays may be used direct from freezer to microwave oven. No porous pottery will stand this treatment without cracking. Any porous clay body, particularly low-temperature earthenware bodies that are likely to be porous, should not be used in a freezer, as it might well crack from the moisture that is in the pores. Pots that are likely to be frozen should be carefully considered. The nature of foods frozen in cooking pots is to expand. The form of the pot needs to be made with this expansion in mind. If they flare out from the base like a truncated cone, the form allows the frozen contents to expand upward, minimizing the internal pressures on the clay. If pots are spherical in form, smaller at the rim than at the base, there will almost certainly be a problem in freezing and thawing food.

Regular Ovens

Whether the heat source is wood, gas, oil, coal, or electricity, the behaviour of pottery in ovens is usually good, and most pottery is quite safe from cracking. The heating is gradual, due to the slow conductivity of pottery. Since the heat surrounds the pot, it all expands at the same rate. This is quite different from the effect of direct cooking on an electric surface element, or a gas ring, where there is an intense heat from below only. In this case, the clay of the base will expand before the clay of the rim, causing cracking. The same problem is likely to occur with heat expansion caused through placing the ware under a high-temperature broiler or grill. Here the rim will expand at a greater rate than the body. Neither of these cooking processes is recommended for vitrified pottery.

Microwave Ovens

The cooking heat in microwave ovens is created through low-frequency waves, similar to radio waves. Microwave energy causes food molecules to vibrate millions of times per second; the resultant friction creates the heat that cooks the food. With conventional cooking, heat is applied only to the outer surface of the food, and then heat must be conducted to the interior. It is the quick penetration of microwave energy into the outer layers of food that makes microwave cooking so fast. Pottery can be a possible problem in microwave ovens (see Pots for Cooking, Chapter 14).

Dishwashers

The dishwashing machine cleans pottery using water and cleansers at temperatures considerably higher than can be generally tolerated by the human hand. The water in dishwashers has a swirling motion throughout the interior, making sure that all parts are equally cleaned. Plates and most bowls stand on edge, while cups, mugs, goblets and glasses are placed upside-down. If any of these pots have a deeply cut foot, it will likely fill with water, and be a possible source of annoyance to the user. The spaces in dishwashers are designed to accommodate average-sized industrially produced tableware. If the potter is concerned about dishwasher use, attention should be given to the depth of bowls, mugs, cups, and plates in order to fit the spacing provided in the racks.

Pots Designed for Stacking

Space in houses and apartments has become much smaller in the last four decades, and in kitchens it is usually at a premium. Kitchen cabinets and storage units seldom have as much space as their owners would like. At the same time space has become depleted, the number of kitchen aids has generally increased, so the congestion in cupboards is likely to be acute. As a result, dishes that stack neatly inside, or on top of, one another are often preferred to those that don't. When making bowls, plates, cups, and saucers, it might be worth considering whether certain forms will stack easily (Fig. 17.1). Even things such as cooking pots and serving bowls can easily be made with stacking principles in mind.

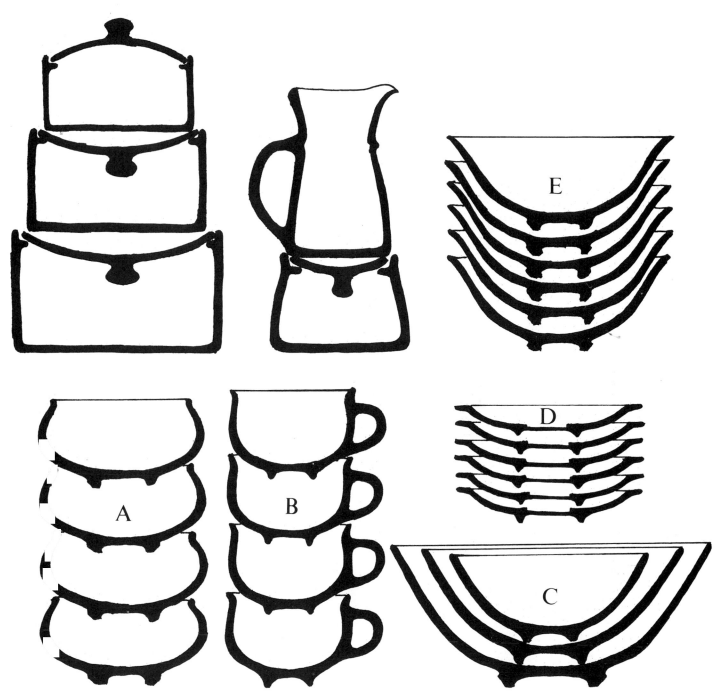

Fig. 17.1 Stacking forms for convenient use of cupboard space. Rounded forms (A, B) stack less efficiently than flaring forms (C, D, E).

The degree to which any clayworker attempts to satisfy the demands and whims of public taste is a purely individual one. I am certainly not going to be dogmatic and state that this is the only way to go about designing and making satisfying objects for use. There are many ways to do it; the use of design analysis is just one, but it is one that works! We, as artists and craftsmen, often complain of what we perceive to be a low level of taste among the general public. But do we do enough to educate the public in what we want to do, and do we listen enough to what they want to say?

SIMPLIFIED TECHNOLOGY FOR THE STUDIO POTTER

Making pottery can be as simple, or as complicated, as one wishes to make it. Sometimes we go overboard in one direction, and cause problems for ourselves in the process. My first book, *The Ceramic Spectrum*, attempted to demystify the problems of glaze and color development and add to an understanding of glaze processes. Much of what would take up valuable space here in relation to glazes and surfaces has already been covered there.

The Ceramic Spectrum doesn't give much space to clays and clay bodies, other than a basic description of what they are and what they are generally used for. There is no space here to give a long discourse on clays either, besides which I feel that other books have said it well, and there is no need for excessive duplication. What I will do here is to state a few observations on both clays and glazes which may assist the reader to better understand the processes he or she is involved in.

Clays

A potter's clay is the most important physical ingredient of his work. A highly skilled clayworker can probably adapt his making methods to work with just about anything, but for those in the learning stages the quality of the clay and its maleability are of paramount importance. If the clay is not good it makes the whole process much more difficult than it need be. What do I mean by good?

Almost any clay has some potential for use

in making functional pottery, depending on what that use is to be. However, most people who are making pots generally seem to rely on clay which they can purchase ready made and all set to go. More often than not, what goes into these clays is secret to the producer, unless one is having clay custom blended. Ready made clays can easily be adjusted to suit the individual by additions of other clays or materials such as grog or sand. Sometimes ready made clay is as hard as bricks, other times it may be like mush. It can always be softened or stiffened to a more workable state, so the potter can adjust for personal preferences. For extended periods of throwing, it is better to use soft clay, as it is less damaging to the skin and muscles of the hand and wrist. Excessive use of hard clay can cause severe damage which may need surgery to correct.

When deciding on a clay to use, there are six basic questions that one should ask oneself before either buying prepared clay or making one's own. They are as follows:

1 What do I want it to do?
2 How do I want it to behave?
3 What color do I want it to be?
4 What temperature do I want it to mature at?
5 What type of kiln and atmosphere will it be fired in?
6 What sort of glazes am I going to use on it?

Question 1 refers to the type of pottery which will be made from the clay. Will it be dinnerware, casseroles, flower vases, or what? *Question 2* asks about the quality of the clay. What is its plasticity? What are its shrinkage and absorption rates? How does it behave in drying? Does it require pampered treatment? Does it have good wet-strength and dry-strength? Do I want to throw or handbuild with it? Up to what size? Do I throw quickly? Will it stand slow use? Do I use a lot of water in throwing? Do I prefer my clay soft or hard? *Question 3* asks, do I want white clay, colored clay, or black clay or any variation in between? Is it earthenware, stoneware, or porcelain? *Question 4* is a basic technical question—clays may be made to mature, or become vitrified, at a variety of temperatures. What do I prefer, or am I at the mercy of my kiln? What amount of cone range do I want my clay to have? *Question 5 probably requires two simple answers. Question 6 might also include further questions, such as will it be decorated? Do I want the color of the clay to show through the glaze? If the body is spotty will it destroy the subtlety of the decoration?*

Armed with these criteria, it is easier to limit the decision to a smaller variety of potential bodies, and thus limit the margin for error. There is little point to the frustration which goes with the quixotic search for the ultimate, perfect body. When you find a clay that will do half of what you want it to, you will probably be well off. The ultimate clay that will do all things for all people just doesn't exist.

If the clay is to be used for making cooking ware, and it is to be fired in a kiln through a reduction cycle, the degree of reduction is critical. If the reduction is excessive, it inhibits the growth of mullite crystals within the matrix or structure of the clay. Mullite is what gives much of the strength, being a network of interlaced, or interconnected, needlelike crystals. The heavy reduction weakens the clay, and makes it prone to cracking when used in the ordinary household oven. *How much reduction is too much?* One cannot be specific here, because there are so many different bodies available, and each one of them may have a different threshold of tolerance. Perhaps two pointers can be these: (1) Has the fired body a densely blackened core? and (2) is the clay heavily colored by iron or manganese? Both of these materials will quickly react with the carbon of reduction and seriously weaken the body.

There are probably many other hypothetical questions that could be asked about clays and their use, and one could fill a whole book with them; several other authors already have. Most questions are specific to each clay user, in each particular place, depending on the availability of materials. Personal research in some of those other books will be quite rewarding, and a list of them is found in the Bibliography.

Glazes

Now there's a subject with some scope! Once again, it is a field with so many questions to it that many people are frightened off, and use the same old tried-and-true solutions that made me ask in *The Ceramic Spectrum*, "Is there life after temmoku, celadon and high alumina matt?" Fortunately there is, and lots of it!

One can make good functional pottery at a range of temperature from about Cone 010 up to Cone 14, depending on such factors as clay, glazes, and kiln. It would be futile for me to even think of suggesting all the wonders and all the problems that this range makes possible, even if I had the ability and knowledge. So many things are relevant to the individual that only the individual can solve them. Making pottery, remember, is a very private affair! If one chooses to use glazes which are dry, matt, vellum, satin, silky, glossy, glassy, pitted, crazed, crawled, bubbled, or volcanic, this is a personal choice of the maker. The public will soon tell the maker if they don't like his or her choice of surface. Whether that glaze is suitable for the use in hand is yet another question.

Without being dogmatic, glazes for functional pottery should really be hygienic. This usually means fault free and sterile. However, if one agrees that crazing, pinholing, and crawling are faults, then how does one reconcile the beautiful oriental uses of glazes which have these faults? Glazes with crackled patterns, shino and temmoku glazes with pitted surfaces, and nuka-type glazes which use crawling to such wonderful effect, what do we do about them? As I said, it is a personal affair and if one can justify the uses of faulty glazes to oneself and one's customers, then that is all that is needed. A good dishwasher will render almost any glaze hygienic, but not everyone has one. The only glaze fault which should not be tolerated under any circumstances is shivering, where the glaze is too large a fit for the clay; it can cause sharp slivers to come off the edges or rims of pots, easily dropping into foods. These could be potentially lethal, particularly to small children. Shivering seems to be most prevalent in glazes with a high content of lithium-bearing materials such as spodumene, lepidolite, petalite, and lithium carbonate.

Other possible problems may occur from the use of certain materials which can develop potentially toxic glazes. Lead compounds, cadmium, selenium, and barium can all produce glazes that are made dangerous by contact with food acids. If in any doubt, do not use glazes containing these materials for pottery designed to be eaten from, drunk from, cooked in, or with acidic materials to be stored in a liquid state. There are safe ways to use these materials, but they are complex and outside the scope of this book. Further information may be found in *The Ceramic Spectrum*, and other books on glazes. Since the problem materials are few, they shouldn't hamper the development of a wide pallette of surface and color.

My personal preference in developing glazes for any temperature is to produce a number of white or colorless glazes which have the type of surfaces I like, or a number of glaze bases having materials which may be interchanged to give great variety in both surface and color. The materials which go into the glazes are sufficiently varied to produce a wide color response when color is added, or when color is used in decoration. *The Ceramic Spectrum* is devoted to simplifying the approach to glaze and color making. The potential pallette is unlimited.

Part Four

Portfolio:
Ways of Working

INTRODUCTION

This portfolio shows the work of eight artists who work with the thrown functional vessel in a diverse range of styles. In selecting these eight for exposure in this way, my aim is to show this diversity and their commitment to it, both on an individual basis and also in contrast to each other. My criterion for selecting these artists is to establish a cross-section view of primarily wheel-made functional pottery currently being made. It stretches from traditional roots at one end of the scale, to fantasy at the other. I wanted a spread of geographic area, as well as variations in the technology of temperature ranges and firing methods in the work itself. Technically, their work covers a range from earthenware to porcelain, and from electric firing to wood-fired and salt-glazed wares. I look at each person's work in this portfolio as being indicative of a certain genre of ceramic expression within the functional vessel format. By keeping to a small number of individuals, it makes it possible to get a better view of each and their particular solutions to the diverse problems of form and function.

The information on each artist is excerpted both from their personal biographies and from their answers to a long questionnaire, designed to find out "what makes them tick, and do what they do." What are their backgrounds, environments, interests, and lifestyles? What music do they like? Where do their ideas come from? Who are their mentors? How long have they been working with clay? What are the special qualities of their work?

The background, experience, and interests of these artists is extremely wide. Their work has achieved a mature state of balance, not in a static way, but with an inner strength and conviction which continues to demand growth and change. Each one's work is truly an amalgam of that person, and their individuality glows through from an inner fire. Their personal interests and likes are integrated into their work, and it is almost impossible to consider the work without the person, or the person without the work, or even the same work being done by another person. These people are their work.

The length of time spent maturing their craft varies from 12 to 30 years. Pottery making is a very personal process, and the knowledge of how these individual clayworkers approach their craft not only gives a better understanding of the relationship between the artist and the work itself, but also the road and diversions that have led to its development. Apart from the basically differing approaches to their work, there are many adjectives that can be used to describe the works. They might be strong, powerful, loose, sophisticated, free, spontaneous, daring, audacious, funny, capricious, tight, joyful, playful, oblique, exuberant, challenging, and having panache.

The sequence that I have chosen to put these artists in goes more or less from the traditional to the fantasy, in itself reflecting continuity and change.

JOHN LEACH

Two large pitchers: 10 pint and 4 pint. Wood-fired stoneware, unglazed exterior. 11½" and 8¼" high. 1984. Photograph by Ian Robson.

One-gallon hot pot and one-quart casserole. Woodfired stoneware, unglazed exterior. 9½" high, 8" diameter. 1985. Photograph by Ian Robson.

Group of six bottles. Woodfired stoneware, unglazed exterior. From 3½" to 10" high. 1985. Photograph by Ian Robson.

GWYN HANSSEN PIGOTT

Children's tea set. Porcelain; blue celadon inside, white outside, blue and gold decoration; gas fired. Mug, 8 cm high; plate, 17 cm diameter. 1964. Photograph by Stuart Collins.

Woodfired porcelain bowl, celadon and shino type. 24 cm diameter. 1984.

Right: Dish, wood-fired porcelain; shino type glaze outside and over the rim, inside cream glaze decorated with blue pigment and, later, gold luster. 31 cm diameter. 1984. Photograph by Stuart Collins.

BRUCE COCHRANE

Teapot. Thrown, gas-fired white stoneware; barium glaze. 8" high, 5" wide. Photographs by Peter Hogan.

Storage jar. Gas-fired stoneware with shino glaze and finger wipes. 12" high, 8" wide.

Storage jar. Thrown, gas-fired stoneware with ash glaze. 20" high, 12" wide.

Baker. Thrown and ovaled red earthenware, oxidation fired, trailed slip. 7" high, 12" long.

 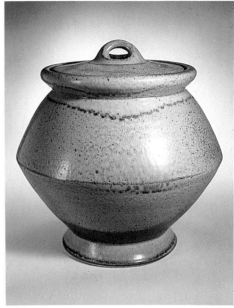

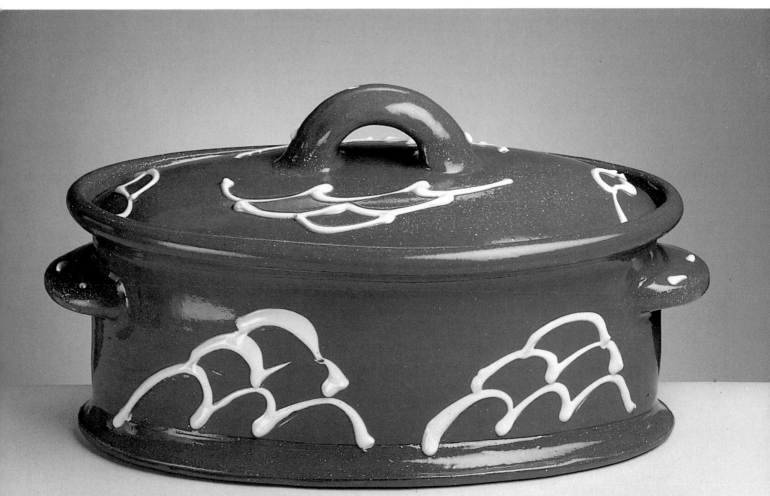

TOM TURNER

Clockwise:

Porcelain perfume bottles. Different copper glazes. 3" high, 2½" wide. Photograph by Marc Braun.

Porcelain lidded jars. Splotchy copper glaze. 2½" high, 4" wide. Photograph by the artist.

Porcelain cap jar. Fake ash glaze sprayed over apple ash glaze. 9" high, 8" wide.

Porcelain cap jar. Fake ash glaze, thick and thin, over wax resist. 21" high, 11" wide. Photograph by the artist.

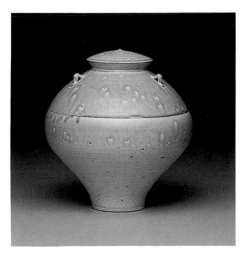

STANLEY MACE ANDERSEN

Salad bowl set. Earthenware, majolica technique. Large bowl, 15" diameter; small bowls, 2¾" high, 6½" wide.

Coffee cups and saucers. Earthenware, majolica technique. 3" high.

Casserole. Earthenware, majolica technique. 8" diameter, 8½" high. Photograph by A. Hawthorne.

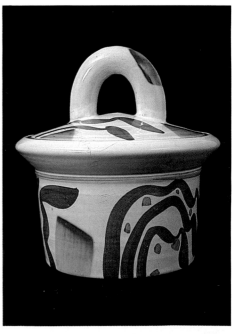

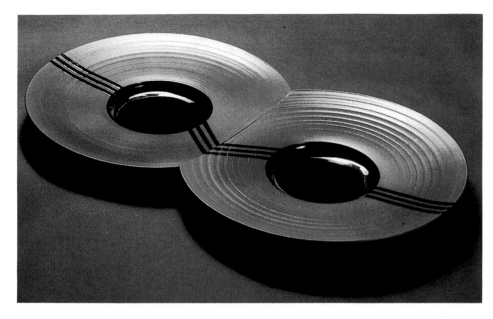

DENISE GOYER AND ALAIN BONNEAU

Siamoise. Two plates, wheel thrown and cut; red earthenware, black and transparent glaze. 39 cm high, 66 cm wide. Designed 1981. Photograph by Alain Bonneau.

Groove bowl. Large serving bowl, wheel thrown; red earthenware, black and transparent glaze. 7 cm high, 37 cm wide. Photograph by Alain Bonneau.

Serving set for sangria, punch, or fruit salad. Wheel thrown, pink earthenware. Large bowl, 16 cm high, 36 cm wide; small bowls, 6 cm high, 11 cm wide. Designed 1981. Photograph by Alain Bonneau.

WALTER KEELER

Opposite:
Large dish with turned foot and cut rim, carved molding. Ash glaze on the inside; pigment sprayed on the rim; salt-glazed. 18" diameter. Photographs by David Cripps.

Flattened teapot. Thrown and distorted, with extruded handle. Sprayed engobe and pigment over cobalt and black underglaze; salt-glazed. Base diameter, 6".

Deep container. Thrown and distorted, with added base; pulled handles. Blue ash glaze inside; sprayed engobe and pigment over cobalt and black underglaze on the outside; salt-glazed. 8" high.

Teapot. Thrown and pushed back, with press-molded spout and extruded handle. Sprayed engobe and pigment over cobalt and black underglaze; salt-glazed. 8½" high.

EILENE SKY

Yellow teapot with flowers. 8½" × 8". Photographs by Burt Sky.

Ballerina bowl; pastels and underglaze. 7" × 6".

Cow platter with drawing and frills. 18" diameter, 4" deep.

Dancer demitasse; multicolored. 5" high.

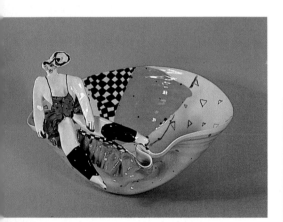

JOHN LEACH

Biography

John Leach is a third generation potter. His grandfather was Bernard Leach, and his father is David Leach, both luminaries in the studio pottery movement of Great Britain. John's wife Elisabeth and their five children help with many of the inevitable jobs around the workshop. They live in a small village in Somerset, England. John is a man of wide tastes in music, films, and literature, from pop to the classics. His involvement with travel is usually concerned with either work or study. His recent study trip to Nigeria has had a significant impact on his thoughts. He is the consummate countryman whose work speaks of the roots of England. If he were not a potter, he says that he would probably be involved in some other bucolic craft, such as basketry, thatching, or leatherwork.

Studio

John has been working with clay for 28 years. Coming from an illustrious potting family he was aware of the craft from an early age, and the future had a sort of inevitability about it. He trained with both his father and grandfather, and for short periods with Ray Finch and Colin Pearson. On average, he works between 50 and 60 hours per week in a rural workshop, employing one full-time assistant, Nick Rees, in addition to the family input. His work is mainly stoneware, using clays from the West of England, and fired in a wood-burning kiln. His palette of glazes is quite small, since the qualities he finds most exciting are those that come from the flame movement, ash runs, and the restrained subtleties of wares sagger-fired in sawdust.

John Leach. Photograph by R. J. Whittick.

Three oval troughs, unglazed exteriors (made with false bottoms). Woodfired stoneware. 9½", 8", 6½" long. 1985. Photograph by John Coles.

Work and Personal Development

Apart from the influences of his father and grandfather, John's work has been primarily influenced by earthenware of seventeenth and eighteenth century England, and by early American folk traditions. His mentors have included Michael Cardew, for his "brilliant modern understanding and rendering of a tradition"; Hans Coper, "whose forms are so exciting, commanding respect"; Lucie Rie, "for her delicate elegance"; Richard Batterham, "for overall strength, power, majesty, and integrity"; Byron Temple, "for subtlety, modesty, simplicity, and freshness"; Wally Keeler, "for his intriguing inventiveness and creativity"; Shoji Hamada, "for his unlabored, unfussy, friendly but deft approach"; Liz Fritsch, "for form, color, pattern and design"; and Clive Bowen, "the most exciting slipware potter in Britain today." He also has great appreciation for craftsmen and artists working in many other media, such as furniture, basketmaking, heavy iron work, toys, and fiber.

John says that his work develops and changes "sometimes in a conscious way when working on a

Opposite: Tall jug, 2 gallons. Unglazed exterior, woodfired stoneware. 16" high. 1985. Photograph by John Coles.

Three cross-handled bottles, two with wood ash glaze and one unglazed exterior. Woodfired stoneware. 6", 7", 10" high. 1985. Photograph by John Coles.

One-gallon hot pot, 3-pint hot pot, 4-pint casserole, and 1-pint casserole. Woodfired stoneware with unglazed exteriors. 1985. Photograph by John Coles.

form idea, and struggling through various shapes and experiments to reach a possible happy conclusion. At other times it is intuitive. Something just happens at the wheel. The fruition of a subconscious design/thought process which has been incubating over the years and suddenly it is born. Thrilling at the time—on the edge of a discovery! I must say this doesn't happen very often." He says, "if a spark of an idea occurs I will worry it, follow it, experiment, work at it, stand back and watch the various stages of growth. This may go on for a period of years. The source of inspiration may be an exhibition, museum, another potter or craft." John doesn't draw ideas, except as a

Tall, open-mouthed flour bin. Woodfired stoneware, unglazed exterior. 17½″ high. 1985. Photograph by John Coles.

Deep bowl, lugged. Sawdust fired in saggar. 9″ high. 1984. Photograph by John Coles.

Opposite: Tall bottle, lugged. Sawdust fired in saggar. 10″ high. 1985. Photograph by John Coles.

Cross-handled bottle. Woodfired stoneware, unglazed exterior. 9½″ high. 1985. Photograph by John Coles.

"memory jogger." Apart from the sources of inspiration already mentioned, he develops three-dimensional ideas from the fullness of flower buds, gourds, or calabashes, and graphic images from frozen mudflats and grasses. His primary concern is with form, with strong lines and sound proportions.

Breadcrock. Woodfired stoneware, unglazed exterior. 14″ high. Photograph by John Coles.

GWYN HANSSEN PIGOTT

Biography

Gwyn Hanssen Pigott was born and grew up in Australia. Her search into her own identity and work has taken her all over the world. She has lived and worked in England, France, and America; she is now back in Australia, living in Brisbane, although she travels extensively. She likes to meditate, which has a significant effect on the tranquility and calmness of her work. Gwyn is a woman of wide tastes in music, film, and literature, depending on mood, although she likes to work in silence. She feels happy living very simply, involved with her work and friends.

Studio

Gwyn has been making pottery for 30 years. She became involved while preparing a thesis, "Pottery in Australia," in the third year of a fine arts degree, after becoming interested in Chinese pots and the work of Bernard Leach and Michael Cardew. After university, she apprenticed for three years with Ivan McMeekin at Sturt Pottery, Mittagong, gaining a particularly strong understanding of the use of local materials. She then went to England and worked with Ray Finch, Leach, and Cardew. She has developed studios in a London basement, rural France, rural Tasmania, and in urban Adelaide and Brisbane. Her work is mainly porcelain or porcellanous stoneware, fired in reduction kilns that are fueled with wood or gas. She also uses an electric kiln for low-fired lusters. Gwyn occasionally takes on trainees, but is currently working on her own.

Gwyn Hanssen Pigott. Photograph by Kate John.

Work and Personal Development

The main influences on her work have been Bernard Leach, Michael Cardew, Ivan McMeekin, Lucie Rie, and Hans Coper; the pottery traditions of China, Korea, Japan, and France; and to some extent the textiles of Africa and the South Pacific. Her husbands, the late poet and potter Louis Hanssen, and John Pigott, have also been strongly influential. Among her favorite artists in clay, she lists Richard Batterham, Elizabeth Fritsch, Alison Britten, Lucie Rie, and David Garland of the U.K.; Steen Kepp and Anne Kjarsgaard of France; Michel Pastore and Evelyne Porret of Switzerland; Clary Illian of the U.S.A.; Mick Henry, John Reeve and Jeannie Mah of Canada; and Ian Mackay, Stephanie Outridge, Stephen Benwell, and John Pigott of Australia. She speaks of them and their work as "alive, alert, committed, sensitive, involved, uncompromising, fresh, strong, surprising, inevitable, and grasping something essential about themselves." She says, "sometimes their depth of vision shocks me, inspires me to dig deeper into myself." She is moved by the paintings of De Stael, David Hockney, William Scott, Rousseau, Matisse, Mark Tobey, Bonnard, Breughel, Bryan Illsley, and Giorgio Morandi.

Gwyn finds that her interest in historical ceramics gravitates toward primitive and peasant wares and genuine folk art, although she is moved by some of the wares of Song Dynasty China, the Ri Dynasty of Korea, tenth and eleventh century Persia, and pre-Columbian American Indian. Her own work draws on her many interests, and slowly evolves from previous pots in an intuitive, unfolding fashion. New ideas and designs sometimes come from a change in materials, firing techniques or newly developed glazes. Although she loves drawing, she never draws pottery ideas on paper. She feels an unconscious affinity with natural forms, although her work is not really evocative of them. Her prime concerns are with function, making pots that she would like to have and use, but form and surface are of paramount importance. "Actually," she says, "it all comes *together*—I see the pots clearly (or the *possibility* of their beauty, their potential) in my head from all the means at my disposal—clay, glaze, fire, and use." Her work is quiet, understated, and deceptively simple.

Partial dinner setting. Gas-fired, celadon and pink-beige. 1981. Photograph by Grant Hancock.

Porcelain teapot, creamer, and sugar bowl. Woodfired, shino type glaze outside, celadon inside. 12 cm high. Photograph by Stuart Collins.

Porcelain teapots, medium size. Woodfired. Photograph by Stuart Collins.

Four mugs. Woodfired porcellanous stoneware. Cream glaze inside, shino type outside. 9 cm high. 1984. Photograph by Stuart Collins.

Part of a child's tea setting. Blue celadon inside, white with blue decoration and gold luster outside. 1984. Photograph by Stuart Collins.

Teapot, woodfired and slightly salted. 15 cm high. 1984. Photograph by Stuart Collins.

Six egg cups. Woodfired porcelain with celadon and shino type glazes. 5 cm high. Photograph by Stuart Collins.

Three translucent boxes. Woodfired, white glaze with luster or celadon on the inside. 8 cm diameter. Photograph by Stuart Collins.

Woodfired porcelain dish with gold luster decoration and blue pigment over calico glaze. Dark amber on the outside. 29.5 cm diameter. Photograph by Stuart Collins.

Porcelain serving dish. Woodfired, blue decoration on grey-white. 31 cm diameter. Photograph by Stuart Collins.

BRUCE COCHRANE

Biography

Bruce Cochrane is a quiet, introspective Canadian who balances his working life between teaching ceramics and potting. He is married to Patti and they have two children, as yet too small to be studio helpers. They live in suburban Toronto, not far from his teaching position at Sheridan College. Bruce is a man of wide musical tastes, but finds little time for films or reading, except books on ceramics and art. He hasn't had much opportunity for travel, but is intent on making travel a priority as soon as possible, so that he may indulge his enjoyment of collecting historical and contemporary ceramics.

Studio

Bruce has been working in clay for 14 years, after choosing ceramics as a college elective on the recommendation of a friend. He was immediately seduced. He studied at John Abbott College, Quebec; Nova Scotia College of Art; and Alfred University, New York. He currently teaches for about 25 hours per week, and does studio work for about 25 hours. He works in an urban environment, with studios both at home and at school. This situation gives him access to a variety of kiln types—electric, wood, gas, and salt. The range of his work includes earthenware, as well as both buff and white stonewares. "I avoid allowing the material to dominate my ideas." Bruce makes clay bodies and chooses firing techniques "to suit the design, function, and feeling" of the pottery that he makes.

Bruce Cochrane.

Work and Personal Development

Bruce credits his early development as a student to encouraging and stimulating teachers. He has always loved the work of Leach, Hamada, and Cardew. "Their pots have a clarity of intent; the forms and surfaces are alive and rich with personality." He also admires the work of Betty Woodman, Peter Voulkos, Robert Turner, Rudio Autio, and John and Andrea Gill. "Their work has vitality, a strong sense of material and process. It innovatively blends historical elements with personal contemporary ideas. . . . The anonymous pottery from various folk traditions serves as an endless source of stimulation." His favorites include current Chinese wares, North American Redware, Medieval English Jugs, and early Italian and Spanish majolica. "These pots achieve a wonderful sense of energy and spirit. They portray a culture and a way of life."

Bruce's ideas for new forms usually evolve indirectly from previous work. He finds that one unrelated form may eventually suggest another, i.e., vase to jar. A specific type of food will also suggest form, texture, or color. Drawing is used as a tool to make these connections but nothing replaces the wheel as a fast method of exploring several variations of an idea.

In his work Bruce aims at achieving a sense of invitation to use, through visual elements in form and surface. Generous volumes, fat comfortable handles and lips, and feet which stabilize and present the form, all contribute to this approachable quality. "The scale of much of my work implies a larger gathering, signifying special occasions. The preparation and presentation of food can be a memorable experience. The associated objects can enrich this experience and enhance the meal."

Casserole. White stoneware, shino type glaze. Reduction fired. 8" high, 12" diameter. Photograph by Peter Hogan.

Mixing bowl set. Salt-fired stoneware. White slip under iron glaze. Large bowl, 7" high, 11" diameter. Photograph by Peter Hogan.

Casserole. Gas-fired white stoneware with overglaze brush work. 8" high, 12" diameter. Photograph by Peter Hogan.

Tureen. Gas-fired white stoneware with shino type glaze. 10" high, 10" wide. Photograph by Peter Hogan.

Fruit basket. Red earthenware, thrown and ovaled with majolica technique and overglaze color. 9" high, 16" long. Photograph by Peter Hogan.

Vase. Wood-fired white stoneware. 15" high, 5" wide. Photograph by Peter Hogan.

Pitcher. Gas-fired stoneware with shino type glaze. 10" high, 4" wide. Photograph by Peter Hogan.

Three pitchers. Wood-fired stoneware. 12", 9", 6" high. Photograph by Peter Hogan.

Coffee pot. Thrown red earthenware, majolica technique with overglaze color. 11" high, 5" wide. Photograph by Peter Hogan.

Teapot. Thrown and ovaled gas-fired stoneware with a shino and iron glaze. 9" high, 5" wide. Photograph by Peter Hogan.

TOM TURNER

Biography

Tom Turner is a quiet and intense man, thoroughly committed to his work. When interviewed, he was living in rural Ohio, but is currently on sabbatical, traveling and visiting potters and schools. The studio isolation causes a yearning for more interaction with people. He enjoys good food, baking and cooking, and soft music from country to classical. He is essentially a romantic at heart, always seeking perfection. Everything about him is gentle, from his musical and literary tastes to the fluid and sensuous forms of his work. Yet there is always an inner fire that exerts continual demands in search of the ultimate. He doesn't usually travel much, except in relation to his guest teaching.

Studio

Tom has been making pots for 24 years. He started "by taking a class in high school and falling madly in love with the medium." His training was at the Illinois State University, followed by two years' Army service. He then taught at Clemson University for five years, completing an M.F.A. during that time. In 1976 he decided to devote all of his energies to his work, and resigned from teaching. He works alone for approximately 60 hours per week in his rural Ohio studio. "I've been terribly isolated. Most potters that I know are. We usually live in the country, and we're always working. This also affects our relationships. A potter must be strong to survive—and so must his or her mate." His idea of an ideal working environment is "on the edge of a city so I can live in the country, but have a city to go to for culture and

Tom Turner. Photograph by Marc Braun.

entertainment." He has been working with porcelain for about twelve years, and prepares his own clay by the filter pressing method. He fires his work in reduction, in a gas-fired car kiln at cone 9. Tom is a superlative technician in the field of glaze and color development, continually doing research in quest for the elusive.

Work and Personal Development

Tom's primary influence was his college teacher, Jim Wozniak. Other strong influences have been Don Reitz, David Shaner, Don Pilcher, Tim Mather, Tom Coleman, Ralph Bacerra, and Otto and Vivika Heino. He is particularly interested in the work

Porcelain cap jar. Fake ash sprayed over apple ash glaze. 9" high, 8" wide. Photograph by Marc Braun.

of David Nelson, Tom Hoadley, David Crane, and Adrian Saxe, as well as woodworker Sam Maloof, and glassworker John Nygren. "They exemplify the magnificence of craft. Their work is a marriage of materials, process, and form, all of the points working and making a solid individual statement." The potters make "potter's pots" and they all make personal statements. Tom's historical attractions are the Chinese Song and Tang dynasties, and also American stoneware of the eighteenth and nineteenth centuries. Talking of his work, he says: "My work grows very slowly over a long period of time through trial and error. I believe it is more subconscious and intuitive." New directions come from the work itself, "today suggests tomorrow." Tom uses mathematics in a minimal way for surface embellishment, but natural forms are used only in the subconscious. The order of his main concerns are form, surface, and function. Tom's work represents an individual classicism, imbued with precision, understanding, impeccable craftsmanship, and concern for the minutest detail.

Porcelain bowls. Apple ash bowl between two temmoku bowls. Left bowl, fluted with saw blade; center fluted with a vegetable peeler; and right bowl is indented. 4" high, 5" wide. Photograph by Marc Braun.

Spouted porcelain vessel. Copper red glaze, handwoven handle. 12" high, 10" wide. Photograph by Marc Braun.

Porcelain cap jar. Copper red glaze. 9" high, 8" wide. Photograph by Marc Braun.

Porcelain cap jars. Copper red on the left and black-brown temmoku on the right. Both 4½" high. Photograph by Marc Braun.

Porcelain bottle vase. Fake ash glaze, thick and thin, over wax resist. Brown dots. 7" × 7". Photograph by Marc Braun.

Porcelain lidded jars and perfume bottle. Barium pink matt on the left, copper red on the center piece, and splotchy copper on the right. 2½" high, 4" wide. Photograph by Marc Braun.

218

Porcelain cap jar. Apple ash and fake ash glazes over sticker resist. Green, white, and brown glaze trailed dots. 14" high, 10" wide. Photograph by Marc Braun.

Porcelain cap jar. Apple ash and fake ash glazes over sticker resist. Green, white, and brown dots glaze trailed. 9½" high, 7½" wide. Photograph by Marc Braun.

Spouted porcelain vessel. Apple ash and fake ash glaze with green, white, and brown glaze trailed dots. 12" high, 10" wide. Photograph by Marc Braun.

STANLEY MACE ANDERSEN

Biography

Stanley Mace Andersen is a man of diverse education, with degrees in philosophy, sociology, library science, and fine arts. He lives with his wife in Bakersville, North Carolina. In the past he has traveled widely through North America, Europe, and North Africa. He has lived in two of the Western world's liveliest cities, Paris and New York, and has spent time in London, Istanbul, Amsterdam, Marrakech, and Venice. Of the places that he has lived, he says, "I think these urban experiences were important in the formation of my aesthetic in that the energy of cities, the colors of cities, and the diversity of visual excitement in cities has fed my own energy and excitement." His taste in music is eclectic, but he primarily listens to rock and roll. His taste in visual entertainment is wide, but he hasn't had time to read since he took up pottery.

Studio

Stan has been making pots since 1973. He says that working in clay suits his personality: "It's not very precise." Clay satisfies both his desire to work with his hands, and his desire to create art. His work in clay started informally at the University of Iowa, and later formally with Chuck Hindes in Iowa. He took classes at Kansas City Art Institute, and gained his M.F.A. at Rhode Island School of Design. His studio is currently in a rural area in North Carolina. His work week averages between 50 and 65 hours. He works alone, and doesn't take apprentices or have assistants. He works in earthenware, which he fires in an electric kiln to cone 03. He has his clay custom made for his temperature range, preferring a smooth plastic clay to work with. He uses the majolica technique of decoration on his work, enjoying the strong colors that he can obtain with commercially prepared stains.

Work and Personal Development

Among the people who have had a strong influence on him are John and Andrea Gill, Norman Schulman, and Jackie Rice. His enjoyment of work by other ceramists includes Jun Kaneko, Charlie Malin, Judith Salomon, Susan Loftin, and Kurt Weiser. Of the work by these artists, he says, "I like strong color, I like imaginative, experimental work that expands our ideas about forms and color. This doesn't mean that I don't like traditional work, but I am more drawn to the other." He is not particularly concerned with ceramic history, nor with mathematics. His work generally develops from

Stanley Mace Andersen. Photograph by Chris Jones.

Opposite: Coffee pot with cups and saucers. Earthenware, majolica technique. Photograph by A. Hawthorne.

Dinnerware place setting. Earthenware, majolica technique. Dinner plate, 11" diameter.

Pitcher. Earthenware, majolica technique. Photograph by A. Hawthorne.

previous work with form, sometimes in an intuitive and sometimes in a conscious way, experimenting on the pots themselves. When he was first developing his work he did drawings, but now feels that his pots are his drawings. Questioned about the content of his work, he says, "I don't have any conscious reference to nature in my work, but since what I mostly see are natural forms I'm sure they are reflected." His main concern is with form. His decorating is casual with an unusual use of strong color, where the painting has an uncompromising directness.

Teapot. Earthenware, majolica technique. Thrown body, handbuilt spout and handle. 9½" high, 6½" diameter. Photograph by Dan Bailey.

Teapot. Earthenware, majolica technique. 12" high, 7½" diameter.

Pitcher. Earthenware, majolica technique. 10"
high, 5" diameter.

Casserole. Earthenware, majolica technique; 2½-
quart capacity. 8½" high, 8¾" diameter. Photo-
graph by Dan Bailey.

Serving bowl. Earthenware, majolica technique.
Photograph by A. Hawthorne.

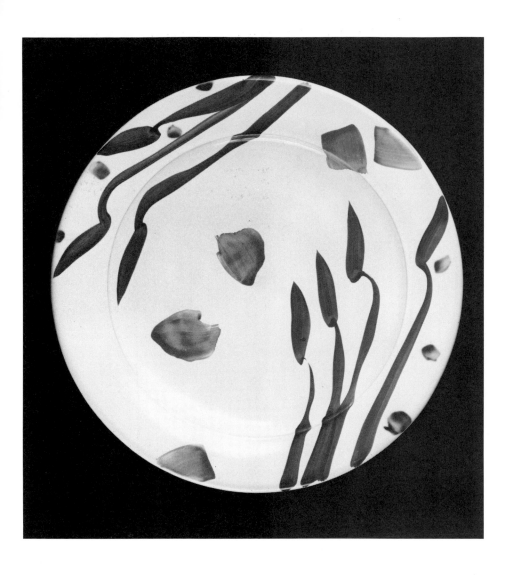

Platter. Earthenware, majolica technique. 15" diameter.

Two casseroles. Earthenware, majolica technique. Large casserole, 9" × 8½"; small casserole, 7" × 6¾".

WALTER KEELER

Biography

Walter Keeler leads a full life. He lives with his wife, Madoline, and their three children in a rural community in Wales. His tastes in music, film, and literature run to the extremes of style and content. His musical tastes go from one extreme to the other, including tribal, ethnic, medieval to Baroque, chamber, orchestral, ecclesiastical, blues, traditional and some modern jazz, pop music of the 30s and 40s, through to rock music. Film and literature (when he has time to read) are about as wide ranging. His interests also take in industrial design, which he would like to explore for the production of tableware. He doesn't get time to travel much, other than in connection with his work, teaching, or committees. If he were not making pots he would like to be a gardener.

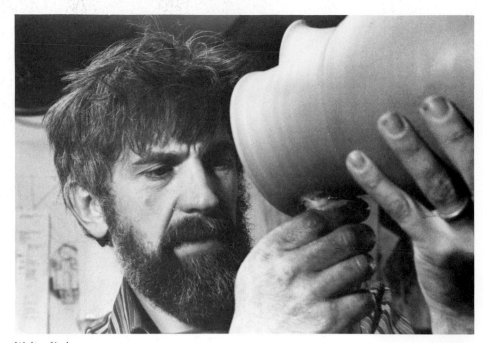

Walter Keeler.

Studio

Walter has been making pots for 27 years. As a child and youth he was interested in archaeology, spending much of his time collecting shards of ancient pots. When he went to art school, pottery seemed an obvious choice. His major studies were at Harrow School of Art, with Victor Margrie and Mick Casson. He works in a rural studio, shared with his wife, for approximately 30 to 40 hours per week, depending on his other commitments. They work independently and have no assistants. Although he has worked in most variations of pottery making, he is currently exploring salt-glazed stoneware as his prime mode of expression. With an agile mind, however, he is quite likely to make major changes in direction to explore new avenues. His work is currently fired in reduction in an oil-fired salt-glaze kiln, at cone 8–9. He often uses simple slips, runny glazes, and sprayed color in addition to the salt-glaze covering, to develop "juicy" surfaces. His preferences for clay are a ball clay with added sand, and a buff stoneware clay, both of which respond well to the salt. He prefers a clay that has strength and "standing-power, rather than plasticity."

Work and Personal Development

The primary influences in Walter's work have been the Romano-British pottery of the first to fourth centuries A.D., late seventeenth century salt glaze, early industrial pottery from Staffordshire and Leeds between 1700 and 1770, and metalwork, especially tinware forms. His appreciation for contemporary clayworkers include Betty Woodman, "for her delicious use of clay and soft glazes"; Richard Slee, "for his eccentric humor"; and Hans Coper, "for classical beauty and spiritual quality." Other artists who have moved him strongly have been Picasso, "for invention, humor, and abstract design"; Matisse, "for freshness, pattern, and color"; Max Ernst, "for mystery and invention"; and Kokoshka, Braque, Dali, Palmer, Constable, Turner, Tobey, Pollock, Monet, Holbein, Bonnard and many others. His work develops in an intuitive, evolutionary way, one thing inevitably leading to another, sometimes from the process itself and sometimes from drawings. "On rare momentous occasions," he says, "I sometimes deliberately launch off into

Salt-glazed stoneware teapot. 1984. Photograph by Tim Hill.

unknown territory." Such a launching was responsible for the development of the most recent phase of his work, evident in the illustrations. When asked about form, function, and surface, he says, "Form and function are often inseparable for me. The notion of pouring, for instance, inevitably suggests form. Although surface comes last, it should enhance the form and at least not impede the function." The uniqueness of his work stems from the combination of "sculptural" considerations with domestic pottery, the notion that pots can be visually challenging as well as useful.

Dish with extruded and cut rim. Grey ash glaze inside. 10″ diameter. Photograph by Keith Morris.

Jug. Thrown, distorted and cut. Added base and extruded handle. Grey salt-glaze. 8″ high. Photograph by Keith Morris.

Salt-glazed stoneware dish. 1982. Photograph by Tim Hill.

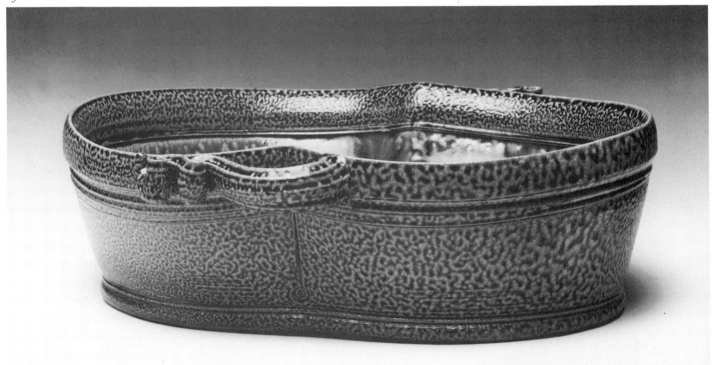

Teapot with press-molded spout and extruded handle. Grey salt glaze. 8½" high. Photograph by Keith Morris.

Three teapots with extruded handles. Salt glazed. 8" × 8½". Photograph by Clint Brown.

Jug. Thrown top, thrown and press-molded base. Extruded handle. Blue-grey salt glaze. 11¾" high.

Large lidded jar, with cut rim on the lid. Salt glazed, 24″ × 8″ × 8″. Photograph by Clint Brown.

Two cups with pulled and twisted handles. Salt-glazed. Photograph by Lutz Dille.

DENISE GOYER
AND ALAIN BONNEAU

Biography

Denise Goyer and Alain Bonneau are a married team with two children, living in a small rural community near Montreal, Canada. They work in total collaboration, with Denise being the visualizer and primary maker, and Alain looking after the technical aspects. Denise answered the questionnaire, although through continual discussion on their work, they obviously work and think very much as one. Their tastes in other arts is eclectic and wide ranging. The appreciation of music varies with the time of day and year, but extends from jazz and classics to New Wave. Their reading choices vary from contemporary technology to general history, geography, and different movements of art history. They like a wide range of well-made films. Denise says that they would like to travel, but at present it is only a dream. If she had had another vocation, she would like to have been an architect on major projects.

Studio

Denise has been working in clay for 20 years, and was drawn to the medium in order to make useful things where she could be in control of the whole process. Alain became her apprentice after four years of study in graphic art. They have no assistants,

Denise Goyer and Alain Bonneau. Photograph by Jean Marc Charron.

La Theiere. Five-cup teapot, colored earthenware, slip cast, black glaze. Height 11 cm high, 23 cm wide. Designed 1976. Photograph by Alain Bonneau.

and work in a small but efficient studio. Denise says that she works about 40 hours per week in the studio, but seldom stops thinking about their work, and spends many hours in discussion with Alain about new directions. The majority of their work is thrown, but they also use casting, both for the purity of line and to keep up with their orders. They work in both earthenware and semiporcelain. They are passionately concerned with the use of local raw materials. Their earthenware clay is a red clay body colored with manganese which they call "terre-noire." The work is fired in both electric and gas-fired kilns, at cone 02 for the earthenware, and cone 10 for the semiporcelain.

Work and Personal Development

Denise's concern has always been to make functional pottery, since it is seen and used on our tables three times a day from childhood. Her main mentor has been Eva Zeisel, a Hungarian ceramist and industrial designer who has produced revolutionary design in Hungary, Germany, the USSR, and the United States since the 1920s. In Quebec, she admires her former teachers, Jacques Garnier "for his tenacity," Gaetan Beaudin, "for his technical expertise," and Maurice Savoie, "for his sense of aesthetics and composition." In general she appreciates artists who dare to venture beyond the norm and commonplace. Her enjoyment of history has given her a strong appreciation of Egyptian and Classical Greek art, and the structures of Art Deco. She feels that they have given her an understanding of the customs and needs of people of different times and civilizations, which she can relate to today's society. She formulates new designs, "Par l'esprit d'abord. Une ligne ça s'exprime. Une forme ça se compose. Une fonction ça s'invente"—first by the spirit, then a line that expresses the spirit, a form that composes the line, and a function that invents itself. Her compositions, which reflect geometry and mathematics, are always developments from drawings, with the final product being a result from creative research into forms, functions, and techniques.

Cream and sugar. Colored earthenware, wheel thrown, black glaze. Cream, 10 cm × 10 cm; sugar, 8 cm × 10 cm. Designed 1976. Photograph by Alain Bonneau.

Grooves Bowl. Serving bowl for soup, salad, cereal, etc.; it can be hung on the wall. Colored earthenware, wheel thrown, black glaze. 5 cm × 17 cm. Designed 1978. Photograph by Alain Bonneau.

The Perfect Setting. Seven-piece place setting. Colored earthenware, wheel thrown and cut, black glaze and resist. Dinner plate, 27 cm wide. Designed 1983. Photograph by Alain Bonneau.

Spinning. Butter dish with stainless steel handle. Colored earthenware, wheel thrown, black glaze with resist. 10 cm × 15 cm. Designed 1982. Photograph by Alain Bonneau.

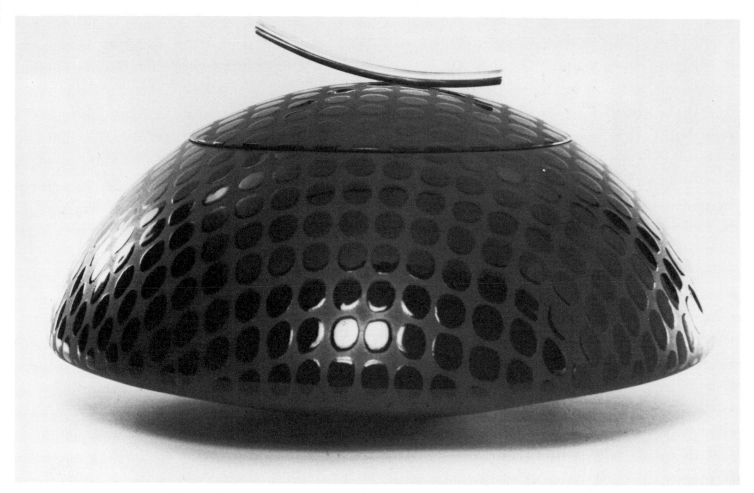

Hors d'Oeuvre. Dip plate or wall hanging. Pink earthenware, wheel thrown, polka dot, green glaze. 3 cm high, 39 cm wide. Designed 1980. Photograph by Alain Bonneau.

French Pea Soup. Soup tureen with solid brass handle; rounded bottom makes it easy to serve from. Slip cast, colored earthenware, polka dot, black glaze. 16½ cm high, 28 cm wide. Designed 1979. Photograph by Alain Bonneau.

Excentrique. Candy or serving bowl (round bottom). Slip cast, colored earthenware, polka dot, black glaze. 4 cm high, 17 cm wide. Designed 1978. Photograph by Alain Bonneau.

"Seule Ou Avec d'Autres," Five-base module, can be stacked or left side by side. Slip cast, colored earthenware, black glaze with resist. All together, 4½ cm high, 50 cm long. Designed in 1983. Photograph by Alain Bonneau.

Fan-Shaped Bowl. Serving bowl, porcelain, wheel thrown, and cut by hand. High-fire, black glaze with yellow slip. 3½ cm high, 30 cm wide. Designed 1982. Photograph by Alain Bonneau.

Eilene Sky.

EILENE SKY

Biography

Eilene Sky is an effervescent woman who is happy to have found the direction in her work that she says "is really me." She comes originally from New York, but her art studies, teaching, and travel have taken her to live in many parts of the United States. She has spent some time living with her husband in a rural area in Texas, but has recently moved to a loft in downtown Dallas. She is happy to be back in the city, her spiritual home. There she is close to the aspects of civilization that feed the imagery of her works of fun and fantasy, for she is a chronicler of her environment, be it cows, clowns, or people. She is totally serious about her work, but communicates joy and laughter, an important part of life so often lacking today.

Studio

Eilene has been working in clay since 1967. She originally studied painting, but seriously questioned her validity in that medium because, as she says, "Painters always had to have something to say, but I pretty much had nothing to say—possibly as a rather undeveloped 18 to 20 year old." She started working in clay at Goddard College, Vermont, and loved it. She likes "doing the same thing over and over, like patterns, and I like the things that a lot of people find irritating (an obsession for order), and have found myself functioning better by accepting my essential nature as "just fine," and working *with* it rather than waste energy trying to be something else." Pottery-wise, she grew up with the back-to-the-earth, "spotty brown stoneware" syndrome. Becoming bored with this genre of pottery she almost gave up, but for fun started to explore her inner fantasies and emerged with a true self in her work. It is a combination of comment and froufrou, where the zany imagery gives rein to the skills of both potter and painter. She works alone, for about 7 to 8 hours per day, 7 days a week. She uses low-fire technology, with commercially prepared white earthenware clay, prepared glazes and colors, and cone 05–06 electric firing.

Work and Personal Development

With a background in both painting and pottery, her work now ties them together. She says: "My early training as a painter re-emerged and made sense. Now I use the piece as a canvas

Plate with woman and frills; multicolored.

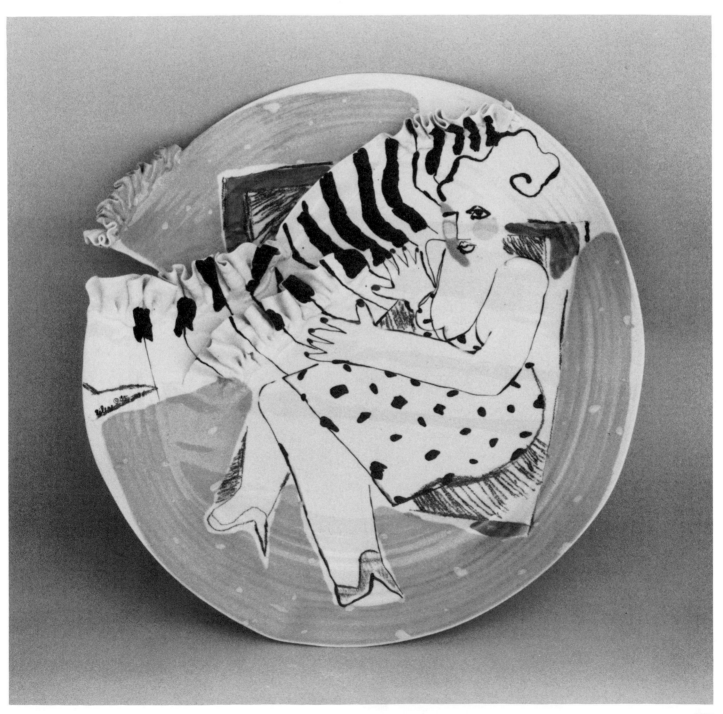

Clown teapot; grey, lime, pink, blue, and green. 8½" high.

for color and pattern. Through no conscious decision, I broke through my preconceptions on how I should approach my work in clay—preconceptions based on a more traditional idea where shape and glaze merge into a harmonious whole, a spiritual approach which eventually got boring! So now I don't think about all that too much. I just let whatever shapes emerge that want to. That way the piece acts as a vehicle for the play of pattern and color that I love. Its softer and looser and much more fun.'' She has never been one for developing ''heroes'' in art, but responds to Lucie

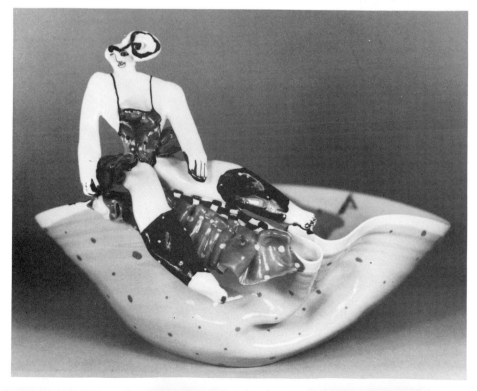

Ballerina bowl; pastels, underglaze. 7" wide, 6" high.

Cow bowl with frills; drawing inside; blue, black, red, and white. 14" wide, 8" deep.

Cow bowl with frills and blocks; grey, pink, black, and white. 7" wide, 6" high.

Cow demitasse; red, blue, black, and white. 4" × 4".

Dancer teapot; underglaze pastels. 8¼″ high, 9″ wide.

Rie's elegance on the one hand, and "the people who rip and tear and paint like crazy and who do funked-up pieces" on the other. The emotional and aesthetic support which has meant most to her development has come from her husband. She instinctively responds to poetry by Ginsberg, painting by De Kooning, to the medium of glass, and to her earlier love—fashion. The historical and formal associations that many other clayworkers thrive on leave her unmoved, although she sees "nature as a wonderful pattern, and that is part of what I do." Her work is a total inte-

Platter with frills and mug. Platter, 12″ diameter; mug, 4″ × 4½″.

Flower teapot, multicolored. 8" wide, 6½" high.

gration of form and surface where "function matters less and less to me. However, everything is really quite useable—but only by very careful people!" She is concerned with making images, and says "My work has more to do with being ideas in space, drawings in space, than it does with perfecting the art of throwing a perfect pot or getting that perfect firing. Images interest me more than making my own clay. I see monumental sculpture in a two-inch figure. The plasticity and softness of clay allow me to make work that I respond to, and that's what it is all about for me."

Clown platter with blocks; multicolored.

Conclusion

Standards and Aesthetics

Every improvement in the standard of work men do is followed swiftly and inevitably by an improvement in the men who do it.

—*William Morris*

What are standards? Do we need them? And, if so, what can they do for us? These are questions that all potters should spend a long time pondering. The word *standards* can pertain to a great many variables, from aesthetics and concept, to details of craftsmanship and execution. The contemporary clayworker finds himself in a position of enormous difficulty in this age, often lacking the roots of a tradition, and yet bombarded by a morass of influences. It is an awesome task to understand our choice of variables, let alone make appropriate decisions on what to say or make, and how to say or make it. The old traditional potter didn't suffer from an overabundance of sources of inspiration; he generally made simple wares for specific functions to satisfy the needs of a pre-plastic society. Dora Billington writes in *The Technique of Pottery*, "The traditional peasant potter, using the materials that were close at hand, developing very slowly the craft that he had inherited, and knowing only one kind of pottery, made according to well-proven and time-honored methods, produced pots which had a logical directness and usually a real, if largely unconscious, beauty."

The potter himself, and his role in today's society, is quite different. He or she is usually a well-educated person, deciding to work in clay for any number of different reasons that seldom have anything to do with either being a peasant, or of following a particular tradition. In essence, he or she is an anomaly, for the main part producing wares to suit functions that are often done better by industry. The potter is more flexible than any machine, and is able to make things that show the indomitable spirit of humanity, which are part of a tradition going back to the very roots of civilization. Although the potter may be working in archaic ways, and is an extension of a living tradition, he or she is capable of challenging and adapting tradition to face new needs. He or she may make unpretentious objects for a strictly utilitarian need, or precious objects which fulfill an often unseen need in everyday life and its rituals. He or she has the opportunity to produce works that transcend the purely utilitarian, becoming usable works of art that can be integrated into daily living, or a central focus in a special occasion. Pottery sometimes has that special quality found in all good art that gradually unfolds itself to the user or viewer. It has a slow release mechanism that seems to expose the work a little at a time—a nuance of color or a change in the form that wasn't noticed before. One probably never knows all that there is to know about a really good piece, in the way that one never really knows all there is to know about a close friend.

The time that it takes to develop a well-rounded clayworker hasn't changed much from the past, and is still generally thought of as being from ten to fifteen years before real mastery or thorough understanding can be achieved. Unfortunately, in our haste to become "instantized" craftsmen, we fall over ourselves trying so many trends and variations to achieve an individual statement. This generally only comes from a prolonged development and understanding gained by the thorough mastery of a relatively narrow parameter of intensive experience. The aim of developing standards of excellence in our work should be paramount, but in today's mad rush society we often have little time to think about, let alone deeply consider, the intrinsic qualities inherent in a given piece or method of working. The imposition of standards, either on the self or on the mass, derives from a desire to establish aesthetic and technical criteria by which one can judge the relative qualities, strengths, or weaknesses of any work. Although it should become intuitive, it seldom reaches that stage because of the plethora of extraneous matter which bombards the senses and obliterates that innate sense of judgment so developed in craftsmen of the past. Our problems are further compounded by technical complexities unknown to the peasant potter. So just how does one establish standards and aesthetic criteria?

Aesthetics, like philosophy, are intangible. They influence and affect the qualities of our lives in many ways. They generally develop over a long period of time from continual viewing, appraising, and evaluating the qualities that objects may possess. If one only uses plastics, watches television, and listens to electronic music, it becomes very hard to relate to the subtleties of ceramics, theatre, or the sound of an oboe. We are seldom surrounded by objects of unconscious and unpretentious beauty, as people were in times prior to the Industrial Revolution. More often than not we are surrounded by ugliness and junk, and that has become the basis for much of the development of our aesthetic. One can only develop out of what one is aware of and memory traces are part of that awareness. The more cognizant we become, the more our aesthetic is challenged, and the more we can intuit that which can be considered satisfying or beautiful. In talking about aesthetics, the whole gamut of verbal complexity comes into play, making a real understanding of the inherent or intrinsic qualities of craft work very difficult to define. To give an accurate, objective, and constructive criticism is one of the most difficult tasks with which a teacher is faced, and there are very few who can do it well. The process of constructive self-criticism is also hard, but necessary, particularly in the light of confused and limited understanding. It is almost impossible to rule out subjectivity in any critical appraisal, because of the closeness that one feels with the object being viewed. Self-criticism shouldn't be thought of as criticizing the self, but merely the object that the self has made, and possibly the thought processes that led to its making. One should learn to be as objective as possible, since it is always possible to rationalize one minor good point over a host of bad ones. The usual divisions of aesthetic appraisal are: form, proportion, function, surface, color, process, intent and content, not necessarily in that order. Aesthetics relate not only to matters of form, function, and surface, but also to cerebral, spiritual, and emotional ideas and ideals (intent and content). These are the most difficult to analyze and to understand. Different cultures have widely differing aesthetic values, and when we consciously borrow from other cultures without at least a basic understanding of those cultures, we obliterate a very important part of the spiritual life of the work. Even when done with great skill, the emerging form will lack the spirit and emotion of the original.

There are many ways to develop pottery forms, both from the point of process and technique, and from visualization and structure. They may be emotionally developed from the reaction to the quality of material, or as calculated as mathematics in proportion and structure. Depending on the individual clayworker, the main approaches to work in clay are either cerebral, where logic, proportion and structure are of paramount importance; or they may be intuitive, where the emotions or "gut reactions" take precedence. It is usually either head or heart which prevails, although there are always some gray overlapping areas. Cerebral works can of course be spiritual, as in the music of Bach. If one's use of clay is cerebral, after a time intuition will often blend with mathematics when the spirit and the head join forces. As with most of the learning processes related to clay, it is a slow evolution. In addition to the cerebral and intuitive, and the selection of influences and inspiration, one has to develop skills and foresight to produce good work. Whether one makes functional or nonfunctional work, some standards are necessary although they will vary according to the object. In truly functional work the prime objective is the function. As Yanagi expresses it in *The Unknown Craftsman*, "Utility is the first principle of beauty." Generally when one analyzes the functional requirements of any object, it is possible to simplify the use to the barest essentials. If one uses this essence and makes the required piece along the lines of simplicity, then a certain beauty will develop in an unconscious way. Once the functional requirements are decided upon, the simpler a thing can be generally the better it functions. A utilitarian piece covered with knobs, blobs, twiddles, and other excesses in the name of individualism only loses its functional attributes by their presence. This is not to say that one shouldn't use decoration, only that the decorative aspects should probably be secondary to the function, and certainly not impede it. Attention to details, combined with skills in surface development, make the difference between quality work and indifferent, mediocre, or badly executed work. If one pays significant attention to details, the time thus spent will quickly pay off. However, it is a trap to become totally seduced by details at the expense of the overall form. I have often seen people exuberant and exhilarated over one square inch of a sumptuous glaze on an otherwise remarkably ugly pot. I usually suggest that they should smash the pot, and keep the shard with the beautiful glaze as a reminder to develop the beautiful glaze on something better. In this way we could eliminate much of the ugliness that surrounds us, and begin to develop a process of self-improvement.

Nonfunctional ceramics, and objects where the function is of a secondary concern, require a different aesthetic judgment. These are emotional and entirely subjective statements, as opposed to the objective and analytical nature of pure function. Often, established criteria of craftsmanship are diminished in favor of the concept behind the work. Unfortunately, this has led to an acceptance of the "laissez-faire" sloppy work which has become commonplace, even in work that can by no means be considered conceptual. If we are to establish a professional acceptance for ourselves, it can only happen when the craftsman accepts the responsibility of professional craftsmanship, work habits, and attitude. The makers of most of the best in conceptual ceramics have very high standards of craftsmanship. It is generally the second-rate artist who produces inferior work which may be acceptable since it is in vogue. Fashion changes quickly, but time will tell where lasting qualities lie.

There are some specific things that one can do to improve one's standards and aesthetics. First, read some or all of the books mentioned in the Bibliography, as this will give a much wider and more experienced view than mine in the understanding of aesthetic problems and solutions. Second, aim to develop a high degree of self-criticism and objective analysis. Third, avoid the pitfall of pretentiousness, and learn something of humility. Finally, remember that a potter's best friend is his hammer, and it is the best arbitrator in the event of aesthetic indecision. Working within the discipline of the ultimate human art form, the potter should be engaged in an endless search, following a line of thought from work to work, with growth from one to the next. With tenacity, one continues to grow and change. One becomes one's work; one's work becomes oneself. The cycle is complete, but the wheel doesn't stop turning.

A journey of ten thousand miles begins with one small step beneath your feet.

—*Lao Tzu*

Bibliography

GENERAL

Berman, Rick. *Teapots*. Self-published: Rick Berman, 1980.

Billington, Dora M. *The Technique of Pottery*. London: B. T. Batsford, 1962.

Cardew, Michael. *Pioneer Pottery*. London: Longmans, 1969.

Casson, Michael. *Pottery in Britain Today*. London: Alec Tiranti, 1967.

———. *The Craft of the Potter*. London: B.B.C. Publications, 1977.

Clark, Garth. *Michael Cardew*. Tokyo: Kodansha, 1976.

Clark, Kenneth. *Practical Pottery & Ceramics*. London: Studio Vista, 1964.

———. *The Potter's Manual*. Secaucus: Chartwell Books, 1983.

Cottier-Angeli, Fiorella. *Ceramics*. New York: Van Nostrand Reinhold, 1974.

Counts, Charles. *Pottery Workshop*. New York: Collier, 1973.

Coyne, John, ed. *The Penland School of Crafts Book of Pottery*. New York: Bobbs-Merrill Co., 1975.

Dodd, A. E. *Dictionary of Ceramics*. Totowa, N.J.: Littlefield, Adams & Co., 1967.

Fournier, Robert. *Illustrated Dictionary of Practical Pottery*. New York: Van Nostrand Reinhold, 1977.

———. *Illustrated Dictionary of Pottery Form*. New York: Van Nostrand Reinhold, 1981.

Green, David. *Pottery: Materials and Techniques*. London: Faber and Faber, 1967.

Hamer, Frank. *The Potter's Dictionary of Materials and Techniques*. London: Pitman, 1975.

Hamilton, David. *Manual of Pottery and Ceramics*. New York: Van Nostrand Reinhold, 1974.

Hogben, Carol. *The Art of Bernard Leach*. New York: Watson-Guptill, 1978.

Kanzaki, Noritake. *Japanese Teapots*. Tokyo: Kodansha International, 1981.

Kriwanek, Franz F. *Keramos, The Teaching of Pottery*. Dubuque: Kendall/Hunt, 1970.

Lakofsky, Charles. *Pottery*. Dubuque: William C. Brown, 1968.

Leach, Bernard. *A Potter's Book*. London: Faber and Faber, 1940.

———. *A Potter's Portfolio*. London: Lund Humphries & Co., 1951.

———. *A Potter's Work*. London: Evelyn, Adams & Mackay, 1967.

———. *Hamada, Potter*. Tokyo: Kodansha International, 1975.

Lenssen, Heidi. *Art and Anatomy*. New York: Barnes & Noble, 1946.

Lucie-Smith, Edward. *The Story of Craft*. New York: Van Nostrand Reinhold, 1984.

Mansfield, Janet, ed. *The Potter's Art*. Canberra: Cassell, 1981.

Miller, Jonathan: *The Body in Question*. New York: Random House, 1978.

Nelson, Glenn C. *Ceramics* (fifth edition). New York: Holt, Rinehart & Winston, 1984.

Norton, F. H. *Ceramics for the Artist Potter*. Reading, Mass.: Addison-Wesley, 1956.

O'Malley, C. and Saunders, F. *Leonardo da Vinci on the Human Body*. New York: Greenwich House, 1982.

Peterson, Susan. *Shoji Hamada, A Potter's Way and Work*. Tokyo: Kodansha International, 1974.

Rose, Muriel. *Artist Potters in England*. London: Faber and Faber, 1955.

Savage, G., and H. Newman. *An Illustrated Dictionary of Ceramics*. New York: Van Nostrand Reinhold, 1974.

Shafer, Thomas. *The Professional Potter*. New York: Watson-Guptill, 1978.

Tipton, Barbara, ed. *Great Ideas for Potters*. Professional Publications, 1983.

HISTORY

Amiet, P. *Art in the Ancient World: A Handbook of Styles and Forms*. New York: Rizzoli, 1981.

Amirau, Ruth. *Ancient Pottery of the Holy Land*. Israel: Massada Press, 1969.

Art Gallery of Victoria. *Ceramics of the Yuan Dynasty*. Victoria: Art Gallery of Greater Victoria, 1980.

Artigas, J. L. *Spanish Folk Ceramics of Today*. Barcelona: Editorial Blume, 1970.

Asian Art Museum. *A Decade of Collecting* (catalog). Tokyo: Kodansha International, 1976.

The Asia Society. *The Art of the Korean Potter*. New York: Asia House Gallery, 1968.

Atil, Esin. *Ceramics from the World of Islam*. Washington: Smithsonian Institution, 1973.

Auboyer, J. *Oriental Art: A Handbook of Styles and Forms*. New York: Rizzoli, 1980.

Boston Museum. *Egypt's Golden Age: 1558–1085 B.C.* Boston: Museum of Fine Arts Boston, 1982.

Bray, W., and D. Trump. *Dictionary of Archaeology*. Middlesex: Penguin, 1970.

Brendel, Otto. *Etruscan Art*. Middlesex: Penguin, 1978.

Bushnell, G. and A. Digby. *Ancient American Pottery*. London: Faber and Faber, 1955.

Caiger-Smith, Alan. *Tin-Glaze Pottery*. London: Faber & Faber, 1973.

Campbell Museum. *The Campbell Museum Collection*. Camden, N.J.: Campbell Museum, 1972.

Charleston, Robert, ed. *World Ceramics*. London: Paul Hamlyn, 1968.

Christe, Y. *Art of the Christian World: A Handbook of Styles and Forms*. New York: Rizzoli, 1982.

Clark, G. and M. Hughto. *A Century of Ceramics in the United States*. New York: E. P. Dutton, 1979.

Cook, B. F. *Greek and Roman Art in the British Museum*. London: British Museum Publications, 1976.

Cooper, Emmanuel. *A History of World Pottery*. New York: Larousse & Co., 1972.

Cotterell, Arthur. *The Encyclopedia of Ancient Civilizations*. New York: Mayflower Books, 1980.

Cox, Warren E. *Pottery and Porcelain* (vol. 1 & 2). New York: Crown Publishers, 1970.

Cuisenier, Jean. *French Folk Art*. Tokyo: Kodansha International, 1977.

Cushion, John P. *Pottery and Porcelain*. New York: Hearst Books, 1972.

———. *Pottery and Porcelain Tablewares*. New York: William Morrow & Co., 1976.

Davaras, Costis. *Phaistos Hagia Triada Gortyn*. Athens: Hannibal.

Egami, Namio. *The Beginnings of Japanese Art*. New York: Weatherhill/Heibonsha, 1973.

Essays. *Mimbres Pottery*. New York: Hudson Hills Press, 1983.

Fleming, J. and H. Honour. *Dictionary of the Decorative Arts*. New York: Harper & Row, 1977.

Frasche, Dean F. *Southeast Asian Ceramics (9th–17th C.)*. New York: Asia House Gallery, 1976.

Fujioka, Ryoichi. *Shino and Oribe Ceramics*. Tokyo: Kodansha International, 1977.

Fukai, Shinji. *Ceramics of Ancient Persia*. New York: Weatherhill/Tankosha, 1980.

Gompertz, G. St. G. M. *Korean Celadon*. London: Faber & Faber, 1963.

Hawkes, Jacquetta. *Dawn of the Gods*. Toronto: Clarke, Irwin & Co., 1968.

Hayashiya S., and H. Tubner. *Chinese Ceramics from Japanese Collections*. New York: Asia House Gallery, 1977.

Hayes, John W. *Roman Pottery*. Toronto: Royal Ontario Museum, 1976.

Hobson and Hetherington. *The Art of the Chinese Potter*. New York: Dover Publications, 1982.

Honour, H., and J. Fleming. *The Visual Arts: A History*. Englewood Cliffs, N.J.: Prentice-Hall, 1982.

Hughes, G. Bernard. *English & Scottish Earthenware*. London: Abbey Fine Arts.

Huxford, Sharon and Bob. *Weller Pottery*. Paducah, Ky.: Collector Books, 1979.

Jenkins, Marilyn: *Islamic Pottery*. New York: Metropolitan Museum of Art, 1983.

Ketchum, William C., Jr. *Pottery and Porcelain*. New York: Alfred A. Knopf, 1983.

Kodansha: *Famous Ceramics of Japan*. 9 vols. Tokyo: Kodansha International, 1983.

Kurtz, Seymour. *The World Guide to Antiquities*. New York: Crown Publishers, 1975.

Lefebvre d'Argence, R. *The Hans Popper Collection of Oriental Art*. Tokyo: Kodansha International, 1973.

Medley, Margaret. *The Chinese Potter*. Oxford: Phaidon, 1976.

Metropolitan Museum. *Spirit and Ritual: The Morse Collection of Ancient Chinese Art*. New York: Metropolitan Museum of Art, 1982.

Mikami, Tsugio. *The Art of Japanese Ceramics*. New York: Weatherhill/Heibonsha, 1972.

Miller, Roy Andrew. *Japanese Ceramics*. Tokyo: Toto Shuppan Co., 1960.

Mingazzini, Paolino. *Greek Pottery Painting*. London: Paul Hamlyn, 1969.

Mino, Yutaka. *Chinese Stonewares*. Toronto: The Royal Ontario Museum, 1974.

———. *Tz'u-chou Type Wares, 960–1600 A.D.* Bloomington: Indiana University Press, 1980.

Mitsuoka, Tadanari. *Ceramic Art of Japan*. Tokyo: Japan Travel Bureau, 1964.

Moes, Robert. *Japanese Ceramics*. New York: Brooklyn Museum, 1979.

Munsterberg, Hugo. *The Ceramic Art of Japan*. Tokyo: Charles E. Tuttle, 1964.

Rackham, Bernard. *Medieval English Pottery*. London: Faber & Faber, 1947.

Rawson, Jessica. *Ancient China: Art and Archaeology*. New York: Harper & Row, 1980.

Robinson, D., and C. Harcum. *Greek Vases in the R.O.M.* 2 vols. Toronto: University of Toronto Press, 1930.

Rosenthal, Ernst. *Pottery and Ceramics*. Middlesex: Penguin, 1949.

Salam-Liebich, Hayat. *Islamic Art*. Montreal: Musee des beaux-arts de Montreal, 1983.

Sanders, Herbert. *The World of Japanese Ceramics*. Tokyo: Kodansha International, 1967.

Savage, George. *Porcelain Through the Ages*. Middlesex: Penguin, 1954.

———. *Pottery Through the Ages*. Middlesex: Penguin, 1959.

Schuster, F., and C. Wolseley. *Vases of the Sea*. London: Anugus & Robertson, 1974.

Shepard, Anna O. *Ceramics for the Archaeologist*. Washington, D.C.: Carnegie Institution of Washington, 1971.

Southeast Asian Society. *Vietnamese Ceramics*. Singapore: Oxford University Press, 1982.

Taggart, Ross E. *English Pottery in the William Rockhill Nelson Gallery*. Kansas City: Nelson Gallery-Atkins Museum, 1967.

Tannahill, Reay. *Food in History*. New York: Stein and Day, 1973.

Till, B. and P. Swart. *The Flowering of Japanese Ceramic Art*. Victoria: Art Gallery of Greater Victoria, 1983.

Tregear, Mary. *Song Ceramics*. New York: Rizzoli, 1982.

Webster, Donald. *Early Canadian Pottery*. Toronto: McClelland and Stewart, 1971.

Yoshida, Mitsukuni. *In Search of Persian Pottery*. New York: Weatherhill/Tankosha, 1972.

Yoshida, Shoya. *Folk Art*. Osaka: Hoikusha, 1971.

AESTHETICS

Arieti, Silvano. *Creativity*. New York: Basic Books, 1976.

Bronowski, J. *The Visionary Eye*. Cambridge: MIT Press, 1978.

———. *The Ascent of Man*. Boston: Little, Brown & Co., 1973.

Carpenter, Rhys. *The Esthetic Basis of Greek Art*. Bloomington: Indiana University Press, 1959.

Clark, Garth, ed. *Ceramic Art: Comment and Review*. New York: E. P. Dutton, 1978.

Hayashiya, T. *Japanese Arts and the Tea Ceremony*. Tokyo: Weatherhill/Heibonsha, 1974.

Iguchi, Kaisen. *Tea Ceremony*. Osaka: Hoikusha Publishing, 1975.

Jung, Carl. *Man and His Symbols*. New York: Doubleday & Co., 1964.

Kakuzo, Okakura. *The Book of Tea*. Rutland: Charles E. Tuttle, 1956.

Knobler, Nathan. *The Visual Dialogue*. New York: Holt, Rinehart and Winston, 1966.

Leach, Bernard. *The Potter's Challenge*. New York: E. P. Dutton, 1975.

de Lucio-Meyer, J. J. *Visual Aesthetics*. New York: Harper & Row, 1973.

Pye, David. *The Nature and Art of Workmanship*. Cambridge: Cambridge University Press, 1968.

———. *The Nature and Aesthetics of Design*. New York: Van Nostrand Reinhold, 1978.

Rawson, Philip. *Ceramics*. London: Oxford University Press, 1971.

Richards, M. C. *Centering*. Middletown, Conn.: Wesleyan University Press, 1962.

Samuels, Mike and Nancy. *Seeing with the Mind's Eye*. New York: Random House, 1975.

Seizo, Hayashiya. *Chanoyu: Japanese Tea Ceremony*. New York: Japan Society, 1979.

Tanaka, Sen'o. *The Tea Ceremony*. Tokyo: Kodansha International, 1973.

Yanagi, Soetsu. *The Unknown Craftsman*. Tokyo: Kodansha International, 1972.

DESIGN AND ARCHITECTURE

Alex, William. *Japanese Architecture*. New York: George Braziller, 1963.

Arnheim, Rudolf. *Art and Visual Perception*. Los Angeles: University of California Press, 1954.

B.B.C. *Ways of Seeing*. London: Penguin Books, 1972.

Bentley, W. and W. Humphreys. *Snow Crystals*. New York: Dover, 1962.

Bergamini, David. *Mathematics*. New York: Time Incorporated, 1963.

Blossfeldt, Karl. *Art Forms in Nature*. New York: Universe Books, 1967.

Caudill, W. and W. Pena. *Architecture and You*. New York: Whitney Library of Design, 1978.

Ching, Francis D. K. *Architecture: Form, Space & Order*. New York: Van Nostrand Reinhold, 1979.

Cooper, J. C. *An Illustrated Encyclopaedia of Traditional Symbols*. London: Thames and Hudson, 1978.

Copplestone, T., ed. *World Architecture*. London: Hamlyn, 1963.

Doczi, Gyorgy. *The Power of Limits*. Boulder: Shambhala, 1981.

Dondis, Donis A. *A Primer of Visual Literacy*. Cambridge: M.I.T. Press, 1973.

Engel, Heinrich. *The Japanese House*. Rutland, Vt.: Charles E. Tuttle, 1964.

Feininger, Andreas. *Roots of Art*. New York: Viking Press, 1975.

Foster, Michael, ed. *Architecture: Style, Structure and Design*. New York: Excalibur Books, 1982.

Gardiner, Stephen. *Inside Architecture*. Englewood Cliffs: Prentice-Hall, 1983.

Grillo, Paul J. *What is Design?* Chicago: Paul Theobald and Co., 1960.

Ivins, William M., Jr. *Art & Geometry*. New York: Dover, 1946.

Kepes, Gyorgy, ed. *Education of Vision*. New York: George Braziller, 1965.

———. *Sign, Image, Symbol*. New York: George Braziller, 1966.

———. *Module, Proportion, Symmetry, Rhythm*. New York: George Braziller, 1966.

———. *Structure in Art and in Science*. New York: George Braziller, 1965.

———. *The Man-Made Object*. New York: George Braziller, 1966.

Kranz, S. and R. Fisher. *The Design Continuum*. New York: Reinhold, 1966.

Le Chateau Dufresne. *Eva Zeisel: Designer for Industry*. Montreal: Le Chateau Dufresne, Inc., Musee des Arts Decoratifs de Montreal, 1984.

Lee, Sherman E. *The Genius of Japanese Design*. Tokyo: Kodansha International, 1981.

Lowry, Bates. *The Visual Experience: An Introduction to Art*. New York: Prentice-Hall & Harry N. Abrams, 1967.

Mainstone, Rowland J. *Developments in Structural Form*. Middlesex: Penguin Books, 1975.

Miles, Walter. *Designs for Craftsmen*. New York: Doubleday & Co., 1962.

Ocvirk, Bone, Stinson, Wigg. *Art Fundamentals: Theory and Practice*. Dubuque: William C. Brown, 1960.

Papanek, Victor. *Design for the Real World*. London: Granada, 1974.

———. *Design for Human Scale*. New York: Van Nostrand Reinhold, 1983.

Papanek, V. and J. Hennessey. *How Things Don't Work*. New York: Pantheon Books, 1977.

Pedoe, Dan. *Geometry and the Visual Arts*. New York: Dover Publications, 1976.

Porter, Tom. *How Architects Visualize*. London: Studio Vista, 1979.

Pye, David. *The Nature of Design*. New York: Reinhold, 1964.

Rasmussen, Steen E. *Experiencing Architecture*. Cambridge: M.I.T. Press, 1959.

Rhodes, Daniel. *Pottery Form*. Radnor: Chilton Book Co., 1976.

Rowland, Kurt. *Looking and Seeing Series* (Books 1–4). London: Ginn and Co., 1964.

Rudofsky, Bernard. *The Prodigious Builders*. New York: Harcourt Brace Jovanovich, 1977.

Stierlin, Henri. *Encyclopedia of World Architecture*. New York: Van Nostrand Reinhold, 1977.

Teague, Walter Dorwin. *Design This Day*. New York: Harcourt, Brace and Co., 1940.

Thomas, Richard K. *Three-Dimensional Design*. New York: Van Nostrand Reinhold, 1969.

Thompson, D'Arcy. *On Growth and Form*. Cambridge: Cambridge University Press, 1966.

Wildenhain, M. *Pottery: Form and Expression*. Palo Alto: Pacific Books, 1959.

Index

Page numbers in *italic* indicate information in illustrations.

testing, 179
Middle East. *See also* Mesopotamia.
    beginnings of potter's wheel in, 128
    pottery beginnings in, 3
Mixing bowls, 160–161
    by Bruce Cochrane, 210
Modular System (Le Corbusier), 88
Molds, for spouts, 148, 148
Morris, William, *The Lesser Life,* xiv
Mortars, 161
Most Favored Triangle, 85
Mouth, anatomy of and pottery
        dimensions, 95–96, 97
Mugs, 163–164
    by Eilene Sky, 242
    from Germany (17 c. A.D.), 13
    by Gwyn Hanssen Pigott, 205
Mullite, 189
Mycenean jar, 6

Nature,
    angular forms in, 60
    curvilinear forms in, 61
    form in, 59
    spiral forms in, 62
Nautilus, relationship to Golden
        Rectangle, 89
Near East, earthenware jar with spout
        (1000 B.C.), 79
Negative shapes, 52, 56, 57
Nelson, David, 216
New Mexico, bowls from Mimbres
        classic period in (1000–1150
        A.D.), 19
Nigeria,
    casserole from, 16
    water jars in, 36
Nonfunctional ceramics, standards for,
        246
Nygren, John, 216

Oil jar, from Tunisia, 66
Oil lamps, 17, 18
Oinochoe, from Greece (750–550 B.C.),
        70
Originals, vs copies, 110
Outridge, Stephanie, 202
Oval, symbolism of, 51
Oval forms, on potter's wheel, 132–134,
        133
Ovens, pottery in, 186

Paddles, 132
Painting, and pottery, 239–240
Panama, pedestal plate from, 44
Parabolas, as major form in pottery, 55
Pastore, Michel, 202
Pearson, Colin, 195
Perfume bottle, by Tom Turner, 218
Perfuming, and pot form, 17–18

Persia,
    handled spouted jar from (13 c. A.D.),
        115
    jug from, 58
    stem bowl from, 12
Peru,
    earthenware vessels from, 83
    pre-Columbian vessels in, 6
    stirrup jar from, 114
Pickling jars, 171
Pigott, John, 202
Pilcher, Don, 214
Pilgrim flasks, 15
Pinch pots, 22
Pinched handles, 153
Pitchers, 173–174
    gas-fired stoneware, by Bruce
        Cochrane, 212
    from Iran (8 c. B.C.), 66
    in majolica technique, by Stanley
        Mace Andersen, 222, 224
    symbolism of, 8
    wood-fired stoneware, by Bruce
        Cochrane, 213
Planting, and pot form, 18–19, 22
Plants, Fibonacci series in, 88
Plastic, vs clay, in storage containers,
        169
Plastic memory, 142
Plates, 161–162
    by Goyer and Bonneau, 236
    by Eilene Sky, 239, 242
    stoneware, from China (14 c. A.D.),
        12
Platter, in majolica technique, by
        Stanley Mace Andersen, 224
Porcelain,
    from China, 38
    from England (1765 A.D.), 34, 35
    from Germany (1770 A.D.), 34
    Gwyn Hanssen Pigott's work with,
        202
    jug of, from England (1775), 76
    spouted vessel of, by Tom Turner,
        216, 219
Porous clay, uses for, 169
Porret, Evelyne, 202
Positive shapes, 52, 56
Potter's wheel, 128
    development of, 23
    and pot shape, 131–132
Potters,
    attitudes toward ceramic history, 2
    development of, 245
    growth of, 109–110
    influences on, 2
    role of, in contemporary society, 244
    styles of, 194
    traditions of, 109
Pottery,
    as art form, xiv
    beginnings of, 2–3

changes in, 37–38
    forms of, 4–9
    methods for creating, and form, 21–23
    role of function vs appearance of, 7–8
Pouring forms, 68–83, 173–175
    edges of, 139, 139
    with lids, 142
    lips for, 26
Practice, defined, 129
Pre-Columbian vessels, in Peru, 6
Press-molded handles, 155
Press-molded spouts, 147–149
Pressmolding, 22
Primal form, development from, 23–24,
        24–25
Process, and pot form, 21–23
Profile, defined, 27
Profile ribs, 136
Proportion, 49
    defined, 84
    in functional pottery, 93
Pulled handles, 152–153, 153
Pure forms, 52
Pyramid forms, 132

Ramekins, 178
Ratios,
    defined, 84
    test for sense of, 84–85
Rawson, Philip, *Ceramics,* 23
Read, Sir Herbert, *The Origins of Form in
        Art,* 93–94
Rectangles,
    as major form in pottery, 54
    symbolism of, 51
Reduction, 189
Reeve, John, 202
Refrigerators, pottery in, 186
Reitz, Don, 214
Religious associations, form
        development and, 4–5
Repoussé metalworking techniques, 38
Rhythm, 110–111
Rhytons,
    from Greece (600–450 B.C.), 12
    from Turkey (1870 B.C.), 44
Rice, Jackie, 220
Rice bowls, 160
Rie, Lucie, 196, 202, 242
Rim, considerations concerning, 184
Rituals,
    of food preparation and eating, 37
    pots for, 181–182
    washing as, 17
Rum pots, 171, 171

Saddle gourd, from China, 32
Salad bowls, 160
Salomon, Judith, 220
Salt-glaze kiln, 226
Salt-glazed stoneware, from Canada
        (19 c.), 125